GRILL IT, BRAISE IT, BROIL IT

American Heart Association®

GRILL IT, BRAISE IT, BROIL IT

AND 9 OTHER EASY TECHNIQUES FOR MAKING HEALTHY MEALS

CLARKSON POTTER/PUBLISHERS

NEW YORK

ACKNOWLEDGMENTS

AMERICAN HEART ASSOCIATION CONSUMER PUBLICATIONS

Director: Linda S. Ball

Managing Editor: Deborah A. Renza

Senior Editor: Robin P. Loveman

Assistant Managing Editor: Roberta W. Sullivan

RECIPE DEVELOPERS

Janice Cole

Nancy S. Hughes

Carol Ritchie

Francine Wolfe Schwartz

NUTRITION ANALYST

Tammi Hancock, R.D.

Published in the United States by Clarkson Potter/Publishers, an imprint of the Crown Publishing Group, a division of Penguin Random House LLC, New York.
www.crownpublishing.com
www.clarksonpotter.com

CLARKSON POTTER is a trademark and POTTER with colophon is a registered trademark of Penguin Random House LLC.

Your contributions to the American Heart Association support research that helps make publications like this possible. For more information, call 1-800-AHA-USA1 (1-800-242-8721) or contact us online at www.heart.org.

Library of Congress Cataloging-in-Publication Data

American Heart Association grill it, braise it, broil it, and other easy techniques and quick recipes for healthy meals / American Heart Association.

        pages   cm

  Summary: "Knowing how to cook healthfully—without sacrificing flavor—is an important step towards improving heart health, weight, and overall well-being. For the first time, American Heart Association offers a primer on 12 easy-to-master heart-healthy cooking techniques (baking, broiling, braising, poaching, grilling, roasting, microwaving, blending, slow cooking, and stewing, to name a few). Once you know these techniques, you'll be able to customize the 175 recipes in this book for an endless supply of delicious meals. Learn the basics and then start experimenting!"—Provided by publisher.

    1. Low-fat diet—Recipes.   2. Heart—Diseases—Diet therapy—Recipes.   3. Cooking. 4. Broiling.   I. American Heart Association.   II. Title: Grill it, braise it, broil it, and other easy techniques and quick recipes for healthy meals.

   RM237.7.A374 2015
   641.5'6311—dc23

ISBN 978-0-307-88809-9
Ebook ISBN 978-0-307-88811-2

Printed in the United States of America

Book design by Jennifer K. Beal Davis
Jacket design by Gabriel Levine
Jacket and insert photography by Lucy Schaeffer

10 9 8 7 6 5 4 3 2 1

First Edition

contents

recipes

resources

preface

At the American Heart Association and American Stroke Association, we know that for you and your family, eating nutritiously is a big part of living a healthier lifestyle, and that cooking more at home is an easy way to achieve this. In this cookbook, we share information about healthy cooking techniques and give you recipes to put these techniques into action. You can trust that each of the recipes not only tastes delicious but also follows the dietary recommendations of the American Heart Association.

Tired of the same tried-and-true baked chicken? Braise it and enjoy Curried Chicken Thighs (page 124), or steam it and serve Stuffed Napa Cabbage Rolls with Orange-Ginger Sauce (page 170). Not sure how to cook fish? Get in your weekly omega-3s through Honeyed Salmon with Spiced Honeydew Salsa (page 187) and Tuna with Tomato-Tarragon Sauce (page 36) from the microwave. Try the unexpected, like broiled Warm Caesar Salad with Tofu "Croutons" (page 202) or Smoky Chicken and Vegetable Lasagna (page 82) cooked on the grill. And, unlike any of our other American Heart Association cookbooks, all the recipes are organized by cooking method.

When you cook at home, you can control the amounts of saturated and trans fats, sodium, and added sugar you consume to help lower cholesterol and blood pressure levels that increase your risk for heart disease and stroke. With *Grill It, Braise It, Broil It,* you'll have a reliable resource to help you make nutritious, simple, and creative meals at home each and every day.

ROSE MARIE ROBERTSON, M.D., FAHA, FACC
Chief Science and Medical Officer
American Heart Association/American Stroke Association

cooking with easy techniques for a healthy heart

Organized by technique, *Grill It, Braise It, Broil It* shows you how to cook using 12 different healthy cooking methods. All of them will help you expand your recipe repertoire. Some styles, such as stir-frying, steaming, and poaching, are quick. Techniques such as roasting and broiling offer distinct flavors and interesting textures; others, like braising and stewing, yield melt-in-your mouth dishes that cook low and slow with little attention needed. Slow cooking, microwaving, blending, and grilling let you utilize some of your favorite cooking appliances and don't heat up your kitchen; some methods, like baking, require no equipment or tools beyond what's in a basic kitchen.

The 175 recipes include snacks, appetizers, salads, soups, entrées, breakfasts, side dishes, and desserts that offer you versatility in the kitchen—from countertop to stovetop to oven. In addition, you'll find information on the techniques such as:

- why they're healthy
- the benefits and advantages
- how they work and tips to cook successfully with them
- what main tools and equipment are needed

In the back of the book, you'll also find a list of nutritious pantry items to keep in stock, basic cooking tools for a well-equipped kitchen, food safety practices, grocery shopping recommendations, and overall good nutrition and healthy lifestyle guidelines.

shopping smart and eating well

To be sure you include enough wholesome foods in your daily eating plan and limit foods that are low in health benefits, keep the following guidelines in mind.

CHOOSE MORE NUTRIENT-RICH FOODS

Include a range of different **VEGETABLES** and **FRUITS** to get the widest variety of nutrients. When buying frozen or canned vegetables and fruits, shop for those with the lowest amounts of sodium or added sugars.

Eat high-fiber **WHOLE GRAINS** rather than refined grain products as often as possible. Serve whole-grain breads, pastas, cereals, and side dishes for the benefits of fiber and other important nutrients. Try to be sure at least half the grains you eat are whole grains. Shop for brown rice, bulgur, quinoa, barley, amaranth, and farro, as well as whole-grain breads, pastas, cereals, and crackers. Check that a whole grain is listed first in the ingredients.

Select **FAT-FREE, 1%,** and **LOW-FAT DAIRY** products and limit full-fat dairy products, such as milk, cheese, and yogurt.

Eat **FISH** at least twice a week, especially fish high in omega-3 fatty acids, such as salmon, tuna, and trout. Seafood is an excellent source of protein. Shop for fresh fish when possible, but also look for canned albacore tuna packed in water with the lowest sodium and canned boneless, skinless salmon as healthy alternatives.

Choose **SKINLESS POULTRY** and **LEAN MEAT,** and prepare them without added unhealthy fats, discarding all visible fat before cooking them. Lean cuts of beef and pork, such as sirloin, extra-lean ground beef, pork tenderloin, and pork loin chops, can be part of a heart-healthy diet if you consume them in moderation.

Add **LEGUMES**, **NUTS**, and **SEEDS** to your diet. Legumes, including beans (such as black and kidney), peas (such as green and chickpeas), lentils, and peanuts, are an excellent source of fiber and meatless protein. Nuts and seeds contain monounsaturated fats, which may help improve blood cholesterol levels when they replace saturated and trans fat in the diet. Look for unsalted nuts and seeds for snacks or to add to salads or homemade whole-grain breads or muffins.

Include **HEALTHY FATS** and **OILS** in your eating plan. Vegetable oils provide heart-healthy unsaturated fats. Use canola, corn, olive, and safflower oils as your main go-to oils in the kitchen. Use these along with nonstick cooking sprays and soft tub margarine rather than hard stick margarine, butter, and shortening.

EAT LESS OF NUTRIENT-POOR FOODS

Cut back on **SODIUM**. Be mindful that most of the sodium you eat comes from packaged and processed foods, including restaurant meals. Watch how much sodium (and added sugars) you add to your meals in the form of condiments, dressings, and sauces. Compare the food labels of similar products to find the ones with less sodium, and be cautious of typically high-sodium foods such as soups, breads, sandwiches, pizza, poultry, and cold cuts. When cooking, season food with herbs, spices, and citrus. Use salt sparingly or not at all. To lower blood pressure, aim to eat no more than 2,400 milligrams (mg) of sodium per day. To reduce blood pressure even further, cut back to a daily sodium intake of 1,500 mg.

Limit **ADDED SUGAR**. Keep your intake of sugar-sweetened beverages to no more than 450 calories, or 36 ounces per week. (If you need fewer than 2,000 calories per day, avoid these beverages altogether.) Also, avoid sugary foods that are low in nutrients but high in calories. Buy them only as occasional treats.

Cut back on foods high in **SATURATED FAT** and **TRANS FAT**. A diet high in these fats increases your risk of heart disease. Saturated fat is found primarily in foods from animals, such as meats, poultry, and full-fat dairy products, or in tropical oils, such as coconut, palm, and palm kernel. Trans fat is present in many manufactured foods that include partially hydrogenated oil. Cut back on trans fat by reading labels when choosing snacks, cakes, cookies, pastries, pies, muffins, and fried foods. To lower cholesterol, reduce your intake of saturated fat to no more than 5 to 6 percent of your total calories, so if you eat a 2,000-calorie diet, aim to consume 13 grams or less of saturated fat a day.

living a healthy lifestyle

Although some risk factors for heart disease and stroke, such as increasing age, family history, and ethnicity, can't be changed, many of the most damaging risk factors are things you can control.

MAINTAIN A HEALTHY WEIGHT

Consistently taking in too many calories will lead to becoming overweight or obese—a risk factor for heart disease and stroke, as well as other diseases including diabetes. You have a much higher risk of heart disease and stroke if you're overweight or obese, even if you have no other risk factors. Losing just 5 to 10 percent of your body weight will help lower some of your risk. Too much body fat—especially at your waist—means that your heart has to work harder and your risk increases for high blood pressure, high cholesterol, and diabetes. You can determine your body mass index (BMI) using the BMI Calculator for Adults at www.heart.org. Also, talk to your healthcare provider about what a healthy BMI and waist measurement are for you. To best manage your weight, eat the right amount of calories for you and engage in regular physical activity.

EXERCISE REGULARLY

The American Heart Association recommends that adults get 30 minutes of moderate-intensity physical activity at least five days a week or 75 minutes of vigorous-intensity activity each week for overall cardiovascular health. Children should aim for at least 60 minutes a day.

DON'T SMOKE OR BREATHE TOBACCO SMOKE

Smoking is the number one preventable cause of premature death in the United States. Smoking is a risk factor for cardiovascular disease. A smoker's risk of developing coronary heart disease is two to four times that of a nonsmoker's. If you smoke, quit now! (To find resources to quit, go to www.heart.org.) When you stop smoking, your risk of heart disease and stroke drops rapidly, no matter how long or how much you've smoked. If you don't smoke, don't start.

DRINK ALCOHOL IN MODERATION—OR NOT AT ALL

Drinking too much alcohol can raise blood pressure, increase risk of heart failure and stroke, produce irregular heartbeats, and contribute to many other diseases. If you drink, do so in moderation—no more than one drink per day for a woman and two drinks for a man. One drink is equal to 12 ounces of beer, 5 ounces of wine, or 1½ ounces of 80-proof spirits. If you don't drink, don't start.

SCHEDULE REGULAR MEDICAL CHECKUPS

Make an appointment with your healthcare professional for a heart checkup to find out your numbers and discuss your personal risk for cardiovascular disease.

slow cooking

Traditionally, cooks have turned to their slow cookers to prepare basic chilis, stews, soups, and dips, but the truth is your slow cooker is capable of so much more! You can use this traditional appliance to enjoy modern healthy dishes that include interesting and complex flavors like Chicken Korma (page 16), an Indian dish chock-full of exotic spices, and Madeira Flank Steak (page 20), which uses wine to create a rich-tasting sauce. You can also use your slow cooker to make delicious dishes that you might not think to use your appliance for, such as Chayote Squash and Pepper Casserole (page 27) and Citrus-Cilantro Salmon (page 14).

Use your slow cooker to put a new twist on familiar family classics, too, such as Chicken Cacciatore with Pasta (page 18) and New Mexican Meat Loaf (page 22). Slow cooking not only helps you prepare healthy meals but also saves you time because the dishes need a minimum of hands-on attention. You shouldn't stir the food (unless a recipe calls for it), and you don't need to watch it or worry about it burning. Throw healthy ingredients into a crock, let them cook low and slow, and serve your family a delicious meal! You can save even more time as well as further reduce your kitchen "footprint" by cooking once and eating twice: make large quantities of your favorite dishes, eat some now, and refrigerate or freeze the rest for a quick meal at another time.

Slow cooking can save you money, too. Because slow cooking breaks down the connective tissue in less-expensive cuts of meat, you won't need to spend a lot to enjoy a savory stew or roast.

So how do slow cookers really work? They surround food with low, steady heat, resulting in long, slow cooking without burning. The moist heat cooks foods until they're falling-apart tender. Covering the crock with the lid creates a moisture-tight seal that ensures that the heat and steam released by the contents remain in the crock. This seal is important to maintain a steady temperature inside, and it also helps distribute and blend flavors as vapor condenses on the lid and returns to the food in the pot.

Tools & Equipment Needed: Slow cooker

TIPS:

- Make the cooker work with your schedule. Try prepping a recipe the night before you plan to cook the food. Cover and refrigerate the prepped food in airtight containers overnight, fill the crock in the morning, and turn on the heat and, if your cooker has one, the timer.

- Prep foods so they will cook the most efficiently and evenly. For example, take care to cut carrots into pieces of the same approximate size so all the carrots in the dish will be done at the same time.

- Trim the visible fat from poultry and lean meats, and in most cases discard the skin before cooking the poultry (if skin isn't discarded before cooking, do so before eating), both to cut down on unhealthy fats in the finished dish and for more even cooking.

- Resist the urge to stir or sneak a peek. Open the lid only when the recipe directs you to, complete the necessary actions, such as adding ingredients, and re-cover the cooker quickly. Every time you break the seal between the cover and the crock, you lose heat.

- See safety tips for slow cooking on page 283.

italian vegetable soup with farro

This hearty soup combines smooth broth and chunky vegetables with tender beans and chewy farro (FAHR-oh), an ancient grain also known as emmer. It all adds up to a rich, comforting one-dish meal with a variety of flavors in every spoonful.

SERVES 6 | 1⅓ cups per serving

. . . .

In a 5- to 7-quart round or oval slow cooker, make one layer each, in order, of the carrots, fennel, onions, zucchini, minced garlic, and sprigs of rosemary. Sprinkle the farro over all. Top with the beans and tomatoes with liquid. Pour in the broth. Cook, covered, on low for 9 to 10 hours or on high for 4½ to 5½ hours.

About 5 minutes before serving time, in a food processor or blender, pulse the remaining 1 garlic clove 5 times, or until finely minced. Add the basil. Pulse 10 times, or until finely chopped. In a small bowl, stir together the basil mixture and Parmesan.

Just before serving, discard the rosemary stems, stirring the leaves back into the soup. Sprinkle the soup with the basil mixture.

2 large carrots, cut into ½-inch slices

1 large fennel bulb, coarsely chopped

2 medium onions, coarsely chopped

2 medium zucchini, halved lengthwise if wide, cut into ½-inch slices

4 large garlic cloves, minced, and 1 medium garlic clove, left whole, divided use

2 sprigs of fresh rosemary

½ cup uncooked farro, rinsed and drained

1 15.5-ounce can no-salt-added cannellini beans, rinsed and drained

1 14.5-ounce can no-salt-added diced tomatoes, undrained

4 cups fat-free, low-sodium vegetable broth

———————

1 cup loosely packed fresh basil

½ cup shredded or grated Parmesan cheese

per serving

calories 215	sodium 214 mg
total fat 3.0 g	carbohydrates 37 g
saturated fat 1.0 g	fiber 8 g
trans fat 0.0 g	sugars 8 g
polyunsaturated fat 0.0 g	protein 12 g
monounsaturated fat 0.5 g	dietary exchanges: 1½ starch,
cholesterol 5 mg	3 vegetable, ½ lean meat

meatball soup with spinach and parmesan

It takes a few extra minutes to brown the meatballs before adding them to the slow cooker, but it will be well worth the effort. The seasoned, caramelized meatballs cook to tender perfection in a soup bursting with the freshness of sweet tomatoes, spinach, and basil. A final sprinkle of Parmesan adds the crowning touch.

SERVES 4 | 1 cup (with 4 meatballs) per serving

. . . .

Lightly spray a 3- to 4½-quart round or oval slow cooker with cooking spray. Set aside.

In a medium bowl, using your hands or a spoon, combine the ground beef, oatmeal, egg white, Italian seasoning, onion powder, and red pepper flakes. Shape into sixteen 1-inch balls. Transfer to a large plate.

In a large nonstick skillet, heat 1 teaspoon oil over medium-high heat, swirling to coat the bottom. Cook the meatballs for 2 to 3 minutes, or until browned on all sides, turning occasionally.

Meanwhile, in the slow cooker, stir together the tomatoes, water, bell pepper, onion, wine, and bouillon.

Gently add the meatballs, spooning some of the tomato mixture over them. Cook, covered, on low for 7½ to 8 hours or on high for 3 hours 45 minutes to 4 hours, or until the bell pepper is very tender.

Cooking spray

8 ounces extra-lean ground beef

⅓ cup uncooked oatmeal

1 large egg white

1 teaspoon dried Italian seasoning, crumbled, or dried oregano, crumbled

½ teaspoon onion powder

¼ to ½ teaspoon crushed red pepper flakes

1 teaspoon olive oil and 2 teaspoons olive oil (extra virgin preferred), divided use

2 cups grape tomatoes, halved

2 cups water

1 large green bell pepper, chopped

1 medium onion, diced

½ cup dry red wine (regular or nonalcoholic)

2 packets (2 teaspoons) salt-free instant beef bouillon

(continued)

Gently stir in the spinach, basil, salt, and the remaining 2 teaspoons oil. Let stand, uncovered, for 10 minutes so the flavors blend. Just before serving, sprinkle the soup with the Parmesan.

1 ounce baby spinach, coarsely chopped (about 1 cup)

¼ cup chopped fresh basil

⅛ teaspoon salt

¼ cup shredded or grated Parmesan cheese

per serving

calories 233	sodium 241 mg
total fat 8.5 g	carbohydrates 17 g
saturated fat 2.5 g	fiber 4 g
trans fat 0.0 g	sugars 7 g
polyunsaturated fat 1.0 g	protein 18 g
monounsaturated fat 4.0 g	dietary exchanges: ½ starch,
cholesterol 35 mg	2 vegetable, 2 lean meat,
	½ fat

COOK'S TIP: To handle the meatballs easily while turning them, use two utensils, such as two spoons or forks, or one of each.

SLOW COOKING BONUS: *Don't put away those oats so fast! Once dinner is done, clean out the slow cooker and get a head start on the morning by making oatmeal overnight. Lightly spray a 3- to 4½-quart round or oval slow cooker with cooking spray. In the slow cooker, stir together 2 cups uncooked oatmeal (steel-cut or rolled) and 4½ cups water. Stir in fruit and seasonings, if desired (for example, chopped apple and ground cinnamon). Cook, covered, on low for 6 to 7 hours, or until the oatmeal is tender and the water is absorbed.*

bayou gumbo

This recipe uses the convenience of the slow cooker but boasts a depth of flavor you can only get by first browning the flour and sautéing the vegetables. Serve over fluffy brown rice.

SERVES 6 | 1 cup per serving

In a large skillet, cook the flour over medium-high heat for 4 to 5 minutes, or until golden brown, stirring frequently. Watch carefully so it doesn't burn. In a medium bowl, whisk together the flour and 1 cup water until completely blended. Pour into a 3- to 4½-quart round or oval slow cooker.

In the same skillet, heat the oil, still over medium-high heat, swirling to coat the bottom. Cook the celery, onion, and bell pepper for 5 to 6 minutes, or until tender-crisp, stirring occasionally. Stir in the okra. Cook for 2 to 3 minutes, or until tender-crisp, stirring occasionally. Transfer the celery mixture to the slow cooker.

Stir in the tomatoes with liquid, seasoning blend, garlic powder, cumin, hot-pepper

⅓ cup all-purpose flour

1 cup water and 1 cup water, divided use

1 tablespoon canola or corn oil

2 medium ribs of celery, chopped

1 small onion, diced

1 medium green bell pepper, diced

2 cups sliced okra

1 14.5-ounce can no-salt-added diced tomatoes, undrained

1 tablespoon salt-free Creole or Cajun seasoning blend

1 teaspoon garlic powder

1 teaspoon ground cumin

½ teaspoon Louisiana-style hot-pepper sauce (optional)

(continued)

sauce, salt, pepper, and the remaining 1 cup water. Cook, covered, on low for 6 to 7 hours or on high for 2½ to 3½ hours. Stir in the fish and shrimp. Cook, covered, on low for 1 hour or on high for 30 minutes, or until the fish flakes easily when tested with a fork and the shrimp are pink on the outside.

¼ teaspoon salt

¼ teaspoon pepper (freshly ground preferred)

8 ounces catfish fillets, rinsed, patted dry, and cut into ¾-inch pieces

8 ounces raw medium shrimp, peeled, rinsed, and patted dry

per serving

calories 152
total fat 4.0 g
  saturated fat 0.5 g
  trans fat 0.0 g
  polyunsaturated fat 1.0 g
  monounsaturated fat 2.0 g
cholesterol 70 mg

sodium 223 mg
carbohydrates 15 g
  fiber 3 g
  sugars 4 g
protein 14 g

dietary exchanges: ½ starch, 2 vegetable, 2 lean meat

COOK'S TIP ON CREOLE OR CAJUN SEASONING BLEND: To make your own salt-free Creole or Cajun seasoning blend, stir together ½ teaspoon each of chili powder, ground cumin, onion powder, garlic powder, paprika, and pepper, and, if you wish, ⅛ teaspoon of cayenne. This makes just over 1 tablespoon of the blend; double or triple the amounts if you like, and keep the extra in a container with a shaker top to use in other seafood, poultry, meat, and vegetable dishes.

citrus-cilantro salmon

Slow cooking is an ideal way to ensure that your salmon is perfectly done every time, and it requires very little cleanup. Sweet, refreshing orange contrasts beautifully with the smokiness of cumin and the heat of chili powder and red pepper flakes.

SERVES 4 | 3 ounces fish per serving

Lightly spray a 3- to 4½-quart round or oval slow cooker with cooking spray. Arrange the orange rounds in the slow cooker, overlapping them slightly. Place the fish on the orange rounds with the skin side down. Brush the oil over the fish. In a small bowl, stir together the chili powder, cumin, salt, and red pepper flakes. Sprinkle the mixture over the fish. Cook, covered, on high for 1 hour to 1 hour 15 minutes, or until the fish is the desired doneness.

Transfer the fish to plates. Sprinkle with the cilantro. Serve with the lemon wedges.

Cooking spray

1 medium orange, cut into 4 rounds

4 salmon fillets with skin (about 5 ounces each), rinsed and patted dry

1 teaspoon canola or corn oil

1 teaspoon chili powder

½ teaspoon ground cumin

¼ teaspoon salt

⅛ teaspoon crushed red pepper flakes

¼ cup chopped fresh cilantro

1 medium lemon or lime, cut into 4 wedges

per serving

calories 161	sodium 244 mg
total fat 6.5 g	carbohydrates 1 g
saturated fat 1.0 g	fiber 0 g
trans fat 0.0 g	sugars 0 g
polyunsaturated fat 1.5 g	protein 24 g
monounsaturated fat 2.5 g	dietary exchanges: 3 lean meat
cholesterol 53 mg	

chilean chicken and vegetable stew

Corn is a popular ingredient in Chilean cuisine and is often used in meat dishes. In this entrée, it also acts as a thickener in the form of cornmeal. Bone-in chicken adds extra flavor to stews, but remember to discard the skin before cooking to eliminate much of the saturated fat.

SERVES 6 | 3 ounces chicken and 1 cup vegetable mixture per serving

. . . .

In a 3- to 4½-quart round or oval slow cooker, make one layer each, in order, of the onion, potatoes, sweet potato, bell pepper, green beans, and corn. Place the chicken on the corn.

In a large bowl, whisk together the remaining ingredients except the cilantro. Pour into the slow cooker. Gently press down on the chicken so it's partially covered by the broth mixture. Cook, covered, on low for 6 to 8 hours or on high for 3 to 4 hours, or until the chicken is no longer pink in the center, the onion is soft, and the vegetables are tender.

Just before serving, sprinkle with the cilantro.

1	large onion, cut into 1-inch wedges
12	ounces small red potatoes, cut into 1-inch wedges
1	large sweet potato, cut into 1½-inch pieces
1	large red bell pepper, cut into 1½-inch pieces
4	ounces green beans, trimmed and cut into 1½-inch pieces
1	cup frozen whole-kernel corn, thawed
1	2½- to 3-pound chicken, cut into serving pieces, skin, all visible fat, neck, and giblets discarded
3	cups fat-free, low-sodium chicken broth
⅓	cup cornmeal
2	tablespoons ground cumin
1	tablespoon ground coriander
½	teaspoon pepper
½	cup chopped fresh cilantro

per serving

calories 296	sodium 155 mg
total fat 4.0 g	carbohydrates 39 g
saturated fat 1.0 g	fiber 6 g
trans fat 0.0 g	sugars 8 g
polyunsaturated fat 1.0 g	protein 28 g
monounsaturated fat 1.0 g	dietary exchanges: 2 starch,
cholesterol 69 mg	2 vegetable, 3 lean meat

chicken korma

Your kitchen will fill with the aroma of exotic spices when you prepare this Indian dish. First, though, the chicken needs to marinate for as little as one hour or as long as overnight. Serve this entrée over basmati rice to catch all the sauce.

SERVES 8 | 3 ounces chicken and ½ cup sauce per serving

. . . .

Lightly spray a 3- to 4½-quart round or oval slow cooker with cooking spray. Set aside.

In a food processor or blender, process the chopped onion, ¼ cup almonds, jalapeño, gingerroot, water, garlic, coriander, and salt until smooth. Transfer to a large bowl.

Put the chicken in a large shallow glass dish. Using a rubber scraper, spread all the chopped onion mixture over both sides of the chicken. Cover the dish tightly and refrigerate for 1 hour to overnight.

In a medium skillet, heat the oil over medium-high heat, swirling to coat the bottom. Cook the sliced onion for 10 minutes, or until golden, stirring frequently and adjusting the heat as necessary so it doesn't burn. Reduce the heat to low.

Stir in the cinnamon stick, curry powder, garam masala, and turmeric. Cook for 1 minute, stirring frequently so the spices don't burn.

Meanwhile, put the cornstarch in a small bowl. Add the broth, whisking to dissolve.

Stir the cornstarch mixture into the sliced onion mixture. Increase the heat to medium

Cooking spray

1 large onion, coarsely chopped, and 1 large onion, thinly sliced, divided use

¼ cup slivered or sliced almonds

1 small fresh jalapeño, seeds and ribs discarded, diced (see Cook's Tip on page 45)

1 1-inch piece peeled gingerroot, sliced crosswise

2 tablespoons water

2 medium garlic cloves, chopped

1 teaspoon ground coriander

⅜ teaspoon salt

8 boneless, skinless chicken breast halves (about 4 ounces each), all visible fat discarded

2 teaspoons canola or corn oil

1 cinnamon stick (about 3 inches long), broken in half

1 tablespoon curry powder

1 teaspoon garam masala

½ teaspoon ground turmeric

2 tablespoons cornstarch

1 cup fat-free, low-sodium chicken broth

(continued)

high. Bring to a boil, stirring constantly. Reduce the heat and simmer for 1 minute, or until the sauce is thickened, stirring constantly.

Arrange half the chicken, including any remaining chopped onion mixture, in the slow cooker. Pour half the sauce over the chicken. Repeat with the remaining chicken and sauce. Cook, covered, on low for 3½ to 5½ hours, or until the chicken is no longer pink in the center.

Quickly pour the peas over the sauce (don't stir) and re-cover the slow cooker. Cook for 30 minutes, or until the peas are tender.

Transfer the chicken to serving bowls, leaving the sauce in the slow cooker. Stir the yogurt into the sauce. Spoon over the chicken. Sprinkle with the remaining 2 tablespoons almonds, then with the cilantro.

per serving	
calories 261	sodium 324 mg
total fat 7.0 g	carbohydrates 18 g
saturated fat 1.0 g	fiber 5 g
trans fat 0.0 g	sugars 7 g
polyunsaturated fat 1.5 g	protein 32 g
monounsaturated fat 3.0 g	dietary exchanges: ½ starch,
cholesterol 73 mg	1 vegetable, 3½ lean meat

16 ounces frozen green peas, thawed

1 cup fat-free plain yogurt (Greek preferred), at room temperature

2 tablespoons sliced almonds, dry-roasted

2 tablespoons chopped fresh cilantro

COOK'S TIP: This recipe calls for the low setting as the only option because the flavors need the longer cooking time to develop.

COOK'S TIP ON GARAM MASALA: Garam masala is an Indian blend of spices usually including pepper, cinnamon, cloves, cumin, and hot chiles. The name means "warm" or "hot," indicating that dishes containing this blend are spicy. It's usually found in the spice or ethnic-foods aisle of grocery stores.

chicken cacciatore with pasta

This Italian mainstay has been updated for today's modern cook. *Buon appetito!*

SERVES 6 | 1½ cups cacciatore and ½ cup pasta per serving

. . . .

Lightly spray a 3- to 4½-quart round or oval slow cooker with cooking spray. Set aside.

In a small bowl, whisk together the flour and vinegar until the mixture forms a smooth paste. Gradually whisk in the wine.

In the slow cooker, stir the remaining cacciatore ingredients together. Stir in the wine mixture. Cook, covered, on low for 7 to 8 hours or on high for 3 to 4 hours.

Shortly before serving time, prepare the pasta using the package directions, omitting the salt. Drain well in a colander.

Serve the cacciatore over the pasta. Sprinkle with the Parmesan.

Cooking spray

CACCIATORE

- 1 tablespoon all-purpose flour
- 1 tablespoon balsamic vinegar
- ½ cup Chianti or other dry red wine (regular or nonalcoholic)
- 1½ pounds boneless, skinless chicken breasts, all visible fat discarded, cut into ¾-inch cubes
- 8 ounces brown (cremini) mushrooms, sliced (about 2½ cups)
- 1 14.5-ounce can no-salt-added stewed tomatoes, undrained
- 1 14.5-ounce can no-salt-added diced tomatoes, undrained
- 6 ounces no-salt-added tomato paste
- 1 medium onion, halved, thinly sliced, and separated into half-rings
- ½ medium green bell pepper, chopped
- 1 tablespoon dried Italian seasoning, crumbled
- 2 large garlic cloves, minced
- 2 teaspoons crushed red pepper flakes
- ¼ teaspoon salt

- 6 ounces dried whole-grain spaghetti
- 2 tablespoons shredded or grated Parmesan cheese

per serving

calories 342	sodium 296 mg
total fat 4.5 g	carbohydrates 41 g
saturated fat 1.0 g	fiber 7 g
trans fat 0.0 g	sugars 14 g
polyunsaturated fat 1.0 g	protein 32 g
monounsaturated fat 1.5 g	
cholesterol 74 mg	dietary exchanges: 1½ starch, 4 vegetable, 3 lean meat

rosemary steak smothered in onions

This recipe takes advantage of the long cooking process to tenderize the round steak. Don't be afraid of the quantity of onions. As they cook, they will wilt and turn golden, creating a silky topping for the steak that will melt in your mouth.

SERVES 4 | 3 ounces beef and ⅓ cup onions per serving

. . . .

Lightly spray a 3- to 4½-quart round or oval slow cooker with cooking spray. Set aside.

Sprinkle the pepper and salt over both sides of the beef.

In a large nonstick skillet, heat the oil over medium-high heat, swirling to coat the bottom. Cook the beef for 3 to 4 minutes, or until browned, turning once halfway through.

Meanwhile, put half the onions in the slow cooker. Place the beef on the onions.

Increase the stovetop heat to high. In the same skillet, bring the water to a boil, scraping to dislodge any browned bits. Boil for 1 to 2 minutes, or until reduced by half (to about 2 tablespoons). Pour over the beef in the slow cooker.

Put the rosemary on the beef. Scatter the remaining onions over the rosemary and beef.

Cook, covered, on low for 4 to 6 hours or on high for 2 to 3 hours, or until the beef is fork-tender.

Discard the rosemary. Serve the beef topped with the onions and drizzled with the cooking juices.

Cooking spray

½ teaspoon pepper

¼ teaspoon salt

1 1-pound boneless round steak, cut into 4 pieces, all visible fat discarded

1½ teaspoons olive oil

2 large sweet onions, such as Vidalia, Maui, or Oso Sweet, sliced (about 4 cups)

¼ cup water

4 sprigs of fresh rosemary

per serving

calories 187	sodium 181 mg
total fat 5.5 g	carbohydrates 7 g
saturated fat 1.5 g	fiber 1 g
trans fat 0.0 g	sugars 3 g
polyunsaturated fat 0.5 g	protein 26 g
monounsaturated fat 2.5 g	dietary exchanges:
cholesterol 64 mg	1 vegetable, 3 lean meat

madeira flank steak

Slow cooking the mushrooms makes them wonderfully velvety. Add Madeira, a fortified wine, to the sauce. It will be so rich-tasting, your guests will think you're a culinary genius!

SERVES 4 | 3 ounces beef and ¼ cup sauce per serving

Lightly spray a 3- to 4½-quart round or oval slow cooker with cooking spray. Set aside.

In a large nonstick skillet, heat 1 teaspoon oil over medium-high heat, swirling to coat the bottom. Cook the beef for 4 minutes. Turn over the beef. Cook for 1 minute. Transfer to a large plate. Cover and refrigerate to chill completely so it won't overcook.

In the same skillet, heat the remaining 1 teaspoon oil, swirling to coat the bottom. Cook the shallots for 3 minutes, or until beginning to brown, stirring frequently. Transfer to the slow cooker. Stir in the mushrooms.

Pour ¼ cup Madeira and the water into the skillet, scraping to dislodge any browned bits. Stir into the shallot mixture in the slow cooker. Cook, covered, on low for 3½ to 4 hours or on high for 1 hour 45 minutes to 2 hours, or until the mushrooms are very soft.

Cooking spray

1 teaspoon canola or corn oil and 1 teaspoon canola or corn oil, divided use

1 1-pound flank steak, all visible fat discarded

4 medium shallots, chopped (about 1 cup)

8 ounces shiitake mushrooms (stems discarded) or mixed exotic mushrooms, thinly sliced

¼ cup Madeira or fat-free, low-sodium beef broth and ¼ cup Madeira or fat-free, low-sodium beef broth, divided use

2 tablespoons water

2 tablespoons light tub margarine

⅛ teaspoon salt

2 tablespoons chopped fresh parsley

If using the low setting, change it to high. Quickly stir in the margarine, salt, and the remaining ¼ cup Madeira. Place the beef on top. Pour in any accumulated juices from the beef. Re-cover the slow cooker. Cook for 20 to 30 minutes, or until the beef is heated through.

Transfer the beef to a cutting board, leaving the sauce in the slow cooker. Change the setting to low. Cut the beef diagonally across the grain into thin slices. Just before serving, spoon the sauce over the beef. Sprinkle with the parsley.

COOK'S TIP: You can use sliced button mushrooms in place of the shiitake or mixed exotic mushrooms, but they will have a bit less flavor.

per serving

calories 274
total fat 11.5 g
  saturated fat 3.0 g
  trans fat 0.0 g
  polyunsaturated fat 1.5 g
  monounsaturated fat 6.0 g
cholesterol 48 mg

sodium 167 mg
carbohydrates 9 g
  fiber 1 g
  sugars 4 g
protein 25 g

dietary exchanges: 1 vegetable, 3 lean meat, ½ fat

new mexican meat loaf

New Mexico is famous for its green-chile cheeseburgers, which were the inspiration for this flavorful meat loaf. It's studded with bits of mild, roasted poblano pepper and provides a surprise of melted cheese in the middle. During the meat loaf's standing time, use your microwave to make Broccoli with Jalapeño and Garlic (page 45) for a spicy side.

SERVES 8 | 1 slice or wedge per serving

. . . .

Fold an 18-inch-long piece of aluminum foil lengthwise in thirds. Place the foil in a 3- to 4½-quart oval slow cooker so it runs the length of the cooker and hangs over the two short sides. The foil will help you remove the cooked meat loaf from the slow cooker later. Lightly spray the foil and the inside of the slow cooker with cooking spray.

Put ½ cup of the tomatoes and all the reserved liquid in a large bowl. Set aside the remaining tomatoes.

Add the beef, onion, bread crumbs, ¼ cup poblano pepper, the egg white, 2 tablespoons cilantro, the ancho powder, oregano, cumin, garlic powder, and salt to the tomato mixture. Using your hands or a spoon, gently combine the ingredients. Transfer half the mixture to a flat surface. Depending on the shape of your slow cooker, shape into a loaf that will fit in the slow cooker and leave about a 1-inch space all around between it and the side of the crock.

Using your fingertips, gently press the loaf to form a 1-inch trough down the center. Put

Cooking spray

1 **14.5-ounce can no-salt-added petite diced tomatoes, liquid reserved, divided use**

1½ **pounds extra-lean ground beef**

½ **cup finely chopped sweet onion, such as Vidalia, Maui, or Oso Sweet**

½ **cup plain dry whole-wheat bread crumbs (lowest sodium available)**

¼ **cup chopped roasted poblano pepper and ¼ cup chopped roasted poblano pepper (about a 4-ounce poblano), divided use (see Cook's Tip on page 45)**

1 **large egg white**

2 **tablespoons chopped fresh cilantro and 2 tablespoons chopped fresh cilantro, divided use**

2 **teaspoons ancho powder or chili powder**

1½ **teaspoons dried oregano, crumbled**

1 **teaspoon ground cumin**

1 **teaspoon garlic powder**

(continued)

the cheese in the trough. Cover the loaf with the remaining half of the beef mixture, gently pressing the edges together to seal well. Transfer to the slow cooker, placing the meat loaf so the foil strip is under the middle of it. Cook, covered, on high for 1 hour. Change the setting to low and cook, covered, for 3 hours.

Meanwhile, in a small bowl, stir together the ketchup and the remaining tomatoes, ¼ cup poblano pepper, and 2 tablespoons cilantro.

When the meat loaf is ready, quickly spoon the ketchup mixture over the top and re-cover the slow cooker. Cook on low for 1 hour, or until the meat loaf registers 160°F on an instant-read thermometer, testing where there is no cheese. Grasping the ends of the foil, carefully lift the meat loaf from the slow cooker. Transfer to a cutting board. Let stand for 10 minutes before slicing or cutting into wedges.

¼ **teaspoon salt**

½ **cup shredded low-fat 4-cheese Mexican blend**

———

¼ **cup no-salt-added ketchup**

COOK'S TIP: If you don't have an oval slow cooker, you can still make this dish. Just make your meat loaf round!

COOK'S TIP ON ROASTING POBLANO PEPPERS: To roast a poblano pepper, preheat the broiler. Halve the pepper lengthwise and discard the seeds and ribs (be sure to wear plastic gloves or to wash your hands thoroughly with warm, soapy water after handling the pepper). Place the halves with the skin side up on a baking sheet lined with aluminum foil. Broil 4 to 5 inches from the heat for 7 to 9 minutes, or until the skin is blackened and blistered. Remove the baking sheet from the oven and wrap the foil around the pepper. Let stand for 15 to 20 minutes, or until cool enough to handle. To remove the skin with ease, pull from the pointed end of the pepper.

per serving

calories 185	sodium 230 mg
total fat 6.0 g	carbohydrates 11 g
saturated fat 2.5 g	fiber 2 g
trans fat 0.5 g	sugars 4 g
polyunsaturated fat 0.5 g	protein 22 g
monounsaturated fat 2.0 g	
cholesterol 51 mg	

dietary exchanges: ½ starch, 3 lean meat

hummus and veggie lasagna roll-ups

Navy bean hummus with lasagna? The garlicky bean mixture makes a surprisingly delicious stand-in for the usual ricotta filling. You can make the hummus and the pasta the day before serving the roll-ups to reduce the hands-on time before firing up the slow cooker.

SERVES 4 | 1 roll-up and ½ cup sauce per serving

Lightly spray a 4- to 6-quart round or oval slow cooker with cooking spray. Put the zucchini, bell pepper, and oil in the slow cooker, stirring to combine. Cook, covered, on low for 5 to 5½ hours or on high for 2½ hours to 2 hours 45 minutes, or until the bell pepper is browned on the edges and very tender.

Meanwhile, prepare the noodles using the package directions, omitting the salt. Drain well in a colander. Spread out on a dish towel. Pat dry with paper towels. Let the noodles cool, about 10 minutes. Transfer them to a container large enough for them to lie flat. (To prevent them from sticking together, separate the noodles with cooking parchment or wax paper or only slightly overlap them.) Cover and refrigerate until needed.

In a food processor or blender, process the beans, water, and garlic until smooth. Transfer the hummus to a large bowl. Stir in the spinach, ½ cup parsley, the egg whites, 2 tablespoons Parmesan, and the basil. Cover and refrigerate until needed.

Shortly before the zucchini mixture is ready, place the noodles on a work surface. Spread

Cooking spray

- 1 medium zucchini, quartered lengthwise and cut crosswise into 1-inch pieces
- 1 medium green bell pepper, cut into 1-inch squares
- 1 teaspoon canola or corn oil
- 4 dried whole-grain lasagna noodles
- 1 15.5-ounce can no-salt-added navy beans, rinsed and drained
- 2 tablespoons water
- 2 medium garlic cloves, minced
- 10 ounces frozen chopped spinach, thawed, drained, and squeezed until very dry
- ½ cup chopped fresh parsley and 2 tablespoons chopped fresh parsley, divided use
- 2 large egg whites
- 2 tablespoons shredded or grated Parmesan cheese and 1 tablespoon shredded or grated Parmesan cheese, divided use
- 1½ tablespoons dried basil, crumbled

(continued)

½ cup hummus on each noodle. Gently roll up from one of the short ends.

When the zucchini mixture has cooked, quickly stir it. Place the roll-ups with the seam side down on the zucchini mixture. Pour the spaghetti sauce over the roll-ups. Re-cover the slow cooker. Cook on low for 2 hours or on high for 1 hour, or until the roll-ups are heated through and the sauce is bubbly around the edge. Sprinkle with the mozzarella and the remaining 2 tablespoons parsley and 1 tablespoon Parmesan. Turn off the slow cooker. Let stand, covered, for 5 to 10 minutes so the cheeses melt slightly.

2 cups meatless spaghetti sauce (lowest sodium available)

¼ cup shredded low-fat mozzarella cheese

COOK'S TIP: Make a double recipe of the hummus so you'll have some to enjoy with baked whole-grain pita wedges or baby carrots.

COOK'S TIP: You can wait until about 45 minutes before the zucchini mixture has finished cooking to boil the noodles and make the hummus, if that works better with your schedule.

SLOW COOKING BONUS: *If you prefer to use dried beans in this and other recipes, they cook up wonderfully in the slow cooker. Rinse and drain dried beans, sorting for stones and shriveled beans. If using kidney beans, boil them in water for 10 minutes to remove toxins that can cause intestinal distress (if you're using other beans, there's no need to boil them first). Put 1 to 2 cups of beans in a 3- to 4½-quart round or oval slow cooker (or make a bigger batch using a larger slow cooker). Pour in enough water to cover the beans by 2 inches. Cook, covered, on low for 6 to 8 hours or on high for 3 to 4 hours.*

per serving

calories 293	sodium 309 mg
total fat 5.0 g	carbohydrates 47 g
saturated fat 1.0 g	fiber 11 g
trans fat 0.0 g	sugars 11 g
polyunsaturated fat 1.0 g	protein 19 g
monounsaturated fat 2.0 g	dietary exchanges:
cholesterol 5 mg	2½ starch, 2 vegetable,
	1½ lean meat

savory lentil stew with polenta

This satisfying, hearty stew served over whole-grain polenta features fiber-rich lentils in a well-seasoned tomato sauce. The slow cooker makes it nearly effortless.

SERVES 6 | 1½ cups stew and ½ cup polenta per serving

. . . .

In a 4- to 6-quart round or oval slow cooker, stir together all the stew ingredients except the vinegar. Cook, covered, on low for 6 to 7 hours or on high for 3 to 4 hours, or until the lentils are very tender.

About 30 minutes before serving time, prepare the polenta. In a large saucepan or stockpot, bring the water to a boil over high heat. Using a long-handled whisk, carefully whisk the water to create a swirl. Slowly pour the cornmeal in a steady stream into the swirl, whisking constantly. After all the cornmeal is added, reduce the heat and simmer for 15 to 20 minutes, or until the polenta is the desired consistency, stirring occasionally. Spoon the polenta into bowls.

Just before serving, stir the balsamic vinegar into the stew. Ladle the stew over the polenta.

STEW

- 1 28-ounce can no-salt-added crushed tomatoes, undrained
- 2 cups fat-free, low-sodium vegetable broth
- 1½ cups brown lentils, sorted for stones and shriveled lentils, rinsed, and drained
- 2 medium onions, sliced
- 2 medium ribs of celery, thinly sliced
- 2 medium carrots, diced
- 1 medium red bell pepper, diced
- ¼ cup dry-packed sun-dried tomatoes, thinly sliced
- 2 tablespoons no-salt-added tomato paste
- 3 medium garlic cloves, minced
- 1 teaspoon dried oregano, crumbled
- 1 tablespoon balsamic vinegar

POLENTA

- 4 cups water
- 1 cup cornmeal

---

per serving

calories 339
total fat 1.0 g
  saturated fat 0.0 g
  trans fat 0.0 g
  polyunsaturated fat 0.5 g
  monounsaturated fat 0.0 g
cholesterol 0 mg

sodium 72 mg
carbohydrates 67 g
  fiber 17 g
  sugars 14 g
protein 18 g

dietary exchanges: 3 starch, 4 vegetable, 1 lean meat

chayote squash and pepper casserole

The chayote (chai-OH-tay) squash is about the size and shape of a large pear and has a relatively neutral taste, so it blends nicely with ingredients that have a more assertive flavor, such as poblano peppers and Parmesan cheese.

SERVES 4 | ¾ cup per serving

Lightly spray a 3- to 4½-quart round or oval slow cooker with cooking spray. In the slow cooker, make one layer each, in order, of the poblano, onion, and squash. Drizzle the oil over all. Sprinkle the oregano and garlic powder over all. Don't stir. Cook, covered, on low for 4½ hours or on high for 2½ hours, or until the squash is tender.

Meanwhile, in a small skillet, toast the panko over medium-high heat for 1 minute, or until beginning to brown, stirring constantly. Watch carefully so it doesn't burn. Transfer to a small bowl. Stir in the Parmesan and salt.

Gently stir together the poblano mixture. Sprinkle with the panko mixture. Let stand for 5 minutes before serving.

Cooking spray

1 large poblano pepper, thinly sliced, or 1 medium green bell pepper, thinly sliced (see Cook's Tip on page 45)

1 cup diced onion

2 medium chayote squash, peeled, halved, pitted, and each half cut lengthwise into 4 wedges

1 tablespoon olive oil (extra virgin preferred)

1 teaspoon dried oregano, crumbled

½ teaspoon garlic powder

2 tablespoons whole-wheat panko (Japanese-style bread crumbs)

2 tablespoons shredded or grated Parmesan cheese

⅛ teaspoon salt

per serving

calories 90	sodium 123 mg
total fat 4.5 g	carbohydrates 12 g
saturated fat 1.0 g	fiber 3 g
trans fat 0.0 g	sugars 4 g
polyunsaturated fat 0.5 g	protein 3 g
monounsaturated fat 2.5 g	dietary exchanges:
cholesterol 2 mg	2 vegetable, 1 fat

southwestern sweet potatoes

Not your run-of-the-mill mashed sweet potatoes, these offer a bit of tanginess and spiciness with the unexpected and exciting addition of lime and chipotle. Serve with Mini Meat Loaves (page 257) or Pork Medallions with Mango Mojo (page 86), or enjoy them as a fuss-free side dish on Thanksgiving.

SERVES 4 | ½ cup per serving

Put the sweet potatoes in a 3- to 4½-quart round or oval slow cooker.

In a small bowl, stir together the remaining ingredients. Pour over the sweet potatoes. Cook, covered, on low for 5 to 6 hours or on high for 2½ to 3 hours, or until the sweet potatoes are very tender. Using a potato masher, mash the sweet potatoes to the desired consistency.

1½ pounds sweet potatoes (about 2 large), cut into 2-inch cubes (about 4½ cups)

⅓ cup fat-free, low-sodium chicken broth or water

1 tablespoon firmly packed light brown sugar

½ teaspoon grated lime zest

1 tablespoon fresh lime juice

2 medium garlic cloves, minced

¼ to ½ teaspoon chipotle powder

⅛ teaspoon salt

per serving

calories 149
total fat 0.0 g
  saturated fat 0.0 g
  trans fat 0.0 g
  polyunsaturated fat 0.0 g
  monounsaturated fat 0.0 g
cholesterol 0 mg

sodium 174 mg
carbohydrates 35 g
  fiber 5 g
  sugars 13 g
protein 3 g

dietary exchanges: 2½ starch

microwaving

Microwave a *meal*? In most kitchens, microwaves are used to reheat leftovers, pop popcorn, or heat frozen meals, but, yes, microwaves can actually *cook* food! Microwave cooking uses moist heat, making it an especially healthy way to prepare vegetables, fruits, and fish. That's because very little liquid is needed, so nutrients are retained. You can cook such a variety of healthy meals in a hurry using the microwave that you may never heat up your oven again. Meat loaf in 15 minutes? Try 15-Minute Turkey Meat Loaf (page 40). Homemade chicken soup in under 20 minutes? Give Chicken Parmesan Soup (page 32) a try. Fish in less than five minutes? You'll see for yourself with Tuna with Tomato-Tarragon Sauce (page 36).

How do microwaves cook food so fast? Contrary to the popular misconception, microwaves don't cook food from the inside out. Rather, they penetrate the food from every direction so food cooks much faster than it would in a traditional oven. Another benefit of microwave cooking is that foods don't stick, so cleanup is easy.

TO MICROWAVE:
Cooking, warming, or thawing food with heat produced as microwaves that cause water molecules in food to vibrate.

Tools & Equipment Needed: Microwave oven*; microwaveable bowls, plates, glass casserole dishes, baking dishes, and pie pan

*The recipes that follow have been tested using a 1,000-watt microwave oven. Cooking times should

be adjusted if yours has a higher or lower wattage. To check, look for a sticker on the doorjamb or the back of the microwave.

TIPS:

- If your microwave doesn't have a rotating plate, be sure to rotate food midway through the microwaving time for more even cooking and to eliminate cold spots where harmful bacteria can survive.

- Cover foods with a lid or microwaveable plastic wrap to trap steam and retain moisture. When the food is done, carefully uncover it away from you to prevent steam burns. If you use plastic wrap, poke a hole in the plastic to allow the steam to escape before removing the wrap.

- Add healthy sauces to microwaved foods such as Chicken with Creamy Arugula Pesto (page 37) to make them look more attractive since the microwave oven doesn't brown food.

- To avoid both overcooking and undercooking meat and poultry, use a meat thermometer to check doneness. Remove the meat or poultry from the oven before inserting the instant-read thermometer. Insert the thermometer into the center, or thickest part, of the meat, making sure the thermometer doesn't touch bone or fat.

- See microwaving safety tips on page 282.

chicken parmesan soup

When you need a nourishing soup in short order, this entrée fits the bill. Brimming with chicken and fresh vegetables, it's best served with crusty whole-grain rolls so you can sop up every delectable drop.

SERVES 4 | 1½ cups per serving

. . . .

In a 2-quart microwaveable casserole dish, stir together the chicken, zucchini, onion, and oil. Microwave, covered, on 100 percent power (high) for 6 minutes, stirring once halfway through (the chicken won't be done at this point).

Stir in the broth, tomatoes, oregano, red pepper flakes, and pepper. Microwave, covered, on 100 percent power (high) for 5 minutes. Stir. Microwave, covered, on 100 percent power (high) for 5 to 7 minutes, or until the chicken is no longer pink in the center and the vegetables are tender.

Just before serving, sprinkle with the Parmesan and basil.

12 ounces boneless, skinless chicken breasts, cut into ½-inch pieces

2 small zucchini, cut into ½-inch pieces

½ small onion, chopped

1 teaspoon olive oil

2 cups fat-free, low-sodium chicken broth

2 large tomatoes, peeled and diced

1 teaspoon dried oregano, crumbled

¼ teaspoon crushed red pepper flakes (optional)

⅛ teaspoon pepper (freshly ground preferred)

½ cup shredded or grated Parmesan cheese

¼ cup loosely packed chiffonade of fresh basil

per serving

calories 185
total fat 6.5 g
  saturated fat 2.5 g
  trans fat 0.0 g
  polyunsaturated fat 0.5 g
  monounsaturated fat 2.5 g
cholesterol 62 mg

sodium 308 mg
carbohydrates 7 g
  fiber 2 g
  sugars 4 g
protein 25 g

dietary exchanges:
1 vegetable, 3 lean meat

COOK'S TIP ON CHIFFONADES: To cut herbs or lettuce into a chiffonade, stack about 10 leaves in a neat pile. Roll up the pile lengthwise into a tight cylinder. Using a sharp knife, cut the cylinder crosswise to create thin strips.

chicken and bulgur salad with feta

This Mediterranean-influenced salad holds its flavor well. It's great to "make and take" for lunch at work or a potluck supper.

SERVES 4 | 1½ cups per serving

. . . .

Lightly spray a medium microwaveable bowl with cooking spray. Microwave the chicken, covered, on 100 percent power (high) for 2 minutes. Stir. Microwave on 100 percent power (high) for 1 minute, or until slightly pink in the center (the chicken will continue to cook while cooling). Drain well in a colander. Transfer to a serving bowl.

In the same medium microwaveable bowl, stir together the water and bulgur. Microwave, covered, on 100 percent power (high) for 7 to 8 minutes, or until the bulgur is just tender and the water is absorbed. Transfer to a fine-mesh sieve. Rinse with cold water to cool completely. Drain well. Return to the bowl. Fluff with a fork.

Stir the bulgur, tomatoes, onion, oil, rosemary, lemon zest, garlic, red pepper flakes, and salt together with the chicken. Gently stir in the feta.

Cooking spray

12 ounces boneless, skinless chicken breasts, all visible fat discarded, cut into bite-size pieces

2 cups hot water

1 cup uncooked instant, or fine-grain, bulgur

1 cup grape tomatoes, quartered

⅓ cup finely chopped red onion

1½ tablespoons olive oil (extra virgin preferred)

1 tablespoon finely chopped fresh rosemary

1 tablespoon grated lemon zest

2 medium garlic cloves, minced

⅛ teaspoon crushed red pepper flakes (optional)

⅛ teaspoon salt

½ cup crumbled low-fat feta cheese

per serving

calories 317	sodium 435 mg
total fat 10.0 g	carbohydrates 32 g
saturated fat 2.5 g	fiber 8 g
trans fat 0.0 g	sugars 3 g
polyunsaturated fat 1.5 g	protein 27 g
monounsaturated fat 5.0 g	dietary exchanges: 2 starch,
cholesterol 61 mg	1 vegetable, 3 lean meat

caribbean snapper with peach salsa

Spicy-sweet peach salsa enhances the delicate flavor of red snapper in this summery dish.

SERVES 4 | 3 ounces fish and ½ cup salsa per serving

In a medium bowl, gently stir together the peaches, bell pepper, shallots, jalapeño, cilantro, lime zest, and lime juice.

Cut eight 12-inch squares of cooking parchment. Place 1 fish fillet in the center of 1 square. Top with ½ cup salsa. Place a second square over the fish. Fold the edges of both squares together several times to seal the packets. Repeat to create the remaining packets.

Transfer the packets to a microwaveable 8-inch square baking dish. Microwave on 100 percent power (high) for 8 minutes. Carefully remove the dish from the microwave. Let stand for 2 minutes. Using the tines of a fork, carefully open a packet away from you (to prevent steam burns). If the fish flakes easily when tested with a fork, carefully open the remaining packets and serve. If the fish isn't cooked enough, reclose the packet and microwave all the packets on 100 percent power (high) for 1 to 2 minutes.

2 medium peaches, peeled and diced

½ medium red bell pepper, minced

2 medium shallots, minced

1 medium fresh jalapeño, seeds and ribs discarded, minced (see Cook's Tip on page 45)

1 tablespoon minced fresh cilantro

1½ teaspoons grated lime zest

1½ tablespoons fresh lime juice

4 red snapper fillets (about 4 ounces each), rinsed and patted dry

COOK'S TIP ON CLEANING AND FRESHENING A MICROWAVE OVEN: In a 2-cup glass measuring cup, stir together 1 cup water and several lemon slices or 2 tablespoons of fresh lemon juice. Microwave on 100 percent power (high) for 3 to 4 minutes, or until the water is boiling. Let the cup stand inside the microwave for 10 minutes. Remove it and wipe the inside of the microwave with paper towels. Repeat the process if necessary.

per serving

calories 152	sodium 51 mg
total fat 1.5 g	carbohydrates 11 g
saturated fat 0.5 g	fiber 2 g
trans fat 0.0 g	sugars 7 g
polyunsaturated fat 0.5 g	protein 24 g
monounsaturated fat 0.5 g	dietary exchanges: 1 fruit,
cholesterol 40 mg	3 lean meat

trout with grape tomato relish

Mild fish is topped with a relish highlighted by briny capers, bright parsley, and refreshing lemon zest. You can prepare the relish up to one day in advance.

SERVES 4 | 3 ounces fish and ¼ cup relish per serving

. . . .

In a small bowl, stir together the relish ingredients. Set aside.

Lightly spray a microwaveable glass casserole dish with a lid with cooking spray. Arrange the fish in a single layer in the dish, making sure that any thick pieces are closer to the edge of the dish. Spoon the lemon juice over the fish. In a small bowl, stir together the paprika, salt, and pepper. Sprinkle over the fish.

Microwave, covered, on 100 percent power (high) for 2 minutes. Let stand, covered, for 2 minutes. Carefully uncover the pan away from you (to prevent steam burns). If the fish flakes easily when tested with a fork, transfer to serving plates. If the fish isn't cooked enough, re-cover the dish and microwave on 100 percent power (high) for 1 minute. Let stand, covered, for 1 minute. Serve with the relish.

RELISH

⅔ cup grape tomatoes, diced

¼ cup finely chopped red onion

3 tablespoons capers, drained

2 tablespoons chopped Italian (flat-leaf) parsley

1 tablespoon olive oil (extra virgin preferred)

2 teaspoons grated lemon zest

————

Cooking spray

4 trout or other mild white fish fillets (about 4 ounces each), rinsed and patted dry

2 to 3 tablespoons fresh lemon juice

¼ teaspoon paprika

¼ teaspoon salt

¼ teaspoon pepper

per serving

calories 182	sodium 377 mg
total fat 7.5 g	carbohydrates 4 g
saturated fat 1.5 g	fiber 1 g
trans fat 0.0 g	sugars 2 g
polyunsaturated fat 2.0 g	protein 24 g
monounsaturated fat 4.0 g	dietary exchanges:
cholesterol 67 mg	1 vegetable, 3 lean meat

tuna with tomato-tarragon sauce

This time-saving recipe features a marinade that doubles as a sauce and keeps the tuna steaks moist while they're microwaved. The crunchy-juicy topping adds a nice contrast to the tangy sauce.

SERVES 4 | 3 ounces fish, 2 tablespoons sauce, and 2 tablespoons celery mixture per serving

In a 1½-quart microwaveable casserole dish, whisk together the tomato sauce, tarragon, horseradish, mustard, lemon juice, paprika, salt, and pepper. Add the fish, turning to coat. Cover and refrigerate for 10 minutes to 1 hour, turning occasionally.

Microwave, covered, on 100 percent power (high) for 4 minutes, or to the desired doneness.

Meanwhile, in a small bowl, stir together the celery, bell pepper, and tomato.

Transfer the fish to serving plates. Just before serving, drizzle the sauce over the fish. Sprinkle with the celery mixture.

½ cup no-salt-added tomato sauce

1 tablespoon chopped fresh tarragon

1 teaspoon bottled white horseradish

1 teaspoon Dijon mustard (lowest sodium available)

1 teaspoon fresh lemon juice

½ teaspoon paprika

¼ teaspoon salt

⅛ teaspoon pepper

4 tuna steaks (about 4 ounces each), about 1 inch thick, rinsed and patted dry

3 tablespoons diced celery

3 tablespoons diced green bell pepper

2 tablespoons diced tomato

per serving

calories 140	sodium 235 mg
total fat 1.0 g	carbohydrates 4 g
saturated fat 0.0 g	fiber 1 g
trans fat 0.0 g	sugars 2 g
polyunsaturated fat 0.0 g	protein 28 g
monounsaturated fat 0.0 g	dietary exchanges: 3 lean meat
cholesterol 44 mg	

chicken with creamy arugula pesto

Make any rushed weeknight special by topping moist microwaved chicken breasts with a yogurt-pesto sauce made with peppery arugula and ground almonds instead of the traditional basil and pine nuts.

SERVES 4 | 3 ounces chicken and 2 tablespoons pesto per serving

....

Put the chicken in a microwaveable 8- or 9-inch round or square baking dish with a lid. Pour the wine over the chicken.

Microwave, covered, on 70 percent power (medium high) for 7 to 9 minutes, or until the chicken is no longer pink in the center. Remove from the microwave. Let stand for 5 minutes (the chicken will continue to cook).

Meanwhile, in a food processor or blender, process the arugula, almonds, and garlic until finely minced. Add the Parmesan and oil. Process until smooth. Transfer the pesto to a medium microwaveable bowl. Stir in the yogurt and pepper. Microwave on 40 percent power (medium low) for 2 to 3 minutes, stirring twice. Spoon over the chicken.

4 **boneless, skinless chicken breast halves (about 4 ounces each), all visible fat discarded**

2 **tablespoons dry white wine (regular or nonalcoholic) or fat-free, low-sodium chicken broth**

½ **cup arugula**

2 **tablespoons unsalted almonds, dry-roasted**

1 **small garlic clove, chopped**

2 **tablespoons shredded or grated Parmesan cheese**

1 **tablespoon olive oil**

½ **cup fat-free plain Greek yogurt**

Pepper to taste (freshly ground preferred)

per serving

calories 212	sodium 186 mg
total fat 9.5 g	carbohydrates 3 g
saturated fat 1.5 g	fiber 1 g
trans fat 0.0 g	sugars 1 g
polyunsaturated fat 1.5 g	protein 29 g
monounsaturated fat 5.0 g	
cholesterol 74 mg	dietary exchanges: 3½ lean meat

COOK'S TIP: This recipe makes extra pesto, which is also delicious with microwave-steamed vegetables such as broccoli, cauliflower, or zucchini.

chicken with citrus-dijon sauce

Chicken comes out tender, juicy, and full of flavor when it's seasoned with fresh herbs and steamed on a bed of green onions. A tangy yogurt sauce tops it off.

SERVES 4 | 3 ounces chicken and 2 tablespoons sauce per serving

Lightly spray a shallow microwaveable 1½-quart casserole dish with cooking spray.

Arrange the green onions in a single layer in the dish. Pour in the broth and sherry.

In a small bowl, stir together the parsley, sage, rosemary, and thyme. In a separate small bowl, whisk together the yogurt, mustard, orange zest, orange juice, and 1 tablespoon of the parsley mixture until combined. Cover and refrigerate until serving time.

Sprinkle the remaining parsley mixture over both sides of the chicken. Place the chicken on the green onions with the smooth side up. In a

Cooking spray

8 medium green onions, ends trimmed

¼ cup fat-free, low-sodium chicken broth

1 tablespoon dry sherry or white wine vinegar

1 tablespoon chopped fresh parsley or 1 teaspoon dried parsley, crumbled

1 tablespoon chopped fresh sage or 1 teaspoon dried rubbed sage

1 tablespoon chopped fresh rosemary or 1 teaspoon dried rosemary, crushed

(continued)

small bowl, stir together the paprika, salt, and pepper. Sprinkle over the top of the chicken.

Microwave, covered, on 100 percent power (high) for 8 to 9 minutes, or until the chicken is no longer pink in the center. Transfer to plates. Spoon the sauce over the chicken. Serve with the orange wedges.

per serving

calories 181	sodium 392 mg
total fat 3.5 g	carbohydrates 8 g
saturated fat 0.5 g	fiber 2 g
trans fat 0.0 g	sugars 5 g
polyunsaturated fat 0.5 g	protein 26 g
monounsaturated fat 1.0 g	
cholesterol 73 mg	dietary exchanges: ½ other carbohydrate, 3 lean meat

1 tablespoon chopped fresh thyme or 1 teaspoon dried thyme, crumbled

½ cup fat-free plain yogurt

1 tablespoon Dijon mustard (lowest sodium available)

1 teaspoon grated orange zest

1 tablespoon fresh orange juice

4 boneless, skinless chicken breast halves (about 4 ounces each), all visible fat discarded, flattened to ½-inch thickness

½ teaspoon paprika

¼ teaspoon salt

¼ teaspoon pepper (freshly ground preferred)

1 medium orange, cut into 8 wedges (optional)

15-minute turkey meat loaf

Even meat loaf can be made in the microwave, saving energy and time, and keeping your kitchen cool. Use the standing time to whip up Broccoli with Jalapeño and Garlic (page 45) or Sugar Snap Peas with Sweet-and-Sour Sauce (page 46).

SERVES 6 | 1 slice per serving

Lightly spray a microwaveable 9-inch pie pan with cooking spray.

In a small bowl, whisk together the tomato sauce, Worcestershire sauce, sugar, and salt.

In a large bowl, using your hands or a spoon, combine half the tomato sauce mixture with the remaining ingredients. Transfer to the pie pan. Shape the mixture into a 6-inch-wide ring with a 2-inch hole in the middle. Spread the remaining tomato sauce mixture over the meat loaf. Microwave, covered, on 100 percent power (high) for 8 to 10 minutes, or until the meat loaf registers 165°F on an instant-read thermometer and is no longer pink in the center. Let stand for 5 minutes before slicing.

Cooking spray

1 8-ounce can no-salt-added tomato sauce

1 tablespoon Worcestershire sauce (lowest sodium available)

2 teaspoons sugar

½ teaspoon salt

1 pound ground skinless turkey breast

1 cup chopped onion

1 medium green bell pepper, chopped

½ cup chopped Italian (flat-leaf) parsley

½ cup quick-cooking oatmeal

¼ cup flax seed meal

2 large egg whites

1 teaspoon dried thyme, crumbled

per serving

calories 178
total fat 3.0 g
  saturated fat 0.5 g
  trans fat 0.0 g
  polyunsaturated fat 1.5 g
  monounsaturated fat 0.5 g
cholesterol 47 mg

sodium 263 mg
carbohydrates 15 g
  fiber 4 g
  sugars 5 g
protein 23 g

dietary exchanges: ½ starch, 2 vegetable, 3 lean meat

COOK'S TIP: Shaping the meat loaf into a ring allows it to cook more evenly in the microwave and keeps the edges from overcooking.

speedy stuffed spuds

These southwestern-style studded spuds are filled with tender beef, fresh tomatoes, a generous amount of green onions, and sharp Cheddar cheese.

SERVES 4 | 1 stuffed potato per serving

Using a fork, pierce each potato in several places. Wrap each in a paper towel. Place on a large microwaveable plate. Microwave on 100 percent power (high) for 10 minutes, or until the tines of a fork inserted into each potato come out easily. Remove from the oven.

Lightly spray a microwaveable 9-inch pie pan with cooking spray. Crumble the beef into the pan. Microwave, covered, on 100 percent power (high) for 6 minutes, or until no longer pink in the center, stirring every 2 minutes. Drain in a colander. Return the beef to the pan. Stir in the chili powder, cumin, and salt. Gently stir in the tomatoes, Cheddar, and green onions.

Halve the potatoes lengthwise. Using a fork, fluff the pulp. Top with the beef mixture. Microwave on 100 percent power (high) for 2 minutes. Top with the sour cream.

4 medium red potatoes (about 6 ounces each)

Cooking spray

8 ounces extra-lean ground beef

1½ teaspoons chili powder

½ teaspoon ground cumin

⅜ teaspoon salt

1 cup diced tomatoes or quartered grape tomatoes

½ cup shredded low-fat sharp Cheddar cheese

3 medium green onions, finely chopped

¼ cup fat-free sour cream (optional)

COOK'S TIP: Use red or Yukon gold potatoes if you prefer a moister potato. Use russets if you prefer a drier, flakier potato.

per serving

calories 237
total fat 4.5 g
  saturated fat 2.0 g
  trans fat 0.0 g
  polyunsaturated fat 0.5 g
  monounsaturated fat 1.5 g
cholesterol 34 mg

sodium 404 mg
carbohydrates 31 g
  fiber 5 g
  sugars 4 g
protein 19 g

dietary exchanges: 2 starch, 2 lean meat

quick and easy chili

This simple recipe is ready in minutes, and most of the ingredients can be found in any well-stocked pantry. The jícama topping adds a unique, slightly sweet crunch to this bowl of red.

SERVES 4 | 1½ cups per serving

. . . .

Lightly spray a 2-quart microwaveable casserole dish with cooking spray. Crumble the beef into the dish. Add the bell pepper and onion. Microwave, covered, on 100 percent power (high) for 8 minutes, or until the beef is no longer pink in the center, stirring every 2 minutes to turn and break up the beef. Drain well in a colander. Return the beef mixture to the dish.

Stir in the beans, tomatoes with liquid, chiles, chili powder, cumin, garlic powder, oregano, paprika, salt, and pepper. Microwave, covered, on 100 percent power (high) for 10 minutes, or until the beans and vegetables are tender, stirring once halfway through.

Just before serving, sprinkle the chili with the red onion, jícama, and Cheddar.

Cooking spray

12 ounces extra-lean ground beef

½ medium green bell pepper, chopped

½ small onion, chopped

1 15.5-ounce can no-salt-added pinto beans, rinsed and drained

1 14.5-ounce can diced tomatoes, undrained

1 4-ounce can diced green chiles, drained

1 tablespoon chili powder

1 teaspoon ground cumin

1 teaspoon garlic powder

1 teaspoon dried oregano, crumbled

½ teaspoon smoked paprika

⅛ teaspoon salt

⅛ teaspoon pepper

½ cup chopped red onion

½ cup diced peeled jícama

½ cup shredded low-fat Cheddar cheese

per serving

calories 292
total fat 6.0 g
  saturated fat 2.5 g
  trans fat 0.3 g
  polyunsaturated fat 0.5 g
  monounsaturated fat 2.0 g
cholesterol 50 mg

sodium 376 mg
carbohydrates 30 g
  fiber 8 g
  sugars 9 g
protein 30 g

dietary exchanges: 1 starch, 3 vegetable, 3 lean meat

COOK'S TIP ON JÍCAMA: When peeling jícama, be sure to remove the fibrous layer just under the skin. Peel until the flesh no longer looks stringy.

black bean chili

This vegetarian chili requires very little prep and is ready in less than 30 minutes, but it still has that satisfying, long-simmered taste. To speed things up even more, buy pre-chopped onion.

SERVES 4 | 1 cup per serving

. . . .

Put the water and onion in a large microwaveable bowl. Microwave, covered, on 100 percent power (high) for 5 minutes, or until the onion is soft. Stir in the beans, tomatoes with liquid, chiles with liquid, chili powder, sugar, and cumin. Microwave, covered, on 100 percent power (high) for 20 minutes, or until the onion is very soft. Remove from the oven. Stir in the oil and salt.

Meanwhile, in a small bowl, stir together the Cheddar, jalapeño, and cilantro. Sprinkle the chili with the Cheddar mixture.

½	cup water
1	cup chopped onion
1	15.5-ounce can no-salt-added black beans, rinsed and drained
1	14.5-ounce can no-salt-added stewed tomatoes, undrained
1	4-ounce can chopped green chiles, undrained
1	tablespoon chili powder
2	teaspoons sugar
1½	teaspoons ground cumin
1	tablespoon olive oil (extra virgin preferred)
⅛	teaspoon salt
¾	cup shredded low-fat sharp Cheddar cheese
2	tablespoons finely chopped fresh jalapeño, seeds and ribs discarded (see Cook's Tip on page 45)
2	tablespoons chopped fresh cilantro

per serving

calories 226
total fat 5.5 g
  saturated fat 1.5 g
  trans fat 0.0 g
  polyunsaturated fat 0.5 g
  monounsaturated fat 3.0 g
cholesterol 5 g

sodium 356 mg
carbohydrates 31 g
  fiber 7 g
  sugars 11 g
protein 13 g

dietary exchanges: 1½ starch, 2 vegetable, 1 lean meat

COOK'S TIP: Adding the oil after microwaving the chili provides another layer of flavor and helps the other flavors to blend.

risotto with edamame

Risotto is notorious for requiring long cooking and continuous stirring. With this version, you need only stir every few minutes, giving your biceps a break.

SERVES 4 | 1½ cups per serving

In a shallow microwaveable 2-quart casserole dish with a lid, stir together the rice, onion, and oil. Microwave, covered, on 100 percent power (high) for 2 to 3 minutes, or until the onion is soft.

Remove the dish from the microwave. Carefully remove the lid away from you (to prevent steam burns). Stir in the broth, thyme, salt, and pepper. Microwave, covered, on 100 percent power (high) for 5 minutes, or until simmering.

Stir in the squash and edamame. Microwave, covered, on 100 percent power (high) for 15 minutes, stirring once every 5 minutes.

Stir in the corn. Microwave, covered, on 100 percent power (high) for 5 minutes. Stir in the spinach and Parmesan. Microwave, covered, on 100 percent power (high) for 1 minute, or until the rice is tender and the spinach is wilted.

¾ cup uncooked Arborio rice

1 small onion, chopped

1 teaspoon olive oil

3 cups fat-free, low-sodium vegetable broth

½ teaspoon dried thyme, crumbled

¼ teaspoon salt

⅛ teaspoon pepper (freshly ground preferred)

2 cups diced butternut squash

1½ cups frozen shelled edamame

1 cup frozen whole-kernel corn

4 cups baby spinach

¼ cup shredded or grated Parmesan cheese

COOK'S TIP: Be careful when removing a covered dish from the microwave. Always remove the lid away from you to prevent steam burns.

COOK'S TIP ON ARBORIO RICE: Arborio rice is more absorbent and has a higher starch content than other types of rice, yielding a flavorful and creamy risotto.

per serving

calories 319
total fat 5.5 g
  saturated fat 1.0 g
  trans fat 0.0 g
  polyunsaturated fat 1.5 g
  monounsaturated fat 2.5 g
cholesterol 4 mg

sodium 281 mg
carbohydrates 54 g
  fiber 7 g
  sugars 6 g
protein 16 g

dietary exchanges:
3½ starch, 1 lean meat

broccoli with jalapeño and garlic

Tender-crisp broccoli tossed with garlic, jalapeño, cumin, and lime juice is a spicy, smoky complement to almost any Tex-Mex or southwestern entrée, including Baja Fish Tacos (page 80) or Citrus-Cilantro Salmon (page 14). If you like a lot of heat, leave the ribs and some of the seeds in the jalapeño when you make this dish.

SERVES 4 | heaping ½ cup per serving

. . . .

Put the broccoli in a medium microwaveable bowl. Microwave, covered, on 100 percent power (high) for 2 minutes, or until just tender-crisp. Remove from the microwave.

Meanwhile, in a medium nonstick skillet, heat the oil over medium-high heat, swirling to coat the bottom. Cook the jalapeño and garlic for 3 minutes, or until the garlic is lightly browned and the jalapeño begins to soften, stirring frequently. Watch carefully so the garlic doesn't burn.

Stir the cumin into the jalapeño mixture. Cook for 1 minute, stirring constantly. Stir in the broccoli, lime juice, and salt.

4	**cups broccoli florets**
2	**teaspoons olive oil**
1	**medium fresh jalapeño, halved lengthwise, seeds and ribs discarded, thinly sliced**
2	**medium garlic cloves, thinly sliced**
⅛	**teaspoon ground cumin**
2	**teaspoons fresh lime juice**
⅛	**teaspoon salt**

COOK'S TIP ON HANDLING HOT CHILES: Hot chiles contain oils that can burn your skin, lips, and eyes. Wear plastic gloves or wash your hands thoroughly with warm, soapy water immediately after handling them.

per serving

calories 44	sodium 92 mg
total fat 2.5 g	carbohydrates 5 g
saturated fat 0.5 g	fiber 2 g
trans fat 0.0 g	sugars 0 g
polyunsaturated fat 0.5 g	protein 2 g
monounsaturated fat 1.5 g	dietary exchanges:
cholesterol 0 mg	1 vegetable, ½ fat

sugar snap peas with sweet-and-sour sauce

In just a couple of minutes, you can enjoy a bright, tasty side dish that's perfect to serve with grilled flank steak or stir-fried chicken tenders.

SERVES 4 | ½ cup peas and 2 tablespoons sauce per serving

In a medium microwaveable bowl, stir together the peas and water.

In a small microwaveable bowl, whisk together the remaining ingredients except the sesame seeds until the cornstarch is dissolved.

Microwave both the peas and sauce, both covered, on 100 percent power (high) for 1½ minutes, or until the peas are cooked and the sauce has thickened and is heated through. Drain the peas well in a colander. Transfer the peas to serving dishes.

Drizzle with the sauce. Sprinkle with the sesame seeds.

8 ounces sugar snap peas, trimmed

3 tablespoons water

¼ cup apricot all-fruit spread

3 tablespoons fresh orange juice

1 tablespoon cider vinegar

½ teaspoon cornstarch

1 teaspoon sesame seeds, dry-roasted (optional)

per serving

calories 72
total fat 0.0 g
  saturated fat 0.0 g
  trans fat 0.0 g
  polyunsaturated fat 0.0 g
  monounsaturated fat 0.0 g
cholesterol 0 mg

sodium 1 mg
carbohydrates 17 g
  fiber 2 g
  sugars 11 g
protein 2 g

dietary exchanges: ½ fruit, 1 vegetable

stuffed "baked" apples

If you're craving a healthy dessert, look no further than this easy recipe, which replicates the warm flavors of oven-baked apples.

SERVES 4 | 1 stuffed apple per serving

In a small bowl, stir together the brown sugar, cranberries, raisins, cinnamon, oil, nutmeg, ginger, and allspice.

Put the apples in a shallow 1-quart microwave-able baking dish with a lid. Spoon the stuffing into the apples. Pour the orange juice around the apples.

Microwave, covered, on 100 percent power (high) for 6 to 7 minutes, or until the apples are soft.

Carefully transfer the apples to serving plates, leaving the juices in the dish. Microwave the remaining juices, uncovered, on 100 percent power (high) for 2 to 3 minutes, or until the mixture is reduced by half (to about ¼ cup).

Just before serving, drizzle the juice mixture over the apples. Sprinkle with the walnuts.

- 2 **tablespoons light brown sugar**
- 2 **tablespoons sweetened dried cranberries**
- 2 **tablespoons golden raisins**
- 1 **teaspoon ground cinnamon**
- 1 **teaspoon olive oil**
- ¼ **teaspoon ground nutmeg**
- ¼ **teaspoon ground ginger**
- ¼ **teaspoon ground allspice**
- 4 **small Granny Smith, Fuji, or Gala apples, halved, cores discarded**
- ½ **cup fresh orange juice**
- 2 **tablespoons chopped walnuts, dry-roasted**

MICROWAVING BONUS: *To dry-roast nuts in the microwave, spread them in a single layer on a microwaveable plate. Microwave on 100 percent power (high) for 1 to 4 minutes, or until the nuts are fragrant, stirring once every minute. Nuts can burn quickly, so check them frequently.*

per serving

calories 182
total fat 4.0 g
  saturated fat 0.5 g
  trans fat 0.0 g
  polyunsaturated fat 2.0 g
  monounsaturated fat 1.0 g
cholesterol 0 mg

sodium 5 mg
carbohydrates 39 g
  fiber 5 g
  sugars 30 g
protein 1 g

dietary exchanges: 2½ fruit, 1 fat

buttermilk-oat pancakes with warm blueberry topping

Think you don't have time to make a homemade breakfast on weekday mornings? Think again. Just prepare the pancake batter ahead of time and microwave individual portions whenever you want. For those in the family who don't like pancakes or are watching their carbs, see the Microwaving Bonus (page 49) to make an individual omelet instead.

SERVES 8 | 1 pancake and 2 tablespoons topping per serving

. . . .

In a medium microwaveable bowl, stir together all the topping ingredients. Microwave, covered, on 100 percent power (high) for 2 minutes. Stir. Microwave, covered, on 100 percent power (high) for 2 minutes. If needed, microwave for 1-minute intervals until the mixture has thickened and is heated through, stirring after each interval. If making the topping in advance, cover and refrigerate for up to three days. To reheat, microwave, covered, on 100 percent power (high) for 30 to 40 seconds, or until heated through.

In a medium bowl, whisk together the buttermilk, ½ cup oatmeal, the egg, and oil. Let stand for 5 minutes.

Meanwhile, in a separate medium bowl, stir together the flour, brown sugar, baking powder, baking soda, cinnamon, and nutmeg.

TOPPING

1½ cups frozen blueberries (about 8 ounces)

2 tablespoons water

1 tablespoon light brown sugar

1 teaspoon grated lemon zest

1 tablespoon fresh lemon juice

2 teaspoons cornstarch

1 teaspoon vanilla extract

PANCAKES

1 cup low-fat buttermilk

½ cup uncooked quick-cooking oatmeal and 2 tablespoons plus 2 teaspoons uncooked quick-cooking oatmeal, divided use

1 large egg

(continued)

Stir the buttermilk mixture into the flour mixture until the batter is just moistened but no flour is visible. Don't overmix; the batter may be slightly lumpy. If making the batter in advance, cover and refrigerate for up to three days.

For each pancake, lightly spray a small microwaveable plate with cooking spray. Ladle ¼ cup batter onto the plate, slightly spreading the mixture with the ladle. Sprinkle 1 teaspoon of the remaining 2 tablespoons plus 2 teaspoons oatmeal over the pancake. Microwave on 100 percent power (high) for 55 seconds to 1 minute, or until a wooden toothpick inserted in the center comes out clean. Spoon the topping over the pancake. Repeat with the remaining batter, oatmeal, and topping.

2 tablespoons canola or corn oil

¾ cup whole-wheat pastry flour

2 teaspoons light brown sugar

1 teaspoon baking powder

½ teaspoon baking soda

¼ teaspoon ground cinnamon

¼ teaspoon ground nutmeg

Cooking spray

MICROWAVING BONUS: *To make a coffee mug omelet, lightly spray a microwaveable mug with cooking spray. In the mug, stir together 4 egg whites (or ¼ cup egg substitute), 3 tablespoons diced vegetables (such as bell pepper, onion, and mushroom), 2 tablespoons shredded spinach, and 1 tablespoon low-fat Cheddar or feta cheese. Microwave, covered, on 100 percent power (high) for 1 minute. Stir. Microwave on 100 percent power (high) for 1 to 1½ minutes, or until the egg whites are set.*

per serving

calories 150	sodium 171 mg
total fat 5.0 g	carbohydrates 22 g
saturated fat 0.5 g	fiber 3 g
trans fat 0.0 g	sugars 7 g
polyunsaturated fat 1.5 g	protein 4 g
monounsaturated fat 2.5 g	dietary exchanges: 1 starch,
cholesterol 25 mg	½ fruit, 1 fat

blending

You may use your blender or food processor only when you want to whip up a frozen drink, but it can also help you easily make healthy snacks, soups, sauces, salad dressings, and desserts. Blending can be an ideal technique to encourage you or your children to increase fruit and vegetable consumption because it transforms foods that are unfamiliar or that you may have avoided. And unlike juicing, blending the whole fruit or vegetable retains the fiber and nutrient content. Because blending compacts the ingredients so well, you can pack a lot of different healthy foods into one serving, maximizing the variety of nutrients you're consuming, such as with Cherry-Berry Slush (page 66), in which you get the health benefits of three different fruits—and carrot. In Almond, Kale, and Blueberry Smoothies (page 64), you combine not only fruits and a vegetable but also dairy and nuts.

Not crazy about the texture of raw shelled peas or tofu? Try Minted Pea Soup with Yogurt Swirl (page 57) or Creamy Tomato-Basil Soup (page 59). Looking for a way to jazz up plain carrot and celery sticks for an office or after-school snack? Whip up Edamame Dip (page 54) or White Bean and Roasted Red Bell Pepper Hummus (page 55). Need a fast dinner? While you're boiling some whole-wheat pasta or sautéing chicken breasts, make Pesto (page 61) or Roasted Bell Pepper and Garlic Sauce (page 62) to put on either one—or both. Craving something to satisfy your sweet tooth? How about Peanut Butter and Banana "Ice Cream" (page 67)?

Blending is also fast, requires no heat, and allows easy cleanup. Just throw a few ingredients into your appliance, flip a switch for a few minutes (or, in some cases, only seconds), and enjoy a medley of whole-food goodness. With such fast results, there's no need to let this versatile kitchen appliance sit idle on your countertop.

Tools & Equipment Needed: Blender or food processor, rubber spatula

TIPS:

- Never operate the blender without the lid. Even the smallest amount of food can create quite a mess if the top isn't secured.

- Regardless of how snug the lid is, you should hold it down while the blender is operating.

- Always leave room for the contents to expand—at least one-third capacity and more for very thin or hot liquids.

- Cut vegetables and other foods into pieces to enable them to circulate around the blade.

- When making smoothies or other cold drinks that call for ice, adding it last can help avoid a watery drink. If you use frozen fruit, you may not need as much ice.

- See safety tips for blending (including important information on blending hot liquids) on page 280.

spinach and artichoke dip

This dip is delicious with crisp vegetables or crunchy baked whole-wheat pita wedges. For a real treat, serve it warm. It's best enjoyed the day you make it; it tends to get watery when refrigerated too long.

SERVES 10 | ¼ cup per serving

. . . .

In a food processor or blender, process all the ingredients until almost smooth but slightly chunky. Serve immediately or cover and refrigerate for 1 to 3 hours to serve chilled.

2 cups baby spinach or 10 ounces frozen chopped spinach, thawed and squeezed dry

12 ounces frozen artichoke hearts, thawed and drained

1 cup fat-free plain Greek yogurt

½ cup coarsely chopped green onions

3 tablespoons low-fat cream cheese

1 tablespoon shredded Parmesan-Asiago cheese blend

1 teaspoon minced or crushed garlic

per serving

calories 45
total fat 1.0 g
  saturated fat 0.5 g
  trans fat 0.0 g
  polyunsaturated fat 0.0 g
  monounsaturated fat 0.0 g
cholesterol 3 mg

sodium 60 mg
carbohydrates 5 g
  fiber 3 g
  sugars 1 g
protein 4 g

dietary exchanges:
1 vegetable

COOK'S TIP: To serve warm, preheat the oven to 350°F. Spoon the dip into a large ramekin or small casserole dish. Bake for 10 to 15 minutes, or until the dip is heated through.

COOK'S TIP ON FROZEN SPINACH: Use a potato ricer to easily and thoroughly squeeze the moisture out of frozen spinach.

edamame dip

This protein-rich dip is ideal as an afternoon pick-me-up snack with a selection of fresh vegetables. The Asian flavors pair especially well with sugar snap peas or strips of red bell pepper.

SERVES 4 | ¼ cup per serving

In a food processor or blender, process the ingredients for 30 seconds, or until smooth. Serve immediately or cover and refrigerate for up to five days.

1½ cups frozen shelled edamame, thawed

½ cup fat-free plain Greek yogurt

2 tablespoons coarsely chopped fresh cilantro

1½ tablespoons fresh lime juice

1 tablespoon soy sauce (lowest sodium available)

2 teaspoons light brown sugar

2 teaspoons toasted sesame oil

½ teaspoon garlic powder

¼ teaspoon pepper

per serving

calories 140
total fat 6.0 g
  saturated fat 1.0 g
  trans fat 0.0 g
  polyunsaturated fat 3.0 g
  monounsaturated fat 1.5 g
cholesterol 0 mg

sodium 117 mg
carbohydrates 11 g
  fiber 4 g
  sugars 5 g
protein 10 g

dietary exchanges: ½ starch, 1 lean meat, ½ fat

white bean and roasted red bell pepper hummus

Roasted garlic adds a delectably nutty flavor to this creamy hummus, while roasted red bell peppers lend color and a sweet smokiness. Served with plenty of crunchy raw veggies, this spread makes an unusual side dish at lunch or a satisfying snack anytime.

SERVES 4 | 3 tablespoons hummus and ½ cup vegetables per serving

In a food processor or blender, process the hummus ingredients except the oil until the desired consistency. Transfer to a small bowl. Stir in the oil. Serve at room temperature with the vegetables or cover and refrigerate for up to two days.

per serving

calories 84	sodium 24 mg
total fat 2.0 g	carbohydrates 13 g
saturated fat 0.5 g	fiber 3 g
trans fat 0.0 g	sugars 4 g
polyunsaturated fat 0.0 g	protein 4 g
monounsaturated fat 1.0 g	
cholesterol 1 mg	dietary exchanges: ½ starch, 1 vegetable

HUMMUS

½   **15.5-ounce can no-salt-added navy beans, rinsed and drained**

2   **tablespoons chopped roasted red bell peppers, drained if bottled**

2   **tablespoons fat-free sour cream**

1½ **teaspoons cider vinegar**

½   **teaspoon dried oregano, crumbled**

½   **teaspoon bottled minced roasted garlic**

¼   **teaspoon liquid smoke (optional)**

1½ **teaspoons olive oil (extra virgin preferred)**

2   **cups vegetables, such as baby carrots, sugar snap peas, sliced red bell peppers, sliced cucumbers, or a combination**

COOK'S TIP: Store unused beans in the refrigerator for up to two days or freeze them in an airtight container for up to one month. Or just use the full can and double the recipe.

butternut squash and apple soup

Nothing says fall has arrived better than a bowlful of this velvety soup. Onion and garlic add a savory touch that highlights the sweetness of the squash and apple, while just a bit of cayenne gives a warm finish.

SERVES 6 | 1 cup per serving

In a stockpot, heat the oil over medium heat, swirling to coat the bottom. Cook the onion for 5 minutes, or until soft, stirring frequently.

Stir in the garlic. Cook for 2 minutes, or until the garlic is fragrant but hasn't begun to brown.

Stir in the remaining ingredients except the lemon juice. Bring to a simmer, still over medium heat. Reduce the heat and simmer for 20 minutes so the flavors blend, stirring occasionally.

In a food processor or blender (vent the blender lid), process the soup in batches until smooth. Carefully return the soup to the pot. Stir in the lemon juice. Cook over medium heat for 3 minutes, or until hot, stirring occasionally.

1 tablespoon canola or corn oil

1 medium onion, chopped

1 medium garlic clove, minced

3 cups fat-free, low-sodium chicken or vegetable broth

24 ounces cubed butternut or other winter squash

1 cup unsweetened apple juice

1 medium Golden Delicious apple, peeled and diced

¼ teaspoon ground nutmeg

¼ teaspoon salt

Pinch of cayenne

1 teaspoon fresh lemon juice

per serving

calories 118	sodium 117 mg
total fat 2.5 g	carbohydrates 24 g
saturated fat 0.0 g	fiber 3 g
trans fat 0.0 g	sugars 11 g
polyunsaturated fat 0.5 g	protein 3 g
monounsaturated fat 1.5 g	
cholesterol 0 mg	dietary exchanges: 1 starch, ½ fruit, ½ fat

COOK'S TIP ON BLENDING HOT LIQUIDS: Be careful when blending hot liquids. Venting the blender lid prevents heat and steam from popping off the lid. Most blender lids have a center section that can be removed. You can even place a kitchen towel over the opening. Begin blending at the lowest speed and increase to the desired speed, holding the lid down firmly. If you have an immersion, or handheld, blender, you can use it instead.

minted pea soup with yogurt swirl

Sweet green peas and fresh mint are a perfect match in this dish. A flourish of creamy yogurt contrasts beautifully with the vibrant green soup.

SERVES 4 | 1 cup per serving

. . . .

In a food processor or blender, pulse the peas, 1 cup broth, the flour, and garlic 5 or 6 times, or until the peas are slightly broken up. Process the mixture for 1 minute, or until slightly chunky. Add the mint, salt, and pepper. Process for 10 seconds, or until the mint is finely chopped.

In a medium saucepan, stir together the pea mixture and the remaining 1½ cups broth. Bring to a simmer over medium-high heat. Cook for 2 minutes, or until the soup thickens, stirring occasionally. Reduce the heat to medium. Cook for 10 minutes, stirring occasionally. Remove from the heat.

Just before serving, spoon 1 tablespoon yogurt onto each serving of soup. Using a wooden toothpick, gently pull it through the yogurt to create a swirl or design of your choice. Serve with the lime wedges.

16 ounces frozen green peas, thawed

1 cup fat-free, low-sodium vegetable broth and 1½ cups fat-free, low-sodium vegetable broth, divided use

2 tablespoons all-purpose flour

1 medium garlic clove

8 medium fresh mint leaves

¼ teaspoon salt

⅛ teaspoon pepper

¼ cup fat-free plain yogurt

1 small lime, cut into 4 wedges

per serving

calories 107
total fat 0.5 g
  saturated fat 0.0 g
  trans fat 0.0 g
  polyunsaturated fat 0.0 g
  monounsaturated fat 0.0 g
cholesterol 0 mg

sodium 186 mg
carbohydrates 18 g
  fiber 7 g
  sugars 4 g
protein 7 g

dietary exchanges: 1 starch, ½ lean meat

yogurt gazpacho

Try our creamy version of this popular cold soup. It makes a protein-packed lunch or refreshing appetizer in summer, when fresh tomatoes are at their finest.

SERVES 5 | 1 cup per serving

In a food processor or blender, process all the ingredients until almost smooth, but with some texture.

4 **cups fat-free plain Greek yogurt**

2 **medium ripe tomatoes, quartered**

3 **medium green onions, quartered**

¼ **cup picante sauce (lowest sodium available)**

⅛ **teaspoon garlic powder**

Coarsely chopped fresh cilantro to taste

per serving

calories 115
total fat 0.0 g
  saturated fat 0.0 g
  trans fat 0.0 g
  polyunsaturated fat 0.0 g
  monounsaturated fat 0.0 g
cholesterol 0 mg

sodium 126 mg
carbohydrates 11 g
  fiber 1 g
  sugars 10 g
protein 16 g

dietary exchanges: 1 fat-free milk, 1 lean meat

Minted Pea Soup with Yogurt Swirl

page 57

Chinese Chicken Salad
page 98

Mediterranean Tuna Kebabs
page 78

Moroccan Beef Stew with Fragrant Couscous
page 148

Eggs with Smoked Sausage, Spinach, and Tomatoes
page 137

Acorn Squash Stuffed with Cranberry-Studded Quinoa

page 267

Pork Tenderloin Stuffed with Spinach, Pine Nuts, and Sun-Dried Tomatoes
page 258

Warm Cinnamon-Raisin Apples
page 114

creamy tomato-basil soup

This soup has all the flavor and creamy texture you love without all the saturated fat—and with a punch of protein from tofu and beans.

SERVES 4 | 1½ cups per serving

. . . .

In a food processor or blender, pulse the beans, tomatoes with liquid, tofu, tomato paste, and garlic 5 or 6 times, or until the beans, tomatoes, and garlic are finely chopped. Using a rubber spatula, scrape the side. Process for 1 minute, or until smooth, scraping the side once halfway through.

Add ½ cup basil, the onion powder, salt, pepper, and red pepper flakes. Process for 15 to 20 seconds, or until the basil is chopped. Pour into a medium saucepan. Stir in the broth and carrot juice. Bring to a simmer over medium-high heat. Reduce the heat and simmer, partially covered, for 5 to 6 minutes, or until the soup is heated through.

Just before serving, garnish with the remaining ¼ cup basil.

1 **15.5-ounce can no-salt-added Great Northern beans, rinsed and drained**

1 **14.5-ounce can no-salt-added diced tomatoes, undrained**

12 **ounces light soft tofu, drained, patted dry, and cut into 1-inch pieces**

2 **tablespoons no-salt-added tomato paste**

1 **medium garlic clove, peeled**

½ **cup loosely packed fresh basil and ¼ cup loosely packed fresh basil, rolled and cut into thin strips, divided use**

1 **teaspoon onion powder**

¼ **teaspoon salt**

¼ **teaspoon pepper (freshly ground preferred)**

¼ **teaspoon crushed red pepper flakes (optional)**

½ **cup fat-free, low-sodium chicken or vegetable broth**

½ **cup 100% carrot juice**

per serving

calories 175
total fat 2.0 g
  saturated fat 0.0 g
  trans fat 0.0 g
  polyunsaturated fat 0.5 g
  monounsaturated fat 0.0 g
cholesterol 0 mg

sodium 298 mg
carbohydrates 27 g
  fiber 8 g
  sugars 7 g
protein 13 g

dietary exchanges: 1 starch, 2 vegetable, 1½ lean meat

greek goddess salad dressing

Greek yogurt updates Green Goddess dressing, which was created in 1923 at a
San Francisco hotel and named after a hit play of the time. This dressing gets
its beautiful hue from parsley and dillweed, with extra flavor from cucumber
and green onion.

SERVES 4 | 2 tablespoons per serving

In a food processor or blender, process all the
ingredients, scraping the side as necessary,
until almost smooth.

per serving

calories 17	sodium 83 mg
total fat 0.0 g	carbohydrates 2 g
saturated fat 0.0 g	fiber 0 g
trans fat 0.0 g	sugars 1 g
polyunsaturated fat 0.0 g	protein 2 g
monounsaturated fat 0.0 g	dietary exchanges: Free
cholesterol 0 mg	

⅓ cup fat-free plain Greek yogurt

¼ cup peeled, seeded, and chopped cucumber

2 tablespoons coarsely chopped fresh parsley

2 teaspoons chopped fresh dillweed or ¼ teaspoon dried dillweed, crumbled

1 medium green onion, cut into 1-inch pieces

1 teaspoon fresh lemon juice

1 teaspoon white wine vinegar

¼ teaspoon garlic powder

¼ teaspoon sugar

⅛ teaspoon salt

⅛ teaspoon pepper

pesto

This versatile sauce makes an excellent topping for pasta or baked potatoes. Try stirring it into fat-free Greek yogurt to make a dip. To change the flavor of this pesto, substitute fresh cilantro for the basil.

SERVES 16 | 2 tablespoons per serving

. . . .

In a food processor or blender, process all the ingredients except the broth until smooth, occasionally scraping down the side. If the mixture doesn't move during processing, slowly drizzle in the broth to loosen it.

2 cups loosely packed fresh basil

½ cup pine nuts or walnuts, dry-roasted

⅓ cup freshly grated Parmesan cheese

⅓ cup olive oil

1 medium garlic clove

¼ to ½ cup fat-free, low-sodium chicken or vegetable broth (optional)

per serving

calories 69	sodium 27 mg
total fat 7.0 g	carbohydrates 1 g
saturated fat 1.0 g	fiber 0 g
trans fat 0.0 g	sugars 0 g
polyunsaturated fat 1.5 g	protein 2 g
monounsaturated fat 4.0 g	
cholesterol 2 mg	dietary exchanges: 1½ fat

COOK'S TIP: Pesto can be made well in advance and refrigerated or frozen in an airtight container. Or, spoon measured portions into an ice cube tray and freeze. When the pesto is frozen, transfer the cubes to a resealable plastic bag and return to the freezer.

COOK'S TIP ON DRY-ROASTING NUTS OR SEEDS IN THE OVEN: To dry-roast a large amount of nuts or seeds at one time, place them in a shallow baking dish. Roast them at 350°F for 10 to 15 minutes, stirring occasionally. You can freeze them in an airtight container or resealable plastic freezer bag after cooling so they can be ready at a moment's notice. You don't even need to thaw them before using them.

roasted bell pepper and garlic sauce

This very versatile sauce of roasted bell peppers and fresh garlic has a hint of smoky heat from the chipotle pepper and cumin. Use it to perk up grilled or steamed entrées and vegetables. It can be served at room temperature or heated.

SERVES 4 | ¼ cup per serving

. . . .

In a food processor or blender, process all the ingredients except the oil until smooth. With the motor still running, slowly drizzle in the oil.

To serve hot, pour the sauce into a small saucepan. Cook over medium heat for 2 to 3 minutes, or until just heated.

6 ounces roasted red bell peppers, drained if bottled

1 medium chipotle pepper canned in adobo sauce

2 teaspoons adobo sauce (from chipotle peppers canned in adobo sauce)

2 teaspoons balsamic vinegar

1 medium garlic clove

⅛ teaspoon ground cumin

2 tablespoons olive oil (extra virgin preferred)

per serving

calories 83
total fat 7.0 g
  saturated fat 1.0 g
  trans fat 0.0 g
  polyunsaturated fat 0.5 g
  monounsaturated fat 5.0 g
cholesterol 0 mg

sodium 181 mg
carbohydrates 4 g
  fiber 0 g
  sugars 1 g
protein 0 g

dietary exchanges:
1 vegetable, 1½ fat

very berry yogurt parfaits

This parfait combines sweet fresh fruit with crunchy fiber-rich cereal and plenty of protein. Prepare the tofu mixture in advance, then assemble the parfaits whenever you're ready.

SERVES 4 | 1 parfait per serving

In a blender, process the tofu, raspberries, yogurt, raspberry spread, and honey for 20 to 30 seconds, or until smooth, stirring once halfway through. In each parfait glass, layer the ingredients as follows: ¼ cup blueberries, ¼ cup tofu mixture, and 2 tablespoons cereal. Repeat the layers.

12 ounces light soft tofu, drained and patted dry

1 cup raspberries

6 ounces fat-free plain Greek yogurt

2 tablespoons all-fruit raspberry spread

1 tablespoon honey

2 cups blueberries, blackberries, sliced hulled strawberries, or sliced bananas

1 cup high-fiber cereal

per serving

calories 178
total fat 2.0 g
  saturated fat 0.0 g
  trans fat 0.0 g
  polyunsaturated fat 0.5 g
  monounsaturated fat 0.5 g
cholesterol 0 mg

sodium 112 mg
carbohydrates 39 g
  fiber 12 g
  sugars 17 g
protein 11 g

dietary exchanges: 1 starch, 1½ fruit, 1 lean meat

almond, kale, and blueberry smoothies

Blueberries combined with kale create a brilliant purple drink that is packed with nutrition; it's sure to please adults and kids alike.

SERVES 2 | 1 cup per serving

. . . .

In a food processor or blender, process the almond milk and almonds until smooth. Add the remaining ingredients. Process until smooth.

- ¾ cup unsweetened vanilla almond milk
- 2 tablespoons slivered almonds, dry-roasted
- 1 cup fresh or frozen blueberries
- ⅔ cup coarsely chopped kale, any large stems discarded
- ½ cup fat-free plain Greek yogurt
- ½ cup ice cubes
- ⅓ cup sliced ripe banana (½ small banana)

per serving

calories 160
total fat 5.0 g
  saturated fat 0.5 g
  trans fat 0.0 g
  polyunsaturated fat 1.0 g
  monounsaturated fat 2.0 g
cholesterol 0 mg

sodium 100 mg
carbohydrates 23 g
  fiber 4 g
  sugars 13 g
protein 8 g

dietary exchanges: 1 fruit, ½ fat-free milk, ½ fat

COOK'S TIP: Blending the almond milk and almonds together before adding the other ingredients yields a smoother finished product.

orange-apricot smoothies

Even if you are lactose intolerant, you can still enjoy this rich and creamy smoothie. Bananas, orange juice concentrate, and apricot nectar give it natural sweetness.

SERVES 6 | 1 scant cup per serving

. . . .

In a food processor or blender, process all the ingredients until smooth.

12 ounces frozen 100% orange juice concentrate, broken into chunks

12 ounces 100% apricot nectar

1½ cups water

 2 medium bananas

½ teaspoon vanilla extract

per serving

calories 182
total fat 0.5 g
  saturated fat 0.0 g
  trans fat 0.0 g
  polyunsaturated fat 0.0 g
  monounsaturated fat 0.0 g
cholesterol 0 mg

sodium 8 mg
carbohydrates 44 g
  fiber 2 g
  sugars 38 g
protein 3 g

dietary exchanges: 3 fruit

cherry-berry slush

This fruit-filled drink gets its extra fiber and body, along with a boost of vitamins, from carrot.

SERVES 4 | 1 cup per serving

In a food processor or blender, process all the ingredients except the ice cubes until smooth. Add the ice cubes. Process until smooth.

1¼ cups 100% cranberry juice

8 ounces frozen unsweetened dark sweet cherries

6 ounces frozen unsweetened raspberries

1 medium carrot, cut into chunks or shredded

1 teaspoon grated orange zest

1 teaspoon vanilla extract

2 teaspoons sugar (optional)

1 cup ice cubes

per serving

calories 111
total fat 0.0 g
 saturated fat 0.0 g
 trans fat 0.0 g
 polyunsaturated fat 0.0 g
 monounsaturated fat 0.0 g
cholesterol 0 mg

sodium 14 mg
carbohydrates 28 g
 fiber 4 g
 sugars 21 g
protein 1 g

dietary exchanges: 2 fruit

COOK'S TIP: You can store any leftover slush in the freezer. To serve it as a drink, let the mixture thaw at room temperature for 15 minutes. Or use a fork to scrape the surface of the frozen slush and serve it as a granita for dessert.

peanut butter and banana "ice cream"

This cold and creamy frozen treat contains no dairy products. Freezing the bananas and then giving them a whirl in a food processor gives them a consistency similar to soft-serve ice cream. Keep some banana slices in your freezer so you can prepare this dish whenever the mood strikes. For a more adult version and a softer texture, use the optional vodka.

SERVES 4 | scant ½ cup per serving

. . . .

Freeze the banana slices for at least 3 to 4 hours to overnight, or until solid.

In a food processor, process the bananas until they are the consistency of soft-serve ice cream.

Add the remaining ingredients. Process until smooth and creamy. Serve immediately or freeze in an airtight freezer container. If frozen, let stand at room temperature for about 5 minutes to thaw slightly before serving.

4 medium ripe bananas, cut crosswise into ¼-inch slices

2 tablespoons finely chopped unsalted peanuts, dry-roasted

1½ tablespoons low-sodium peanut butter (smooth or crunchy)

1 to 3 tablespoons vodka (optional)

1 tablespoon honey

1 teaspoon vanilla extract

¼ teaspoon ground cinnamon

¼ teaspoon freshly grated or ground nutmeg

per serving

calories 187	sodium 3 mg
total fat 5.5 g	carbohydrates 34 mg
saturated fat 1.0 g	fiber 4 g
trans fat 0.0 g	sugars 20 g
polyunsaturated fat 1.5 g	protein 4 g
monounsaturated fat 2.5 g	
cholesterol 0 mg	dietary exchanges: 2 fruit, 1 fat

COOK'S TIP: Adding the vodka will keep the "ice cream" a little softer when it freezes.

strawberry granita

A granita is a semi-frozen dessert made with water, often sugar or a simple syrup, fruit, and a liquid that adds flavor, such as juice, coffee, tea, or wine. This sweet treat is deceptively creamy although it contains no dairy or added fat. Store a batch in the freezer for a dessert that's ready when you are.

SERVES 6 | ½ cup per serving

In a food processor or blender, process the strawberries until smooth. Stir in the strawberry spread and lemon juice. Strain through a fine-mesh sieve into an 8-inch square pan. Freeze for about 1 hour, or until slushy.

Return the mixture to the food processor. Process until smooth and creamy. Return to the pan and freeze again until solid.

Remove the pan from the freezer. Let stand at room temperature for 15 minutes. Using a fork, scrape the granita into dessert dishes or small bowls.

1 **quart strawberries, hulled**

½ **cup all-fruit strawberry spread**

1 **tablespoon fresh lemon juice**

per serving

calories 85
total fat 0.5 g
  saturated fat 0.0 g
  trans fat 0.0 g
  polyunsaturated fat 0.0 g
  monounsaturated fat 0.0 g
cholesterol 0 mg

sodium 1 mg
carbohydrates 21 g
  fiber 2 g
  sugars 15 g
protein 1 g

dietary exchanges: 1½ fruit

grilling

Grilling is an easy way to cook quick, healthy meals. Grilled foods cook fast so they retain their moisture and excess unhealthy fats drip away into the grill. The intense, direct heat provides a crisp, browned crust and a moist, tender interior, and the quick cooking lets you get dinner on the table in short order. You can use the surface of the grill to cook both your entrée and side dishes—and even your dessert.

Although lean meats and poultry are popular grilling choices, you can also use this healthy cooking technique to incorporate a variety of food groups into your meals, including seafood, vegetables, and fruit such as Island Halibut with Papaya and Strawberry Salsa (page 76) or Honey-Balsamic Brussels Sprouts with Goat Cheese (page 90). Grilling brings out such unique, natural sweet flavors that it's a perfect opportunity to try foods you may not have eaten before or may have avoided because you don't want their aromas to fill your house.

Marinades, rubs, and sauces are good flavor enhancers for grilled foods. Just be sure to look for those that are low in sodium, saturated and trans fats, and added sugar. Rubs impart a stronger flavor than marinades but can burn when grilled, so they work particularly well with foods that will be cooked with indirect heat or for a short time, such as fish. Sauces should be put on foods toward the end of grilling (about 5 minutes for each side before removing) to prevent them from burning as well.

Tools & Equipment Needed: Grill (the recipes in this cookbook are for an outdoor gas grill), grilling tools, wire cleaning brush, basting brushes, instant-read thermometer, skewers, grill baskets or perforated grill sheets, kitchen timer

TIPS:

- To adapt outdoor grilling recipes for a countertop double-sided contact grill, cut the cooking time in half. For stovetop grill pans, cook the food longer because these pans don't get as hot as outdoor grills and aren't covered. These are general rules of thumb, but be sure to watch for visual cues that indicate the food is done.

- Cut vegetables thickly so they don't fall through the grate. Place asparagus and zucchini spears perpendicular to the grates or thread them crosswise onto two skewers.

- Use skewers, grill baskets, or perforated grill sheets for smaller vegetables such as button mushrooms and cherry tomatoes.

- When grilling a variety of veggies, group them according to the cooking time they'll need rather than in one mixed bunch.

- Try adding lemon wedges to your fish or vegetable kebabs. Grilling tames their tartness and adds citrus flavor to the foods sharing the skewer.

- Trim and discard all visible fat from poultry and meats before grilling; this will both cut down on saturated fat and help prevent flare-ups.

- Select boneless (and lean) cuts of chicken, beef, and pork, which cook more evenly.

- Instead of turning kebabs, use a spatula to roll them over.

- Marinate for only the recommended time on a recipe; marinating longer won't necessarily mean better flavor and may give the food an unpleasant texture.

- Most marinades contain an acid—such as vinegar or citrus juice—that helps to tenderize the food and add moisture, so be sure to use a nonreactive container like a glass or stainless steel dish or a resealable plastic bag.

- If you use cooking spray to keep food from sticking, be sure to spray the grate before it is heated.

- To lightly oil a hot grate, soak a paper towel in water, then dip it in oil and hold it with long tongs.

- To clean the grill, preheat it on high for 10 to 15 minutes to burn off most of the residue. Use a grill brush to remove any leftover food. (If you don't have a grill brush, you can use a ball of crumpled heavy-duty aluminum foil held with long tongs.)

- To avoid both overcooking and undercooking meat and poultry, use a meat thermometer to check doneness. Remove the meat or poultry from the grill before inserting the instant-read thermometer. Insert the thermometer into the center, or thickest part, of the meat, making sure the thermometer doesn't touch bone or fat.

- See safety tips for grilling on page 281.

corn and black bean salad

Grilled corn is a treat, but this brightly colored entrée salad steps things up a notch, adding tender black beans, juicy tomatoes, and mild queso fresco.

SERVES 4 | 1½ cups per serving

. . . .

Preheat the grill on medium high. Cut four 5-inch-square pieces of aluminum foil. Lightly spray the corn with cooking spray. Place each ear diagonally in the center of a piece of foil. Roll the foil around the ear. Twist the ends to seal loosely.

Grill the corn for 15 to 20 minutes, or until tender-crisp, turning occasionally. Remove from the grill. Let stand for 10 minutes so the corn cools slightly.

In a small bowl, whisk together the dressing ingredients. Unwrap the corn, discarding the foil. Cut the kernels off the cob. In a large bowl, stir together the corn and the remaining ingredients. Pour the dressing over the salad, tossing gently to coat.

4 large ears of corn, husks and silk discarded

Cooking spray

DRESSING

1 tablespoon olive oil (extra virgin preferred)

1 tablespoon cider vinegar

1 tablespoon fresh lime juice

1 medium garlic clove, minced

½ teaspoon salt

¼ teaspoon pepper

———

1 15.5-ounce can no-salt-added black beans, rinsed and drained

1 cup grape tomatoes, quartered

½ cup chopped fresh cilantro

4 ounces queso fresco or farmer cheese, crumbled

per serving

calories 303	sodium 356 mg
total fat 8.0 g	carbohydrates 49 g
saturated fat 2.5 g	fiber 8 g
trans fat 0.0 g	sugars 14 g
polyunsaturated fat 1.0 g	protein 15 g
monounsaturated fat 4.0 g	
cholesterol 9 mg	dietary exchanges: 3 starch, 1 vegetable, 1 lean meat, ½ fat

COOK'S TIP ON CORN: To remove corn kernels from a cob, place one end of the cob in the hole in the center of a tube or Bundt pan. As you cut downward along the cob, the kernels will fall into the pan.

shrimp and watermelon salad with cucumber-lime vinaigrette

An unusual combination of spiced watermelon, tender shrimp, and peppery arugula, this salad is topped with a dressing that's literally as cool as a cucumber. Juice from a grilled lime adds a slightly smoky flavor to the dressing. This will be your go-to salad all summer.

SERVES 4 | 1 watermelon wedge, ½ cup arugula, 2 ounces shrimp, and 2 tablespoons dressing per serving

. . . .

Soak four 6-inch wooden skewers for at least 10 minutes in cold water to keep them from charring, or use metal skewers. Lightly spray the grill rack with cooking spray. Preheat the grill on medium high.

Grate 1 teaspoon of zest from the lime. Set the zest aside. Halve the lime.

Grill the lime halves with the cut sides down for 2 minutes, or until the cut sides are light golden brown and the limes are heated through. Transfer to a plate. Let cool for 5 minutes.

Juice the lime halves. In a food processor or blender, process the cucumber, honey, lime juice, and reserved lime zest for 30 seconds, or until smooth, scraping the side as necessary. Set the dressing aside.

Thread the shrimp onto the skewers. Sprinkle ½ teaspoon chili powder and the pepper over both sides of the shrimp. Lightly spray both sides of the shrimp with cooking spray.

Olive oil cooking spray

1 small lime

½ medium cucumber, peeled, seeded, and cut into 1-inch pieces

1 tablespoon honey

10 ounces raw medium shrimp (thawed if frozen), peeled, rinsed, and patted dry

½ teaspoon chili powder and ½ teaspoon chili powder, divided use

⅛ teaspoon pepper (freshly ground preferred)

¼ teaspoon salt

1 round slice of watermelon (about 1 inch thick) with rind, cut into 4 wedges

2 cups loosely packed arugula

Sprinkle the salt and the remaining ½ teaspoon chili powder over both sides of the watermelon. Lightly spray both sides of the watermelon with cooking spray.

Grill the shrimp for 2 minutes on each side, or until pink on the outside. Grill the watermelon for 1½ minutes on each side, or until it has light grill marks and is heated through. Transfer the watermelon to plates. Remove the shrimp from the skewers. Arrange on the watermelon.

Using a grill rack or wok-style grilling basket, grill the arugula for 15 to 20 seconds, or until the arugula is slightly wilted, stirring frequently with tongs.

Top the shrimp with the arugula. Drizzle the dressing over the salad.

per serving

calories 92	sodium 319 mg
total fat 1.0 g	carbohydrates 11 g
saturated fat 0.0 g	fiber 1 g
trans fat 0.0 g	sugars 9 g
polyunsaturated fat 0.0 g	protein 11 g
monounsaturated fat 0.0 g	dietary exchanges: ½ fruit,
cholesterol 89 mg	2 lean meat

island halibut with papaya and strawberry salsa

Grilling enhances fruit's natural sweetness by caramelizing its sugar, while grilled jalapeño adds a smoky heat to this unusual salsa. Spooned over flaky halibut marinated in pineapple juice, it will bring a taste of the tropics to your next barbecue.

SERVES 4 | 3 ounces fish and ¼ cup salsa per serving

Soak one 8-inch wooden skewer for at least 10 minutes in cold water to keep it from charring, or use a metal skewer.

In a shallow glass baking dish, whisk together the pineapple juice and pepper. Add the fish, turning to coat. Cover and refrigerate for 10 to 30 minutes, turning every 10 minutes.

Meanwhile, lightly spray a perforated grill sheet with cooking spray and place on the grill rack. Preheat the grill on medium high.

Using a sharp knife, make a series of crosshatch cuts in the papaya, being careful not to cut all the way through the flesh to the peel. Lightly spray the cut side with cooking spray. Thread the strawberries onto the skewer. Lightly spray them with cooking spray.

Lightly spray the jalapeño with cooking spray. Grill for 4 to 5 minutes, or until slightly charred, turning occasionally. Grill the papaya with the cut side down for 2 to 3 minutes, or until the flesh is golden brown. Grill the strawberries for 2 to 3 minutes, or until

¼ cup 100% pineapple juice

¼ teaspoon pepper (freshly ground preferred)

4 halibut fillets with skin (about 5 ounces each), rinsed and patted dry

Cooking spray

½ small papaya, seeds discarded

4 medium hulled strawberries

1 small fresh jalapeño

1 tablespoon chopped fresh mint

1 teaspoon grated lime zest

1 tablespoon fresh lime juice

4 sprigs of fresh mint (optional)

slightly golden and heated through, turning once halfway through. Transfer the jalapeño, papaya, and strawberries to a cutting board. Let stand for 5 minutes to cool.

Using a spoon, scoop out the flesh of the papaya. Transfer to a medium bowl. Chop the strawberries. Add the strawberries to the papaya. Discard the seeds and ribs of the jalapeño (see Cook's Tip on page 45). Chop it. Gently stir the jalapeño, chopped mint, lime zest, and lime juice into the papaya mixture.

Drain the fish, discarding the marinade. Grill the fish for 4 to 5 minutes on each side, or until it flakes easily when tested with a fork. Transfer to plates. Top with the salsa. Garnish with the sprigs of mint.

per serving

calories 118	sodium 80 mg
total fat 1.5 g	carbohydrates 4 g
saturated fat 0.5 g	fiber 1 g
trans fat 0.0 g	sugars 2 g
polyunsaturated fat 0.5 g	protein 21 g
monounsaturated fat 0.5 g	dietary exchanges: 3 lean meat
cholesterol 56 mg	

mediterranean tuna kebabs

A fresh tomato-saffron sauce doubles as a marinade to give the kebabs twice the flavor. Serve them with brown rice or whole-wheat couscous. *(See photo insert.)*

SERVES 4 | 1 kebab per serving

Soak four 12-inch wooden skewers for at least 10 minutes in cold water to keep them from charring, or use metal skewers.

In a small glass bowl, whisk together the hot water and saffron. In a food processor or blender, process the saffron mixture, tomatoes, oil, vinegar, and garlic for 1 minute, or until smooth. Transfer ⅓ cup of the mixture to the bowl. Cover and refrigerate until 10 to 15 minutes before serving time.

For each kebab, thread each skewer with 3 tuna cubes, 3 onion wedges, 3 bell pepper strips, and 3 zucchini slices. Put the kebabs on a rimmed baking sheet. Brush all sides of the kebabs generously with the marinade. Cover and refrigerate for 30 minutes to 1 hour.

¼ cup hot water

Pinch of saffron (optional)

⅔ cup chopped Italian plum (Roma) tomatoes (about 2 small)

2 teaspoons olive oil (extra virgin preferred)

1 teaspoon red wine vinegar

1 small garlic clove

1 pound tuna steaks, rinsed, patted dry, and cut into 12 1-inch cubes

1 medium onion, cut into 12 ½-inch wedges

1 medium red or yellow bell pepper, cut into 12 strips

1 medium zucchini, cut crosswise into 12 slices

Cooking spray

Lightly spray the grill rack with cooking spray. Preheat the grill on medium high.

Meanwhile, remove the reserved saffron mixture from the refrigerator. Let stand at room temperature for 10 to 15 minutes.

Lightly spray the kebabs with cooking spray. Grill the kebabs, covered, for about 4 minutes, or until the fish is the desired doneness and the vegetables are tender-crisp, turning frequently. Serve with the reserved saffron mixture.

per serving

calories 179	sodium 60 mg
total fat 3.0 g	carbohydrates 8 g
saturated fat 0.5 g	fiber 2 g
trans fat 0.0 g	sugars 5 g
polyunsaturated fat 0.5 g	protein 29 g
monounsaturated fat 2.0 g	dietary exchanges:
cholesterol 44 mg	2 vegetable, 3 lean meat

COOK'S TIP: When threading the kebabs, angle the zucchini slices so they lie slightly flat during grilling for more even cooking.

COOK'S TIP ON KEBABS: Instead of turning kebabs, you can use a metal spatula to roll them over.

COOK'S TIP ON SAFFRON: You can buy saffron in powder form or as threads; the threads are fresher and more flavorful. They can be expensive, but a little goes a long way. Crush them just before you use them.

baja fish tacos

The Baja Peninsula, in northwestern Mexico, is famous for fish tacos. Though haddock is featured in this recipe, any firm-fleshed fish will work well for grilling. Set out the cooked fish and topping ingredients and let everyone build his or her own tacos.

4 SERVINGS | 2 tacos per serving

In a small bowl, stir together the chili powder, oregano, thyme, and cumin. Stir in the oil. Spread the mixture over both sides of the fish. Cover and refrigerate for 15 to 20 minutes.

Meanwhile preheat the grill on high. Lightly spray the fish with cooking spray. Grill the fish with the sprayed side down for 5 to 6 minutes, or until it flakes easily when tested with a fork. Don't turn it over.

Using a metal spatula, transfer the fish to a large plate. Let cool for 3 to 5 minutes. Break the fish into 1-inch pieces.

Put the fish on the tortillas. Dice the avocado. Top the fish with the avocado, tomatoes, romaine, and salsa. Serve with the lime wedges.

1 teaspoon chili powder (ancho powder preferred)

1 teaspoon dried oregano, crumbled

½ teaspoon dried thyme, crumbled

½ teaspoon ground cumin

1 tablespoon canola or corn oil

4 haddock fillets (about 4 ounces each), rinsed and patted dry

Cooking spray

8 6-inch corn tortillas

1 medium avocado

2 medium Italian plum (Roma) tomatoes, seeded and diced

1 cup shredded romaine

¼ cup salsa verde (lowest sodium available)

2 medium limes, each cut into 4 wedges

per serving

calories 275
total fat 12.5 g
　saturated fat 1.5 g
　trans fat 0.0 g
　polyunsaturated fat 2.5 g
　monounsaturated fat 7.5 g
cholesterol 61 mg

sodium 352 mg
carbohydrates 21 g
　fiber 6 g
　sugars 2 g
protein 22 g

dietary exchanges: 1 starch, 1 vegetable, 3 lean meat, ½ fat

chicken with red raspberry glaze

Super-simple to put together, this sweet and tart dish uses only five ingredients. You can have it on the table in less than 30 minutes, making it the perfect entrée for a busy summer night.

SERVES 4 | 3 ounces chicken per serving

Lightly spray the grill rack with cooking spray. Preheat the grill on medium high.

In a small bowl, whisk together the raspberry spread, honey mustard, and cayenne. Spoon ¼ cup of the glaze into a separate small bowl. Set aside. Lightly brush both sides of the chicken with the remaining glaze.

Grill the chicken for 5 to 7 minutes on each side, or until no longer pink in the center.

Meanwhile, add the raspberries to the reserved glaze, stirring gently to coat. Just before serving, spoon over the chicken.

Cooking spray

¾ cup all-fruit seedless red raspberry spread

2 tablespoons honey mustard (lowest sodium available)

¼ teaspoon cayenne

4 boneless, skinless chicken breast halves (about 4 ounces each), all visible fat discarded, pounded to ½-inch thickness

6 ounces red raspberries

COOK'S TIP ON CHICKEN BREASTS: Flattened chicken breasts are more uniform in thickness so they cook more evenly. They also cook faster, which makes them less likely to dry out or become tough.

per serving

calories 242
total fat 3.0 g
  saturated fat 0.5 g
  trans fat 0.0 g
  polyunsaturated fat 0.5 g
  monounsaturated fat 1.0 g
cholesterol 73 mg

sodium 137 mg
carbohydrates 27 g
  fiber 3 g
  sugars 20 g
protein 25 g

dietary exchanges: 2 fruit, 3 lean meat

smoky chicken and vegetable lasagna

This unusual recipe takes lasagna out of the oven and into the outdoors. The components are grilled, adding a rich smokiness to the dish, which is also finished on the grill. Round out your meal with a simple salad or some extra grilled vegetables.

SERVES 8 | one 3 x 4½-inch piece per serving

In a shallow glass bowl, stir together the rosemary, vinegar, garlic, salt, and pepper. Add the chicken, turning to coat. Cover and refrigerate for at least 10 minutes, or up to 8 hours, turning occasionally.

Lightly spray the grill rack with cooking spray. Preheat the grill on medium high.

Drain the chicken, discarding the marinade. Lightly spray both sides of the chicken with cooking spray. Grill for 6 to 8 minutes on each side, or until the chicken is no longer pink in the center. Transfer to a cutting board. Let cool. Coarsely chop the chicken.

Meanwhile, lightly spray both sides of the noodles with cooking spray. Grill for 1½ to 2 minutes on each side, or until they have golden-brown grill marks. Remove from the grill.

Put the tomatoes, zucchini, bell pepper, and onion on a baking sheet or platter. Lightly spray with cooking spray. Sprinkle with half the seasoning blend. Turn over the vegetables. Lightly spray with cooking spray. Sprinkle with the remaining seasoning blend.

2 tablespoons chopped fresh rosemary

1 tablespoon white wine vinegar

2 medium garlic cloves, minced

¼ teaspoon salt

¼ teaspoon pepper (freshly ground preferred)

1 pound boneless, skinless chicken breasts, all visible fat discarded

Cooking spray

9 dried whole-grain lasagna noodles

4 medium tomatoes, halved

2 medium zucchini, cut lengthwise into ¾-inch-thick slices

1 large orange bell pepper, cut into ½-inch rings

1 medium red onion, cut into ½-inch slices and separated into rings

1 tablespoon salt-free all-purpose seasoning blend

1 teaspoon dried oregano, crumbled

15 ounces fat-free ricotta cheese

1 cup shredded low-fat mozzarella cheese

Using a perforated grill sheet, grill the vegetables for 2 to 3 minutes on each side. Remove from the grill. In a large bowl, stir together the chopped chicken and grilled zucchini, bell pepper, and onion.

In a food processor or blender, process the tomatoes and oregano for 1½ to 2 minutes, or until the sauce is slightly chunky.

Lightly spray a 13 x 9 x 2-inch metal pan with cooking spray.

In the pan, layer as follows: ½ cup tomato sauce, 3 noodles, half the chicken mixture, half the ricotta, and half the mozzarella. Repeat the layers, finishing with the remaining 3 noodles. Spread the remaining tomato sauce on top. Cover the pan with aluminum foil.

Grill, covered, for 20 to 25 minutes, or until the mozzarella has melted and the lasagna is heated through.

per serving

calories 238
total fat 3.5 g
  saturated fat 1.0 g
  trans fat 0.0 g
  polyunsaturated fat 0.5 g
  monounsaturated fat 1.0 g
cholesterol 46 mg

sodium 350 mg
carbohydrates 25 g
  fiber 5 g
  sugars 7 g
protein 27 g

dietary exchanges: 1 starch, 2 vegetable, 3 lean meat

teriyaki chicken and vegetable kebabs

Juicy chicken and a variety of vegetables are marinated in a spicy-sweet sauce before being grilled to tender perfection. Follow dinner with Chai-Spiced Pineapple Spears (page 93) for dessert.

SERVES 4 | 2 skewers per serving

In a shallow glass baking dish, whisk together the brown sugar, sherry, soy sauce, canola oil, ginger, and chili oil. Add the chicken, onions, mushrooms, tomatoes, and zucchini, stirring to coat. Cover and refrigerate for 1 hour, turning occasionally.

Meanwhile, soak eight 8-inch bamboo skewers for at least 10 minutes in cold water to keep them from charring, or use metal skewers.

Lightly spray the grill rack with cooking spray. Preheat the grill on high.

For each kebab, thread each skewer with 2 chicken cubes, 1 onion wedge, 1 mushroom, 1 tomato, and 1 zucchini slice. Grill for 3 minutes on each side, or until the chicken is no longer pink in the center.

2½ **tablespoons light brown sugar**

2 **tablespoons sherry or fresh orange juice**

1 **tablespoon soy sauce (lowest sodium available)**

2 **teaspoons canola or corn oil**

½ **teaspoon ground ginger**

½ **teaspoon hot chili oil**

1 **pound boneless, skinless chicken breasts, all visible fat discarded, cut into 16 1½-inch cubes**

2 **medium onions, cut into 4 wedges each**

8 **medium button mushrooms**

8 **cherry or grape tomatoes**

1 **medium zucchini, cut crosswise into 8 slices**

Cooking spray

per serving

calories 177
total fat 3.5 g
  saturated fat 0.5 g
  trans fat 0.0 g
  polyunsaturated fat 0.5 g
  monounsaturated fat 1.0 g
cholesterol 73 mg

sodium 239 mg
carbohydrates 11 g
  fiber 3 g
  sugars 8 g
protein 27 g

dietary exchanges:
2 vegetable, 3 lean meat

flank steak with chimichurri sauce

Chimichurri, a garlicky herb sauce, is like the ketchup of Argentina. It's commonly served with all types of grilled or roasted meats. Try this with a side of Beets with Orange Gremolata (page 92).

4 SERVINGS | 3 ounces beef and 1 tablespoon sauce per serving

In a food processor or blender, process the sauce ingredients except the oil for 1 to 2 minutes, or until finely chopped. Add the oil, pulsing 2 or 3 times, or until just smooth. Pour half the sauce into a small glass bowl. Cover and refrigerate.

Pour the remaining sauce into a large glass baking dish. Add the beef, turning to coat. Refrigerate, covered, for 2 hours, turning occasionally. Remove the dish from the refrigerator. Let stand for 20 minutes. Remove the reserved sauce from the refrigerator. Let stand for 30 minutes.

Meanwhile, preheat the grill on high.

Drain the beef, discarding the marinade. Grill the beef for 4 to 5 minutes on each side, or to the desired doneness. Transfer to a cutting board. Let stand for 15 minutes before thinly slicing. Serve with the reserved sauce.

SAUCE

1½ cups Italian (flat-leaf) parsley, coarsely chopped

2 medium shallots, coarsely chopped

2 tablespoons coarsely chopped fresh basil

2 tablespoons fresh lime juice

2 tablespoons water

6 medium garlic cloves, coarsely chopped

1 tablespoon coarsely chopped fresh cilantro (optional)

¼ teaspoon pepper (freshly ground preferred)

2 tablespoons olive oil

1 1-pound flank steak, all visible fat and silver skin discarded

per serving

calories 198
total fat 10.0 g
  saturated fat 3.5 g
  trans fat 0.0 g
  polyunsaturated fat 0.5 g
  monounsaturated fat 5.0 g
cholesterol 65 mg

sodium 53 mg
carbohydrates 3 g
  fiber 1 g
  sugars 0 g
protein 23 g

dietary exchanges: 3 lean meat

pork medallions with mango mojo

A traditional Caribbean mango mojo (MO-ho) includes puréed mango. Grilling the mango and chopping it adds texture and a hint of smoke to the sweet sauce.

SERVES 4 | 3 medallions and 3 tablespoons sauce per serving

. . . .

Using the palm of your hand, gently flatten any thick slices of pork for more even cooking. Arrange the pork on a large rimmed baking sheet. In a small dish, stir together the shallots, lime zest, and pepper. Sprinkle all over the pork. Pour 2 tablespoons lime juice and the oil on top. Sprinkle 2 tablespoons cilantro all over the pork. Let stand for 30 minutes.

Meanwhile, lightly spray the grill rack with cooking spray. Preheat the grill on medium. Grill the mango for 2 minutes on each side. Let cool to room temperature. Finely chop. In a small bowl, stir together the mango and the remaining mojo ingredients.

Grill the pork, covered, for 4 to 6 minutes, or until it registers 145°F on an instant-read thermometer, turning once. Transfer to plates. Let stand for 3 minutes. Serve with the mojo.

1 1-pound pork tenderloin, all visible fat discarded, cut diagonally across the grain into 12 medallions

2 tablespoons minced shallots

1 teaspoon grated lime zest

2 tablespoons fresh lime juice

¼ teaspoon pepper (freshly ground preferred)

1 teaspoon olive oil

2 tablespoons chopped fresh cilantro

Cooking spray

MOJO

1 medium mango, cut lengthwise into ½-inch-thick slices

1½ tablespoons lime juice

1 tablespoon chopped fresh cilantro

1 small garlic clove, minced

¼ teaspoon red hot-pepper sauce

per serving

calories 186
total fat 4.5 g
  saturated fat 1.0 g
  trans fat 0.0 g
  polyunsaturated fat 0.5 g
  monounsaturated fat 2.0 g
cholesterol 60 mg

sodium 51 mg
carbohydrates 15 g
  fiber 2 g
  sugars 12 g
protein 22 g

dietary exchanges: 1 fruit, 3 lean meat

seitan stacks

Seitan (SAY-tan) is a meatlike, protein-rich food made from wheat gluten. In this dish, it's layered with hearty vegetables and gooey mozzarella.

SERVES 4 | 1 stack per serving

. . . .

In a small bowl, stir together the chopped rosemary, oregano, basil, and pepper.

Arrange the eggplant, squash, bell peppers, and seitan in a single layer on a rimmed baking sheet. Drizzle with half the lemon juice and oil. Sprinkle with half the rosemary mixture. Turn over the vegetables and seitan. Repeat with the remaining lemon juice, oil, and rosemary mixture.

Lightly spray the grill rack with cooking spray. Preheat the grill on medium high. Using a perforated grill sheet, grill the vegetables and seitan for 2 to 3 minutes on each side. Remove from the grill. Put 4 slices of eggplant on a platter. Top each with 1 bell pepper ring, 4 squash rounds, 3 seitan strips, and 2 tablespoons mozzarella. Repeat the layers. Spoon the sauce over the stacks. Garnish with the rosemary.

1 tablespoon chopped fresh rosemary or 1 teaspoon dried rosemary, crushed

1 teaspoon dried oregano, crumbled

1 teaspoon dried basil, crumbled

½ teaspoon pepper

1 1-pound eggplant, cut into 8 ½-inch slices

2 medium yellow summer squash, each cut into 16 ½-inch rounds

2 medium red bell peppers, each cut into 4 ½-inch rings

8 ounces seitan strips or chunks, patted dry

2 tablespoons fresh lemon juice

1 tablespoon olive oil

   Olive oil cooking spray

1 cup shredded low-fat mozzarella cheese

½ cup marinara sauce (lowest sodium available), heated

4 small sprigs of fresh rosemary (optional)

per serving

calories 243	sodium 447 mg
total fat 8.0 g	carbohydrates 20 g
saturated fat 1.5 g	fiber 7 g
trans fat 0.0 g	sugars 11 g
polyunsaturated fat 1.5 g	protein 24 g
monounsaturated fat 4.0 g	
cholesterol 10 mg	dietary exchanges:
	4 vegetable, 3 lean meat

mushroom-zucchini nachos with smoky crema

There's no need to feel guilty about eating nachos for dinner when the homemade grilled tortilla chips are topped with veggies and tofu. Seasoned with a zesty spice mix and garnished with a Mexican-style sour cream, these nachos pop with flavor. Remember to allow enough time to press the tofu for easier grilling.

SERVES 4 | 1½ cups per serving

Put the tofu on a cutting board lined with four layers of paper towels. Cover with four layers of paper towels. Place a large, heavy baking dish on top. Let stand for 30 minutes so the tofu releases its excess moisture, replacing the paper towels if necessary.

Meanwhile, arrange the tortilla wedges in a single layer on a large rimmed baking sheet. Let stand for 30 minutes to 1 hour, or until slightly dried and curled. Transfer to a large bowl.

In a small bowl, stir together the cumin, oregano, and garlic powder. Set aside.

In a separate small bowl, whisk together the sour cream, milk, and paprika. Cover and refrigerate.

Lightly spray the grill with cooking spray. Preheat the grill on medium.

Meanwhile, using paper towels, pat dry the tofu. Cut it crosswise into 4 thin slabs. Transfer to the baking sheet. Arrange the mushrooms and zucchini in a single layer on a separate large rimmed baking sheet. Lightly spray the

14 ounces light extra-firm or firm tofu, drained and patted dry

4 6-inch corn tortillas, each cut into 6 wedges

2 teaspoons ground cumin

½ teaspoon dried oregano (Mexican preferred), crumbled

½ teaspoon garlic powder

⅓ cup fat-free sour cream

3 tablespoons fat-free milk

¼ teaspoon smoked paprika
Cooking spray

2 medium portobello mushroom caps, cut into ½-inch slices

1 medium zucchini, cut lengthwise into ½-inch slices

¾ cup cherry tomatoes, halved

½ cup crumbled queso fresco or farmer cheese

⅓ cup chopped fresh cilantro

tofu, mushrooms, and zucchini on all sides with cooking spray. Sprinkle the cumin mixture over all sides of the tofu and vegetables. Using your fingertips, gently press the mixture so it adheres to the tofu and vegetables.

Place the tofu lengthwise so it's perpendicular to the grates of the grill. Grill, covered, for 8 to 10 minutes, or until lightly browned, turning once halfway through. Place the mushrooms and zucchini so they're perpendicular to the grates of the grill. Grill, covered, for 6 to 9 minutes, or until lightly browned and tender, turning occasionally. Grill the tortilla wedges, covered, for 5 to 8 minutes, or until lightly crisp, turning occasionally. Transfer the tofu, mushrooms, and zucchini to a cutting board. Transfer the tortilla wedges to serving plates.

Coarsely chop the tofu, mushrooms, and zucchini, keeping the ingredients separate. Top the tortilla wedges with, in order, the mushrooms, zucchini, tofu, tomatoes, queso fresco, and cilantro. Drizzle with the sour cream mixture.

COOK'S TIP: Pressing the tofu helps release its excess moisture, making it firmer and easier to grill. Use a large pancake turner or spatula to turn the tofu while it grills.

per serving

calories 206	sodium 134 mg
total fat 6.0 g	carbohydrates 22 g
saturated fat 1.5 g	fiber 4 g
trans fat 0.0 g	sugars 5 g
polyunsaturated fat 1.5 g	protein 17 g
monounsaturated fat 2.0 g	dietary exchanges: 1 starch,
cholesterol 14 mg	1 vegetable, 2 lean meat

GRILLING

honey-balsamic brussels sprouts with goat cheese

The gentle tartness of the balsamic mixture accents the flavor of the sprouts. Try these even if you think you don't like brussels sprouts; grilling imparts a sweet smokiness and tames the bitterness.

SERVES 4 | ½ cup per serving

. . . .

Soak four 6- to 8-inch wooden skewers for at least 10 minutes in cold water to keep them from charring, or use metal skewers.

Using a sharp knife, trim the stems of the brussels sprouts. Hold each brussels sprout with the stem end up. Cut halfway through each (to help them absorb the marinade).

In a large shallow glass bowl, whisk together the vinegar, honey, oil, and garlic. Set aside 1 tablespoon of the mixture. Cover and refrigerate the reserved mixture.

Add the brussels sprouts to the marinade in the bowl, stirring to coat. Cover and refrigerate for 15 minutes to 8 hours, turning occasionally.

12   **medium brussels sprouts (about 8 ounces)**

3   **tablespoons balsamic vinegar**

1   **tablespoon honey**

1   **teaspoon olive oil**

1   **medium garlic clove, minced**

    Cooking spray

2   **tablespoons goat cheese crumbles or crumbled fat-free feta cheese**

Lightly spray the grill rack with cooking spray. Preheat the grill on medium.

Piercing the stem ends of the brussels sprouts first, thread them onto the skewers. Grill, covered, for 20 to 25 minutes, or until they are golden brown and can easily be pierced with the tip of a sharp knife, turning every 5 minutes to brown on all sides.

Transfer to a serving platter or plates. Drizzle with the reserved vinegar mixture. Arrange the goat cheese crumbles around the brussels sprouts.

COOK'S TIP: If your grocer carries brussels sprouts on the stalk, you can skip the skewers. Cut halfway through each sprout from the top and brush the marinade on each. Grill as directed, turning the stalk every 5 minutes. To serve, cut the grilled sprouts off the stalk.

per serving

calories 80
total fat 3.0 g
  saturated fat 1.0 g
  trans fat 0.0 g
  polyunsaturated fat 0.0 g
  monounsaturated fat 1.0 g
cholesterol 3 mg

sodium 43 mg
carbohydrates 12 g
  fiber 2 g
  sugars 8 g
protein 3 g

dietary exchanges:
1 vegetable, ½ other
carbohydrate, ½ fat

beets with orange gremolata

A gremolata is a garnish usually made with parsley, lemon zest, and garlic. This one uses orange zest, drops the garlic, and adds almonds for crunch and bits of orange to enhance the sweetness of the grill-caramelized beets.

SERVES 4 | ½ cup beets and 2 tablespoons gremolata per serving

Lightly spray the grill rack with cooking spray. Preheat the grill on medium.

In a small bowl, stir together the thyme, pepper, and salt. Lightly spray both sides of the beets with cooking spray. Sprinkle the thyme mixture over both sides of the beets. Using your fingertips, gently press the mixture so it adheres to the beets.

Using tongs, place the beets about 1 inch apart on the grill rack. Grill, covered, for 15 minutes. Turn over the beets. Grill, covered, for 10 to 15 minutes, or until tender when pierced with the tip of a knife.

Meanwhile, in a small bowl, stir together the remaining ingredients.

Transfer the beets to a platter. Top with the gremolata.

Olive oil cooking spray

1 tablespoon chopped fresh thyme or 1 teaspoon dried thyme, crumbled

¼ teaspoon pepper (freshly ground preferred)

⅛ teaspoon salt

1 pound (5 to 6 medium) beets, cut into ½-inch slices

1 teaspoon grated orange zest

1 large orange, cut into ½-inch pieces

1 tablespoon chopped fresh parsley

1 tablespoon chopped almonds, dry-roasted

per serving

calories 83
total fat 1.0 g
  saturated fat 0.0 g
  trans fat 0.0 g
  polyunsaturated fat 0.5 g
  monounsaturated fat 0.5 g
cholesterol 0 mg

sodium 162 mg
carbohydrates 17 g
  fiber 5 g
  sugars 12 g
protein 3 g

dietary exchanges:
2 vegetable, ½ fruit

chai-spiced pineapple spears

Warm Indian spices complement the natural sweetness of the fruit. Delicious for dessert, this pineapple also pairs well with grilled fish or meat.

4 SERVINGS | 2 spears per serving

In a small bowl, stir together the brown sugar, cinnamon, nutmeg, and cloves.

Preheat the grill on medium. Line a rimmed baking sheet or a large baking dish with aluminum foil.

Put the pineapple on the foil. Lightly spray the pineapple with cooking spray. Sprinkle the brown sugar mixture over all sides of the pineapple. Using your fingertips, gently press the mixture so it adheres to the pineapple.

Place the pineapple spears lengthwise so they are perpendicular to the grates of the grill. Grill for 8 to 10 minutes, or until caramelized, turning them frequently so they don't burn.

1 tablespoon brown sugar

1 teaspoon ground cinnamon

½ teaspoon ground nutmeg (freshly grated preferred)

⅛ teaspoon ground cloves (optional)

1 medium pineapple, peeled and cored, cut into 8 spears, and patted dry

Cooking spray

COOK'S TIP: For convenience, many grocery stores sell peeled and cored whole pineapple in the produce section.

per serving

calories 129
total fat 0.5 g
  saturated fat 0.0 g
  trans fat 0.0 g
  polyunsaturated fat 0.0 g
  monounsaturated fat 0.0 g
cholesterol 0 mg

sodium 3 mg
carbohydrates 34 g
  fiber 4 g
  sugars 26 g
protein 1 g

dietary exchanges: 2 fruit

stir-frying

Stir-frying is a healthy, quick, cost-conscious, and efficient cooking method. Within minutes, a nutritious meal can be put together complete with plenty of vegetables and a protein such as fish, poultry, meat, tofu, or lentils. Stir-fries lend themselves to including more than one type of vegetable in a dish, such as Summertime Stir-Fry (page 101), allowing for a variety of nutrients and the opportunity to include different vegetables in your eating plan. You can easily make substitutions, too, when stir-frying. If you don't have broccoli, then you can add cauliflower instead. If you don't have a particular type of mushroom on hand, use another. Stir-frying requires a minimum of hot oil, and this fast, high-heat method of cooking seals in the natural juices of meats and seafood and preserves the nutrients, texture, and color of vegetables.

Stir-frying offers ethnic variety, too. It's not just for Asian dishes; try Mediterranean Mushrooms and Bell Peppers (page 113) or Taco Time Pork (page 107) to see how versatile this method can be. You can even cook fruit in your wok, such as Warm Cinnamon-Raisin Apples (page 114).

When choosing a wok, look for carbon steel and avoid nonstick coatings, which should not be used when cooking on high heat. Before using your wok, you'll need to "season" it. First, clean the wok inside and out, using a stainless-steel scouring pad and plenty of hot, soapy water, to remove the antirust coating. Rinse the wok well and heat it over low heat for 1 to 2 minutes, or until the water has evaporated (be sure to ventilate the kitchen well because any remaining coating might emit fumes). Allow the wok to cool, then heat it over high heat until a bead of water dropped into the wok evaporates within 1 to 2 seconds. Pour in 2 tablespoons peanut or canola oil, swirling to coat the wok. Reduce the heat to medium. To further season the wok, cook ½ cup sliced unpeeled ginger and one bunch of green onions (sliced into 2-inch pieces) for 20 minutes, or until brown and crusty, stirring frequently and using a spatula to press the ginger mixture all over the inside of the wok. Remove from the heat, discarding the ginger mixture. Wash the wok with hot water but no soap (from this point on, you'll never use soap to wash your wok). Heat the wok over low heat until the water evaporates. To clean the wok after cooking, use hot water and, if needed, a nonabrasive scouring pad. Heat the cleaned wok over low heat until completely dry, to prevent rusting.

HERE'S HOW THIS TECHNIQUE USUALLY WORKS:

1. PREHEAT the pan over high heat. (The pan is hot enough when a bead of water vaporizes within 1 to 2 seconds of contact.)

2. ADD oil to the hot pan (this will help keep the oil from smoking and the food from sticking) and swirl the pan to be sure oil coats the surface.

3. STIR-FRY aromatics such as garlic and ginger (these ingredients should sizzle as soon as they're added).

4. ADD the protein in one layer to sear it (sometimes the protein is cooked before the aromatics).

5. ADD the vegetables.

6. Finally, ADD any liquids and additional seasonings.

7. While the food is cooking, be sure to STIR it around the pan constantly.

Tools & Equipment Needed: 14-inch wok or 12-inch skillet (when you're cooking food for four people, which is the common serving number for the recipes in this cookbook, these sizes will work best to avoid crowding the food; it will be harder to keep a larger wok or skillet uniformly hot), spatulas, wooden spoons, kitchen timer

TO STIR-FRY:
To quickly cook small pieces of food in a large pan over very high heat while constantly and briskly stirring the food.

TIPS:

- Because stir-frying moves so quickly, it's best to use the classic technique called *mise en place*, which means having all the ingredients prepared and measured before you begin cooking.

- Cook in a well-ventilated area.

- When adding oil, quickly tilt the pan back and forth to allow the oil to coat the entire bottom.

- If the pan is hot enough, you'll see the oil shimmer when you add it.

- Start with foods that require the longest cooking times, such as onions and carrots, and finish with those that need to cook for only a few minutes.

- Make sure all the meat, poultry, or fish and vegetables are dry before adding them to the wok.

- Discard all visible fat and skin from meat and poultry.

- Be sure to listen for a constant sizzle throughout the cooking process, as this sound will tell you if the pan is hot enough.

chinese chicken salad

A sweet-hot dressing highlights the juicy chicken and crisp vegetables in this stir-fried salad. If you're too hungry to wait for it to chill, serve this entrée hot over steamed brown rice.

SERVES 5 | 1 cup per serving

Heat a wok over medium-high heat. Pour in 1 tablespoon chili oil and the sesame oil, swirling to coat the bottom. Cook the garlic and gingerroot for 1 minute, stirring constantly. Increase the heat to high. Stir in the chicken. Cook for 4 minutes, or until the chicken is lightly browned, stirring constantly. Stir in the bell pepper, water chestnuts, snow peas, and water. Cook for 3 minutes, or until the water evaporates, stirring constantly. Stir in the green onions. Cook for 1 minute, stirring constantly. Remove the wok from the heat.

In a small bowl, whisk together the soy sauce, honey, vinegar, and the remaining 1 teaspoon chili oil. Pour over the chicken mixture, stirring to coat. Cover and refrigerate for at least 2 hours, or until chilled.

1 tablespoon hot chili oil and 1 teaspoon hot chili oil, divided use

1 tablespoon toasted sesame oil

3 or 4 medium garlic cloves, minced

1½ teaspoons grated peeled gingerroot

1 pound boneless, skinless chicken breasts, all visible fat discarded, patted dry, and cut into ½-inch cubes

1 cup thinly sliced red bell pepper strips

1 8-ounce can sliced water chestnuts, drained and cut into thin strips

6 ounces snow peas, trimmed, halved if large

2 tablespoons water

⅓ cup thinly sliced green onions

2 tablespoons soy sauce (lowest sodium available)

1 tablespoon honey

1 tablespoon rice vinegar

per serving

calories 221	sodium 271 mg
total fat 9.0 g	carbohydrates 13 g
saturated fat 1.0 g	fiber 3 g
trans fat 0.0 g	sugars 8 g
polyunsaturated fat 2.5 g	protein 21 g
monounsaturated fat 4.0 g	dietary exchanges:
cholesterol 58 mg	2 vegetable, 2½ lean meat

sunny seafood mélange

Speedy stir-frying is a perfect technique to let the fresh flavors of the sun-kissed Mediterranean shine. Serve this medley of sweet scallops, lean grouper, and tender vegetables over a bed of whole-grain pasta or couscous.

SERVES 4 | 1 cup per serving

. . . .

Heat a wok over high heat. Pour in 1 teaspoon oil, swirling to coat the wok. Cook the zucchini, mushrooms, bell pepper, onion, and garlic for 1½ to 2½ minutes, or until tender-crisp, stirring constantly. Transfer to a bowl.

Heat the remaining 1 teaspoon oil, still over high heat, swirling to coat the wok. Cook the fish and scallops for 2 to 3 minutes, gently stirring constantly (the fish and scallops won't be done at this point).

Stir in the zucchini mixture and the remaining ingredients. Cook for 1 to 2 minutes, or until the fish flakes easily when tested with a fork and the scallops are opaque, stirring constantly. Be careful not to overcook or the scallops will become rubbery.

1	teaspoon canola or corn oil and 1 teaspoon canola or corn oil, divided use
1	small zucchini, cut into ¼-inch slices
4	ounces sliced brown (cremini) mushrooms
½	medium red bell pepper, diced
½	medium onion, diced
1	medium garlic clove, minced
12	ounces grouper, redfish, mahi mahi, or salmon fillets, rinsed, patted dry, and cut into ¾-inch pieces
4	ounces bay scallops, rinsed and patted dry
1	large tomato, peeled and diced
½	teaspoon dried oregano, crumbled
½	teaspoon dried basil, crumbled
¼	teaspoon salt
⅛	teaspoon pepper

per serving

calories 151
total fat 3.5 g
  saturated fat 0.5 g
  trans fat 0.0 g
  polyunsaturated fat 1.0 g
  monounsaturated fat 1.5 g
cholesterol 38 mg

sodium 309 mg
carbohydrates 7 g
  fiber 2 g
  sugars 4 g
protein 22 g

dietary exchanges:
1 vegetable, 3 lean meat

tex-mex chicken

After marinating in the bright flavors of lime, chili powder, and cumin, juicy chicken teams up with poblano pepper, tomatoes, and cheese in this easy dish.

SERVES 4 | 1 cup per serving

In a large shallow bowl or a baking dish, whisk together the lime zest, lime juice, chili powder, cumin, salt, and pepper. Add the chicken, turning to coat. Cover and refrigerate for 15 minutes to 8 hours, turning occasionally. Drain the chicken, discarding the marinade. Pat it dry.

Heat a wok over high heat. Pour in 1 teaspoon oil, swirling to coat the wok. Cook the chicken for 3 to 4 minutes, or until the chicken is no longer pink in the center, stirring constantly. Transfer to a bowl. Heat the remaining 1 teaspoon oil, still over high heat, swirling to coat the wok. Cook the onion for 2 to 3 minutes, or until tender-crisp, stirring constantly. Stir in the poblano. Cook for 1 minute, stirring constantly. Stir in the chicken and tomatoes. Cook for 30 seconds, or until the tomatoes are hot, stirring constantly. Just before serving, sprinkle with the Cotija.

1 teaspoon grated lime zest

2 tablespoons fresh lime juice

1 teaspoon chili powder

1 teaspoon ground cumin

¼ teaspoon salt

¼ teaspoon pepper

1 pound boneless, skinless chicken breasts, all visible fat discarded, cut into ½-inch pieces

1 teaspoon canola or corn oil and 1 teaspoon canola or corn oil, divided use

1 small red onion, thinly sliced

¼ cup chopped poblano pepper (roasted preferred; see Cook's Tip on page 45)

1 cup halved cherry tomatoes

½ cup shredded low-fat Cotija cheese or low-fat Monterey Jack cheese

per serving

calories 221
total fat 9.0 g
  saturated fat 3.0 g
  trans fat 0.0 g
  polyunsaturated fat 1.5 g
  monounsaturated fat 3.0 g
cholesterol 82 mg

sodium 375 mg
carbohydrates 6 g
  fiber 2 g
  sugars 3 g
protein 29 g

dietary exchanges:
1 vegetable, 3½ lean meat

COOK'S TIP ON COTIJA CHEESE: Cotija is a Mexican cheese made from cow's or goat's milk. It doesn't melt, so it's often sprinkled on salads or cooked dishes.

summertime stir-fry

This entrée is a step above what you'd find on most takeout menus, thanks to the addition of fresh lemon zest and cherry tomatoes.

SERVES 4 | 1 cup stir-fry and ½ cup rice per serving

Put 1 tablespoon cornstarch in a medium shallow glass dish. Add 1 tablespoon soy sauce, whisking to dissolve. Add the chicken, turning to coat. Cover and refrigerate for 10 minutes to 8 hours, turning occasionally. Drain the chicken, discarding the marinade. Pat it dry.

In a medium bowl, whisk together 1¼ cups broth, the lemon zest, and the remaining 1 tablespoon cornstarch and 1 tablespoon soy sauce.

Prepare the rice using the package directions, omitting the salt and margarine and substituting the remaining 1 cup broth for the water.

Meanwhile, heat a wok over high heat. Pour in the oil, swirling to coat the bottom. Cook the chicken for 3 to 4 minutes on each side, or until almost cooked through. Stir in the broccoli. Cook for 2 to 3 minutes, stirring constantly. Stir in the reserved broth mixture. Reduce the heat and simmer, covered, for 5 minutes. Stir in the peas and tomatoes. Remove from the heat. Let stand for 30 seconds. Serve the stir-fry over the rice.

- 1 tablespoon cornstarch and 1 tablespoon cornstarch, divided use
- 1 tablespoon soy sauce and 1 tablespoon soy sauce (lowest sodium available), divided use
- 1 pound chicken tenders, all visible fat discarded
- 1¼ cups fat-free, low-sodium chicken broth and 1 cup fat-free, low-sodium chicken broth, divided use
- ½ teaspoon grated lemon zest
- ½ cup uncooked instant brown rice
- 1 teaspoon canola or corn oil
- 2 cups small broccoli florets
- 1 cup sugar snap peas, trimmed
- 1 cup cherry tomatoes

per serving

calories 247
total fat 5.0 g
  saturated fat 1.0 g
  trans fat 0.0 g
  polyunsaturated fat 1.0 g
  monounsaturated fat 2.0 g
cholesterol 73 mg

sodium 364 mg
carbohydrates 22 g
  fiber 3 g
  sugars 4 g
protein 29 g

dietary exchanges: 1 starch, 2 vegetable, 3 lean meat

chicken with napa cabbage and rice noodles

A delectable sauce spiced with sriracha and sweetened with honey coats a ginger-scented mixture of chicken, rice noodles, and fresh vegetables in this one-dish meal.

SERVES 4 | 1½ cups per serving

. . . .

In a small bowl, whisk together the sauce ingredients. Set aside.

Put the noodles in a large bowl. Pour in boiling water to cover. Let stand for 5 to 7 minutes, or until tender. Drain well in a colander.

Meanwhile, heat a wok over high heat. Pour in the oil, swirling to coat the wok. Cook the chicken for 5 minutes, or until lightly browned, stirring frequently. Transfer to a plate (the chicken won't be done at this point).

Cook the gingerroot for 30 seconds, still over high heat, stirring constantly. Stir in the bell pepper and carrot. Cook for 2 to 3 minutes, or until slightly softened, stirring constantly (add a little water if the vegetables are sticking). Stir in the cabbage. Cook for 1 minute, stirring

SAUCE

2 tablespoons soy sauce (lowest sodium available)

2 teaspoons honey

1 teaspoon plain rice vinegar

½ teaspoon cornstarch

¼ teaspoon hot chile sauce (sriracha preferred)

———

4 ounces dried medium Asian rice stick noodles, broken in half

1 tablespoon toasted sesame oil

1 pound boneless skinless chicken breasts, all visible fat discarded, patted dry, and cut into ½-inch strips

(continued)

constantly. Stir in the green onions, chicken, and sauce. Cook for 1 minute, or until the chicken is no longer pink in the center and the vegetables are tender-crisp, stirring constantly. Stir in the noodles. Just before serving, sprinkle with the cilantro and peanuts.

per serving

calories 373	sodium 415 mg
total fat 11.0 g	carbohydrates 36 g
saturated fat 2.0 g	fiber 4 g
trans fat 0.0 g	sugars 7 g
polyunsaturated fat 3.5 g	protein 29 g
monounsaturated fat 4.5 g	
cholesterol 73 mg	dietary exchanges: 2 starch, 1 vegetable, 3 lean meat

1½ tablespoons minced peeled gingerroot

1 medium red bell pepper, chopped

½ cup matchstick-size carrot strips

4 cups thinly sliced napa cabbage

¾ cup sliced green onions (dark green part only)

¼ cup chopped fresh cilantro

¼ cup chopped unsalted peanuts, dry-roasted

COOK'S TIP ON RICE STICK NOODLES: Rice stick noodles come in various sizes, from thin vermicelli-like strands to wide, hearty noodles. For this recipe, look for noodles that are about the width of spaghetti or linguine. They are available in Asian specialty markets and in the Asian aisle of some supermarkets.

shredded beef with bok choy and carrots

This is so good that you might want to double the recipe and have leftovers. For a change from brown rice, try serving this entrée over another whole grain, such as bulgur or farro.

SERVES 4 | 1 heaping cup per serving

. . . .

In a large glass baking dish, stir together the sherry, soy sauce, gingerroot, garlic, and chili paste. Add the beef, turning to coat. Let stand for 10 minutes.

Drain the beef, discarding the marinade. Pat it dry.

Heat a wok over high heat. Pour in 1½ teaspoons oil, swirling to coat the bottom. Cook the beef for 2 minutes, or until just cooked, stirring constantly. Using a slotted spoon, transfer the beef to a plate.

If the wok is dry, heat the remaining 1½ teaspoons oil, swirling to coat the bottom. Cook the bok choy and carrots for 2 to 3 minutes, stirring constantly. Stir in the beef and broth.

3 tablespoons dry sherry

1 tablespoon soy sauce (lowest sodium available)

2 teaspoons grated peeled gingerroot

2 to 3 medium garlic cloves, crushed or minced

½ teaspoon red chili paste

1 pound flank steak, all visible fat discarded, sliced across the grain into ⅛-inch strips

1½ teaspoons canola or peanut oil and 1½ teaspoons canola or peanut oil (if needed), divided use

6 stalks bok choy, thinly sliced

5 medium carrots, cut into matchstick-size strips

(continued)

Working quickly, put the cornstarch in a small bowl. Add the water, whisking to dissolve. Stir into the beef mixture. Cook for 1 minute, or until the sauce thickens, stirring constantly.

½ cup fat-free, low-sodium beef broth

1 tablespoon cornstarch

2 tablespoons water

per serving

calories 256	sodium 279 mg
total fat 9.5 g	carbohydrates 12 g
saturated fat 2.5 g	fiber 3 g
trans fat 0.0 g	sugars 5 g
polyunsaturated fat 1.5 g	protein 27 g
monounsaturated fat 4.5 g	dietary exchanges:
cholesterol 69 mg	2 vegetable, 3 lean meat

COOK'S TIP: The flank steak will be easier to slice if it's partially frozen. To avoid diluting the flavors, thaw the slices before adding them to the marinade.

COOK'S TIP ON CUTTING MATCHSTICK-SIZE STRIPS: A mandoline slicer is a handy tool to use when you have a lot of vegetables to cut. Most can make thin or thick slices, as well as matchstick-size strips and crinkle or waffle cuts.

japanese stir-fry

This dish has all the flavors of sukiyaki, a Japanese dish that is usually cooked at the table, with all the ingredients kept separate. We simplify the process by stir-frying everything together.

SERVES 4 | 1⅓ cups per serving

. . . .

Prepare the soba noodles using the package directions, omitting the salt. Set aside.

Meanwhile, in a small bowl, whisk together the broth, sherry, brown sugar, soy sauce, gingerroot, chili oil, and pepper. Set aside.

Heat a wok over high heat. Pour in the canola oil, swirling to coat the wok. Cook the beef for 3 to 4 minutes, or until just cooked, stirring constantly. Using a slotted spoon, transfer the beef to a plate. Discard the accumulated juices from the beef.

Cook the cabbage, mushrooms, celery, green onions, and bamboo shoots for 3 to 4 minutes, stirring constantly. Stir in the noodles, beef, and broth mixture. Cook for 2 to 3 minutes, or until heated through, stirring frequently. Serve immediately.

7 ounces dried soba (buckwheat) noodles

½ cup fat-free, low-sodium beef broth

½ cup dry sherry or fresh orange juice

2 tablespoons light brown sugar

2 tablespoons soy sauce (lowest sodium available)

2 teaspoons grated peeled gingerroot

1 to 1½ teaspoons hot chili oil

½ teaspoon pepper

1 teaspoon canola or corn oil

1 pound boneless top round steak, all visible fat discarded, patted dry, and sliced across the grain into strips 2 to 3 inches long and ½ to 1 inch wide

2 cups thinly sliced napa cabbage

1 cup thinly sliced shiitake mushrooms, stems discarded

1 cup diagonally sliced celery

½ cup diagonally sliced green onions

1 8-ounce can bamboo shoots, drained and slivered

per serving

calories 267
total fat 4.0 g
  saturated fat 1.0 g
  trans fat 0.0 g
  polyunsaturated fat 1.0 g
  monounsaturated fat 2.0 g
cholesterol 39 mg

sodium 281 mg
carbohydrates 33 g
  fiber 3 g
  sugars 9 g
protein 24 g

dietary exchanges: 2 starch, 1 vegetable, 2½ lean meat

taco time pork

A Mexican-inspired dish cooked in a wok? Why not? The sizzling pork and vegetables are reminiscent of fajitas.

SERVES 4 | 2 tacos per serving

. . . .

In a medium bowl, stir together the chili powder, cumin, and pepper. Add the pork, stirring to coat.

Heat a wok over high heat. Pour in 2 teaspoons oil, swirling to coat the wok. Cook half the pork for 2 minutes, or until browned (the pork won't be done at this point), stirring constantly. Transfer to a plate. Repeat the process.

Heat the remaining 2 teaspoons oil, swirling to coat the wok. Cook the squash, onion, and Anaheim peppers for 3 minutes, stirring frequently. Stir in the pork, any juices, and the salt. Cook for 1 minute, or until the pork is no longer pink in the center, stirring frequently.

Warm the tortillas using the package directions. For each taco, put ⅔ cup pork mixture on a tortilla. Top with the romaine and sour cream.

- 1 **tablespoon chili powder**
- 2 **teaspoons ground cumin**
- ½ **teaspoon pepper**
- 1 **pound pork tenderloin, all visible fat discarded, patted dry, and cut into thin strips**
- 2 **teaspoons canola or corn oil, 2 teaspoons canola or corn oil, and 2 teaspoons canola or corn oil, divided use**
- 1 **medium yellow summer squash, halved lengthwise and thinly sliced**
- 1 **cup chopped onion**
- 2 **medium Anaheim peppers, seeds and ribs discarded, thinly sliced (see Cook's Tip on page 45)**
- ½ **teaspoon salt**
- 8 **6-inch corn tortillas**
- 3 **cups shredded romaine**
- ½ **cup fat-free sour cream (optional)**

per serving

calories 295	sodium 437 mg
total fat 11.0 g	carbohydrates 23 g
saturated fat 1.5 g	fiber 5 g
trans fat 0.0 g	sugars 5 g
polyunsaturated fat 3.0 g	protein 28 g
monounsaturated fat 5.5 g	
cholesterol 74 mg	dietary exchanges: 1 starch, 2 vegetable, 3 lean meat

plum-sauced pork with asian vegetables

Chinese plum sauce lends its subtly sweet flavor to this dish, while sesame oil adds a nutty flavor. With succulent pork tenderloin, crisp vegetables, and plenty of tender noodles, this delicious meal can be on the table in minutes.

SERVES 4 | 1 cup stir-fry and ½ cup noodles per serving

. . . .

Prepare the noodles using the package directions, omitting the salt. Drain well in a colander. Return the noodles to the pan. Stir in the sesame oil. Set aside.

Meanwhile, put the cornstarch in a small bowl. Add the broth, whisking to dissolve. Whisk in the plum sauce, soy sauce, vinegar, and brown sugar. Set aside.

Heat a wok over high heat. Pour in the canola oil, swirling to coat the wok. Cook the pork for 2 to 3 minutes, or until no longer pink on the outside, stirring frequently. Transfer to a plate. Set aside.

4 ounces uncooked wide lo mein or other Asian noodles

½ to 1 teaspoon toasted sesame oil

1 tablespoon cornstarch

½ cup fat-free, low-sodium vegetable broth or water

¼ cup Chinese plum sauce

2 tablespoons soy sauce (lowest sodium available)

2 tablespoons plain rice vinegar or cider vinegar

1 tablespoon light brown sugar

(continued)

In the wok, still over high heat, cook the vegetables, gingerroot, and garlic for 2 to 3 minutes, or until tender, stirring frequently. Stir in the pork and any accumulated juices. Cook for 1 minute. Stir the plum sauce mixture, then stir it into the pork mixture. Cook for about 1 minute, or until the sauce thickens and bubbles, stirring constantly.

Serve the pork mixture over the noodles. Sprinkle with the almonds.

1 tablespoon canola or corn oil

1 pound pork tenderloin, all visible fat discarded, patted dry, and sliced into 2 x ¼ inch-strips

16 ounces frozen stir-fry Asian vegetable blend

1½ teaspoons grated peeled gingerroot

1 large garlic clove, minced

¼ cup slivered almonds, dry-roasted

per serving

calories 387	sodium 361 mg
total fat 10.5 g	carbohydrates 45 g
saturated fat 1.5 g	fiber 4 g
trans fat 0.0 g	sugars 12 g
polyunsaturated fat 2.5 g	protein 29 g
monounsaturated fat 5.5 g	dietary exchanges:
cholesterol 60 mg	2½ starch, 2 vegetable, 3 lean meat

COOK'S TIP: Read the labels when you buy Asian noodles. Some have very little if any sodium, but others have almost 500 milligrams of sodium per serving.

STIR-FRYING BONUS: *If you're cutting back on sugar or can't find plum sauce, try this simple stir-fry sauce that works with nearly any combination of protein and vegetables: In a small bowl stir together 2½ teaspoons plain rice vinegar, 1½ teaspoons soy sauce (lowest sodium available), 1 teaspoon minced garlic, and 1 teaspoon grated peeled gingerroot.*

vegetarian fried rice

This vegan version of fried rice gets a protein boost from tofu rather than egg. It makes a delicious entrée, or serve ½ cup as a side dish.

SERVES 4 | 1½ cups per serving

. . . .

Prepare the rice using the package directions, omitting the salt and margarine. Set aside.

Heat a wok over high heat. Pour in the canola oil, swirling to coat the wok. Cook the tofu, mushrooms, snow peas, and green onion for 1 to 2 minutes, or until the mushrooms are soft and the snow peas and green onion are slightly wilted, stirring constantly. Stir in the green peas, soy sauce, and sesame oil. Stir in the rice. Cook until heated through, stirring constantly.

1½ cups uncooked brown rice

1 tablespoon canola or peanut oil

8 ounces light firm tofu, patted dry and crumbled

1 cup sliced button mushrooms

1 cup snow peas, trimmed

1 medium green onion, thinly sliced

½ cup frozen green peas, thawed

1 tablespoon soy sauce (lowest sodium available)

1 teaspoon toasted sesame oil

per serving

calories 231
total fat 7.0 g
  saturated fat 0.5 g
  trans fat 0.0 g
  polyunsaturated fat 2.5 g
  monounsaturated fat 3.5 g
cholesterol 0 mg

sodium 146 mg
carbohydrates 32 g
  fiber 4 g
  sugars 3 g
protein 10 g

dietary exchanges: 2 starch, 1 lean meat, ½ fat

lentils with mushrooms, tomatoes, and kale

Earthy cremini mushrooms, hearty lentils, fresh kale, and juicy tomatoes make a meatless meal that's brimming with flavor.

SERVES 4 | 1½ cups per serving

. . . .

In a medium saucepan, bring 2 cups broth to a boil over high heat. Stir in the lentils. Reduce the heat and simmer, covered, for 30 minutes, or until tender. Drain well in a fine-mesh sieve.

Heat a wok over high heat. Pour in the oil, swirling to coat the wok. Cook the onion for 1½ minutes, stirring constantly. Stir in the mushrooms. Cook for 2 to 3 minutes, or until slightly golden brown, stirring frequently. Stir in the wine. Cook for 2 to 3 minutes, stirring constantly. Stir in the kale. Cook for 1 to 2 minutes, or until wilted, stirring constantly. Stir in the lentils, tomatoes, seasoning blend, and the remaining ½ cup broth. Cook for 2 to 3 minutes, stirring frequently. Just before serving, sprinkle with the almonds.

2 cups fat-free, low-sodium vegetable broth and ½ cup fat-free, low-sodium vegetable broth, divided use

1 cup dried lentils, sorted for stones and shriveled lentils, rinsed, and drained

2 teaspoons canola or corn oil

1 small onion, thinly sliced

8 ounces brown (cremini) mushrooms, thinly sliced

¼ cup dry red wine (regular or nonalcoholic)

4 cups coarsely chopped kale, any large stems and ribs discarded

2 medium tomatoes, peeled and diced

1 teaspoon salt-free all-purpose seasoning blend

¼ cup slivered almonds, dry-roasted

per serving

calories 301	sodium 50 mg
total fat 7.0 g	carbohydrates 42 g
saturated fat 0.5 g	fiber 15 g
trans fat 0.0 g	sugars 6 g
polyunsaturated fat 2.0 g	protein 20 g
monounsaturated fat 3.5 g	dietary exchanges: 2 starch,
cholesterol 0 mg	2 vegetable, 1½ lean meat

green beans in spicy sauce

These hot and zesty green beans pair perfectly with nearly any stir-fried dish.

SERVES 4 | ¾ cup per serving

Put the cornstarch in a small bowl. Add the water, stirring to dissolve. Whisk in the remaining sauce ingredients. Set aside.

Heat a wok over high heat. Pour in 1 teaspoon canola oil, swirling to coat the wok. When a wisp of white smoke appears, stir in the green beans. Cook for 2 minutes, or until softened, stirring constantly. Using a slotted spoon, transfer the green beans to a colander.

Pour the remaining 1 teaspoon canola oil into the wok. Stir in the chiles, gingerroot, and garlic. Cook for 1 minute, still over high heat, stirring constantly. Stir in the green beans. Cook for 1 minute, stirring constantly. Make a well in the center of the green beans. Stir the sauce, then pour it into the well. Quickly stir the green beans and sauce together. When the sauce thickens, remove from the heat. Serve immediately.

SAUCE

- 1 teaspoon cornstarch
- 3 tablespoons water
- 1 teaspoon canola or peanut oil
- 1 teaspoon soy sauce (lowest sodium available)
- ½ teaspoon sugar
- ½ teaspoon toasted sesame oil
- ½ teaspoon white vinegar
- ½ teaspoon dry sherry (optional)
  Pinch of pepper (white preferred)

- 1 teaspoon canola or peanut oil and 1 teaspoon canola or peanut oil, divided use
- 12 ounces green beans, trimmed
- 2 small fresh red hot chiles, such as serranos, minced (see Cook's Tip on page 45)
- 2 teaspoons grated peeled gingerroot
- 2 teaspoons minced garlic

per serving

calories 71
total fat 4.5 g
  saturated fat 0.5 g
  trans fat 0.0 g
  polyunsaturated fat 1.5 g
  monounsaturated fat 2.5 g
cholesterol 0 mg

sodium 39 mg
carbohydrates 8 g
  fiber 2 g
  sugars 4 g
protein 2 g

dietary exchanges:
1 vegetable, 1 fat

mediterranean mushrooms and bell peppers

This vegetable dish features plenty of fresh basil, garlic, and lemon zest. You can use just one color of bell pepper if you'd like, but it's prettier and more flavorful if you use several colors. Serve it as a side dish, or use it to top pasta or homemade pizza.

SERVES 4 | ¾ cup per serving

Heat a wok over medium heat. Pour in the oil, swirling to coat the wok. Cook the garlic for 1 minute, stirring frequently. Stir in the mushrooms and salt. Cook for 5 minutes, stirring occasionally.

Increase the heat to high. Stir in the bell peppers. Cook for 7 to 8 minutes, or until tender-crisp, stirring frequently. Stir in the zest. Cook for 1 minute, stirring frequently. Stir in the basil and pepper.

2 teaspoons olive oil

3 medium garlic cloves, minced

8 ounces button mushrooms, thinly sliced

⅛ teaspoon salt

1 medium red bell pepper, cut into thin strips

1 medium green bell pepper, cut into thin strips

1 medium yellow bell pepper, cut into thin strips

1½ teaspoons grated lemon zest

½ cup fresh basil, minced

Pepper to taste (freshly ground preferred)

per serving

calories 61	sodium 79 mg
total fat 2.5 g	carbohydrates 8 g
saturated fat 0.5 g	fiber 2 g
trans fat 0.0 g	sugars 4 g
polyunsaturated fat 0.5 g	protein 3 g
monounsaturated fat 1.5 g	dietary exchanges:
cholesterol 0 mg	2 vegetable, ½ fat

warm cinnamon-raisin apples

The wok isn't just for savory dishes. For this sweet stir-fried dessert, sizzling apples are combined with a sauce that's fragrant with cinnamon and nutmeg. Serve this on its own or atop a scoop of fat-free frozen vanilla yogurt.

SERVES 4 | ½ cup per serving

In a small bowl, stir together the brown sugar, cornstarch, cinnamon, and nutmeg. Stir in ⅓ cup apple juice. Set aside.

Heat a wok over high heat. Pour in the oil, swirling to coat the wok. Cook the apples for 2 to 3 minutes, or until tender and lightly browned, stirring constantly.

Stir in the raisins and the remaining ⅔ cup apple juice. Stir in the brown sugar mixture. Cook for 4 to 6 minutes, or until the sauce is thickened, stirring constantly. Just before serving, sprinkle with the walnuts.

1 tablespoon light or dark brown sugar

2 teaspoons cornstarch

1 teaspoon ground cinnamon

¼ teaspoon ground nutmeg (freshly grated preferred)

⅓ cup 100% apple juice and ⅔ cup 100% apple juice, divided use

2 teaspoons canola or corn oil

2 medium Braeburn, Rome Beauty, or Golden Delicious apples, peeled if desired, thinly sliced, and patted dry

2 tablespoons golden raisins

¼ cup chopped walnuts, dry-roasted

per serving

calories 172
total fat 7.5 g
  saturated fat 0.5 g
  trans fat 0.0 g
  polyunsaturated fat 4.0 g
  monounsaturated fat 2.0 g
cholesterol 0 mg

sodium 4 mg
carbohydrates 28 g
  fiber 2 g
  sugars 21 g
protein 2 g

dietary exchanges: 2 fruit, 1½ fat

braising

Braising is perhaps one of the least familiar techniques to many American home cooks. If you fall into this category, you'll wonder why you haven't tried braising sooner once you've experienced the delicious food it creates. Braising involves layering flavors in a heavy pot. It often begins with a foundation of caramelized meat or poultry to which herbs, aromatics, and vegetables are added before the whole dish is simmered in a fragrant liquid such as wine, beer, broth, vinegar, or fruit juice. Because herbs and aromatics are an important element in braising, little salt—if any—is needed.

Another benefit of braising is that an entire meal can be cooked in the same skillet, so you're easily able to include vegetables in your main dish, such as with Moroccan-Spiced Lentils and Vegetables (page 130) and Eggs with Smoked Sausage, Spinach, and Tomatoes (page 137). The braising liquid is often used to make a sauce that enhances the flavor of the dish and helps retain the nutrients in the ingredients.

If you're a cook who doesn't want to spend a lot of time in the kitchen, braising is an ideal cooking technique that you'll want to use again and again. In fact, you might think of a braising pot as a heavy slow cooker without a plug. And much like a slow cooker, the food cooks low and slow without much tending. Because the dish cooks in one skillet, cleanup is easy, too.

Braising doesn't call for perfect timing, either. The food is cooked gently over low heat, making it a forgiving method.

HERE'S HOW THIS TECHNIQUE WORKS*:

1. For many recipes, first BROWN the food on all sides, using a small amount of healthy oil (or cooking spray). To do this, heat the oil in the pan and then add the meat or vegetables. (Be sure the food is dry; otherwise, moisture will cause it to steam rather than brown.) Then let it sit—without moving it—until the bottom is seared; if you turn the food before that, it will stick to the pan and the surface won't caramelize. Turn to brown all sides. In many braising recipes, the meat is removed from the pot at this point and then returned later.

2. Next, ADD herbs and aromatics such as onion and garlic. Match the herbs and aromatics to the cooking time; a longer cooking time requires bigger pieces so they don't break down while cooking.

3. STIR IN the vegetables, beans, and/or legumes. Return the meat to the pan if it was removed earlier.

4. ADD a small amount of liquid. (The liquid should not cover the meat, fish, or poultry.) The food is gently simmered on the stovetop or in the oven at a low temperature, tightly covered.

5. After the food is cooked, it can REST in the braising liquid. Once it's removed, the braising liquid can be reduced to make a rich, flavorful sauce.

*Sometimes the order of the steps varies

Tools & Equipment Needed: Pot with a tight-fitting lid (such as a Dutch oven or deep skillet)—the pot should be heavy so as to maintain an even temperature and small enough to hold the food snugly, with sides

> **TO BRAISE:**
> To cook food in a small amount of liquid on low heat and tightly covered (on the stovetop or in the oven), often browning it first.

BRAISING

high enough to contain the braising liquid; oven thermometer; instant-read thermometer; oven mitts and pot holders; kitchen timer

TIPS:

- You need to have a tight lid for your pot to keep the steam and vapors—and flavor—close to the food. If the pot lid isn't snug, you can wrap aluminum foil around the edge to seal it. You can also place a sheet of cooking parchment, a little larger than the pot, over the ingredients. Press down until it is just touching the food, with the edges outside the pot, then top with the lid.

- Almost any liquid can be used for braising to add its own unique flavor to the dish. Most braises use broth or wine, but you can also try beer or cider, or add a splash of 100 percent fruit juice to the pot. In more delicate dishes, water is all that's needed.

- A constant simmer is not always easy to regulate, especially on a gas stovetop, so our recipes don't state at what temperature to simmer. Even at the lowest setting on some stovetops, the heat may be too intense, which will cause the liquid to boil (try using a burner plate, sometimes called a simmer plate, which helps diffuse the heat). When simmering, a bubble should break through the surface of the liquid every second or two. If more bubbles rise to the surface, then lower the heat or shift the pot to one side of the burner.

spicy catfish with potatoes and tomatoes

Tender potato wedges, spicy chiles, and sweet grape tomatoes create a savory base for delicate catfish fillets. Serve this entrée in shallow soup bowls so you can enjoy all the broth.

SERVES 4 | 3 ounces fish and 1 cup potato mixture per serving

. . . .

In a large, heavy skillet, heat 1 tablespoon oil over medium-high heat, swirling to coat the bottom. Cook the potatoes, onion, poblano, and ¼ teaspoon salt, covered, for about 7 minutes, or until the potatoes are just tender-crisp, stirring occasionally.

Stir in the tomatoes and broth. Place the fish in the mixture. Bring to a boil, still over medium-high heat. Reduce the heat and simmer, covered, for 12 minutes, or until the fish flakes easily when tested with a fork. Drizzle with the remaining 1 tablespoon oil. Sprinkle with the cilantro, pepper, and the remaining ¼ teaspoon salt.

- 1 tablespoon olive oil and 1 tablespoon olive oil (extra virgin preferred), divided use
- 1 pound red potatoes, quartered
- ½ cup chopped onion
- 1 medium poblano pepper, seeds and ribs discarded, chopped (see Cook's Tip on page 45)
- ¼ teaspoon salt and ¼ teaspoon salt, divided use
- 1 cup grape tomatoes
- ½ cup fat-free, low-sodium chicken broth
- 4 catfish or tilapia fillets (about 4 ounces each), rinsed and patted dry
- ¼ cup chopped fresh cilantro
- ¼ teaspoon pepper

per serving

calories 272	sodium 375 mg
total fat 10.0 g	carbohydrates 24 g
saturated fat 2.0 g	fiber 3 g
trans fat 0.0 g	sugars 4 g
polyunsaturated fat 2.0 g	protein 22 g
monounsaturated fat 6.0 g	dietary exchanges: 1 starch,
cholesterol 66 mg	1 vegetable, 3 lean meat

cod with fennel, tomatoes, and orange

Braising is a perfect technique for cooking meaty fish like cod because the braising liquid keeps the fish moist.

SERVES 4 | 3 ounces fish and ¾ cup fennel mixture per serving

In a large, heavy skillet, heat the oil over medium heat, swirling to coat the bottom. Cook the onion for about 3 minutes, or until beginning to soften, stirring frequently. Stir in the fennel. Cook for 1 minute, stirring constantly. Stir in the garlic. Cook for 30 seconds, stirring constantly.

Stir in the tomatoes with liquid, water, orange juice, and thyme. Increase the heat to high and bring to a boil. Reduce the heat and simmer, covered, for 4 to 5 minutes, or until the fennel is almost tender.

Stir in the orange zest and pepper. Place the fish in the mixture. Simmer, covered, for 6 to 9 minutes, or until the fish flakes easily when tested with a fork.

2 teaspoons olive oil

1½ cups chopped onion

1 medium fennel bulb, halved crosswise, then cut lengthwise into thin slices

3 large garlic cloves, minced

1 14.5-ounce can no-salt-added diced tomatoes, undrained

¼ cup water

1 teaspoon grated orange zest

¼ cup fresh orange juice

2 teaspoons chopped fresh thyme

¼ teaspoon pepper (freshly ground preferred)

4 cod fillets (about 4 ounces each), rinsed and patted dry

per serving

calories 180
total fat 3.0 g
  saturated fat 0.5 g
  trans fat 0.0 g
  polyunsaturated fat 0.5 g
  monounsaturated fat 2.0 g
cholesterol 43 mg

sodium 107 mg
carbohydrates 17 g
  fiber 4 g
  sugars 7 g
protein 20 g

dietary exchanges:
3 vegetable, 3 lean meat

shrimp and grits with greens

This lighter version of a Southern classic proves you don't have to braise greens for a long time. A sauté with a short braise keeps them bright and crisp.

SERVES 4 | 2 ounces shrimp, ⅔ cup vegetable mixture, and ½ cup grits per serving

In a Dutch oven, cook the bacon over medium heat for 2 to 3 minutes, or until browned, stirring frequently. Pour in the oil. Stir in the onions. Cook for 3 minutes, or until the onion begins to soften, stirring occasionally. Stir in the bell peppers. Cook for 1 minute, or until slightly softened, stirring occasionally.

Stir in the greens. Cook for 2 minutes, or until bright green, stirring occasionally. Stir in the vinegar. Bring to a boil. Stir in the broth, wine, and thyme. Return to a boil. Reduce the heat and simmer, covered, for 7 to 10 minutes, or until the greens are tender-crisp. Add the shrimp. Cook, covered, for 2 to 3 minutes, or until pink on the outside. Stir in the hot-pepper sauce. Meanwhile, prepare the grits using the package directions. Spoon into shallow serving bowls. Top with the shrimp mixture.

3 slices turkey bacon, chopped

2 teaspoons olive oil

1½ cups chopped onions

1¼ cups chopped red bell peppers

2 cups chopped collard greens (any tough stems discarded), mustard greens, turnip greens, or baby kale

1 tablespoon cider vinegar

1 cup fat-free, low-sodium chicken or vegetable broth

¼ cup dry white wine (regular or nonalcoholic)

2 teaspoons chopped fresh thyme

12 ounces raw medium shrimp (thawed if frozen), peeled, rinsed, and patted dry

1 teaspoon Louisiana-style hot-pepper sauce

½ cup uncooked quick-cooking grits

per serving

calories 231	sodium 348 mg
total fat 4.5 g	carbohydrates 26 g
saturated fat 1.0 g	fiber 3 g
trans fat 0.0 g	sugars 5 g
polyunsaturated fat 1.0 g	protein 17 g
monounsaturated fat 2.5 g	dietary exchanges: 1 starch,
cholesterol 115 mg	2 vegetable, 2 lean meat

chicken with 40 cloves of garlic

If you're concerned about all that garlic, don't be! As the chicken braises in the oven, so does the garlic, giving it a sweet flavor and soft texture.

SERVES 6 | 3 ounces chicken per serving

Preheat the oven to 325°F. In a Dutch oven, heat the oil over medium-high heat, swirling to coat the bottom. Cook the chicken for 2 minutes on each side, or until browned. Add the garlic. Cook for 1 to 2 minutes, or until lightly browned, stirring frequently. Stir in the wine and thyme. Bring to a boil over high heat. Remove from the heat.

Bake, covered, for 25 to 30 minutes, or until the chicken is no longer pink in the center. Transfer the chicken and garlic to a platter. Cover to keep warm. Pour the cooking liquid into a measuring cup. Add enough of the ⅓ cup broth to measure 1 cup. Return the liquid to the pot. Bring to a boil over high heat. Reduce the heat to medium. Put the flour in a bowl. Add the remaining ¼ cup broth, stirring to dissolve. Stir into the cooking liquid. Cook for 4 to 5 minutes, or until thickened, stirring constantly.

2 teaspoons olive oil

6 boneless, skinless chicken breast halves (about 4 ounces each), all visible fat discarded

40 medium garlic cloves (from 3 to 4 heads)

½ cup dry white wine (regular or nonalcoholic)

1½ teaspoons fresh thyme or ½ teaspoon dried thyme, crumbled

⅓ cup fat-free, low-sodium chicken broth, if needed, and ¼ cup fat-free, low-sodium chicken broth or water, divided use

2 tablespoons white whole-wheat flour

COOK'S TIP: This recipe uses a lot of garlic, so look for containers of whole peeled garlic in the produce section of your grocery store to save yourself time and effort.

per serving

calories 186
total fat 4.5 g
  saturated fat 1.0 g
  trans fat 0.0 g
  polyunsaturated fat 0.5 g
  monounsaturated fat 2.0 g
cholesterol 73 mg

sodium 141 mg
carbohydrates 8 g
  fiber 1 g
  sugars 0 g
protein 26 g

dietary exchanges:
1 vegetable, 3 lean meat

chicken with dried plums and sage

A hint of sweetness from dried fruit balances the tang of Dijon mustard and slight bitterness of sage in this lightly seasoned dish.

SERVES 4 | 3 ounces chicken and ¼ cup vegetables and fruit per serving

. . . .

In a large, heavy, nonstick skillet, heat 1 teaspoon oil over medium-high heat, swirling to coat the bottom. Cook the chicken for 2 minutes on each side, or until browned. Transfer to a large plate.

In the same skillet, still over medium-high heat, heat the remaining 2 teaspoons oil, swirling to coat the bottom. Cook the onion and carrot for about 3 minutes, stirring frequently.

Stir in the remaining ingredients. Bring to a boil. Add the chicken, turning to coat. Reduce the heat and simmer, covered, for 10 to 12 minutes, or until the chicken is no longer pink in the center. Transfer the chicken to a platter.

Increase the heat to medium high and bring to a boil. Boil for 2 minutes, or until the onion mixture is slightly thickened, stirring occasionally. Spoon over the chicken.

- 1 teaspoon canola or corn oil and 2 teaspoons canola or corn oil, divided use
- 4 boneless, skinless chicken breast halves (about 4 ounces each), all visible fat discarded
- 1 medium onion, thinly sliced
- 1 large carrot, thinly sliced
- ½ cup fat-free, low-sodium chicken broth
- 4 medium dried plums, quartered
- 1 tablespoon coarse-grain Dijon mustard (lowest sodium available)
- ½ teaspoon dried rubbed sage
- ¼ teaspoon salt
- ¼ teaspoon pepper

per serving

calories 279	sodium 376 mg
total fat 7.0 g	carbohydrates 31 g
saturated fat 1.0 g	fiber 6 g
trans fat 0.0 g	sugars 23 g
polyunsaturated fat 1.5 g	protein 26 g
monounsaturated fat 3.0 g	dietary exchanges: ½ fruit,
cholesterol 73 mg	3 lean meat

curried chicken thighs

Simmering chicken thighs in a spiced tomato-coconut sauce yields exotic flavor with little effort. Serve the curry with brown basmati rice.

SERVES 4 | 1 thigh and 1 cup vegetables per serving

In a Dutch oven, heat the oil over medium heat, swirling to coat the bottom. Cook the onion for 3 minutes, stirring frequently. Stir in the gingerroot, curry powder, garlic, and cumin. Cook for 30 seconds, stirring constantly.

Stir in the tomatoes with liquid, coconut milk, and broth. Bring to a boil. Add the chicken and sweet potatoes. Return to a boil. Reduce the heat and simmer, covered, for 15 minutes. Turn over the chicken. Stir in the chard. Cook, covered, for 10 to 15 minutes, or until the chicken is no longer pink in the center.

Transfer the chicken and vegetables to a serving bowl. Bring the sauce to a boil over high heat. Boil for 3 to 5 minutes, stirring frequently. Stir in the cilantro. Pour the sauce over all.

1 teaspoon olive oil

1 large onion, halved, then cut into ¾-inch wedges

1 tablespoon minced peeled gingerroot

2½ teaspoons curry powder

3 large garlic cloves, minced

½ teaspoon ground cumin

1 14.5-ounce can no-salt-added diced tomatoes, undrained

½ cup lite coconut milk

½ cup fat-free, low-sodium chicken broth

4 bone-in, skinless chicken thighs (about 5 ounces each), all visible fat discarded

2 medium sweet potatoes, peeled and cubed

2 cups chopped rainbow chard, tough stems discarded

⅓ cup chopped fresh cilantro

per serving

calories 346
total fat 12.5 g
  saturated fat 4.0 g
  trans fat 0.0 g
  polyunsaturated fat 2.5 g
  monounsaturated fat 4.5 g
cholesterol 86 mg

sodium 191 mg
carbohydrates 30 g
  fiber 5 g
  sugars 11 g
protein 28 g

dietary exchanges: 1½ starch, 2 vegetable, 3 lean meat, ½ fat

beer-braised beef with molasses

Tender beef is cooked "low and slow" in a heady combination of beer, molasses, tomatoes, and bell pepper, with just a hint of zippy mustard. Try it over whole-grain, no-yolk noodles or low-fat mashed potatoes.

SERVES 6 | ¾ cup per serving

In a Dutch oven, heat the oil over medium-high heat, swirling to coat the bottom. Cook half the beef for 2 minutes on each side, or until browned. Transfer the beef to a plate. Repeat with the remaining beef.

Stir in the remaining ingredients except the salt. Increase the heat to high and bring to a boil. Return the beef and any accumulated juices to the Dutch oven, pressing down lightly so that the beef is partially covered. Reduce the heat and simmer, covered, for 2 to 2½ hours, or until the beef is very tender and falling apart when pierced with a fork. Using two forks, shred the beef. Stir in the salt.

1 tablespoon canola or corn oil

1½ pounds boneless bottom round steak, halved, all visible fat discarded

1 14.5-ounce can no-salt-added stewed tomatoes, undrained

6 ounces light beer (regular or nonalcoholic)

2 medium green bell peppers, chopped

1½ cups chopped onions

2 teaspoons dried basil, crumbled

2 medium garlic cloves, minced

2 tablespoons dark molasses

1 tablespoon yellow mustard (lowest sodium available)

½ teaspoon salt

per serving

calories 242
total fat 6.5 g
  saturated fat 2.0 g
  trans fat 0.0 g
  polyunsaturated fat 1.0 g
  monounsaturated fat 4.0 g
cholesterol 61 mg

sodium 273 mg
carbohydrates 15 g
  fiber 2 g
  sugars 9 g
protein 27 g

dietary exchanges:
2 vegetable, ½ other carbohydrate, 3 lean meat

sauerbraten

Be sure to plan ahead for this popular sweet-and-sour German dish that will feed a crowd or provide plenty of leftovers, because the beef marinates for two to three days before cooking. We've added roasted red bell peppers for color and a modern twist.

SERVES 12 | 3 ounces beef per serving

In a medium saucepan, stir together the wine, vinegar, water, carrots, onion, cloves, peppercorns, bay leaves, caraway seeds, and coriander. Bring to a boil over high heat. Reduce the heat and simmer for 5 minutes. Remove from the heat. Let stand until cool.

Using a fork, pierce the beef all over. Transfer to a large bowl or baking dish.

Pour the marinade over the beef, turning to coat. Cover and refrigerate for two to three days, turning occasionally.

Drain the beef, reserving the marinade. Pat the beef dry with paper towels.

1½ cups dry red wine (regular or nonalcoholic)

1½ cups red wine vinegar

1 cup water

2 medium carrots, sliced

1 medium onion, sliced

6 whole cloves

4 black peppercorns, crushed using a mortar and pestle

2 medium dried bay leaves

½ teaspoon caraway seeds

¼ teaspoon ground coriander

(continued)

Lightly spray a Dutch oven with cooking spray. Heat over medium-high heat. Cook the beef for 10 minutes, turning to brown it on all sides. Pour in the marinade. Bring to a boil over high heat. Boil for 5 minutes (this destroys harmful bacteria). Reduce the heat and simmer, covered, for 2 hours, or until the beef is tender. Transfer the beef to a cutting board. Let stand for 10 minutes before slicing.

Meanwhile, strain the cooking liquid through a fine-mesh sieve or colander placed over a bowl. Discard the solids. Skim off the fat and return the liquid to the Dutch oven. Stir in the gingersnaps and roasted peppers. Cook over medium heat for 10 minutes, or until bubbly, stirring frequently. Serve with the beef.

1 **3-pound boneless beef rump roast, all visible fat discarded**

Cooking spray

½ **cup crushed low-fat gingersnaps (about 7)**

7 **ounces chopped roasted red bell peppers, drained if bottled**

per serving

calories 164
total fat 4.0 g
  saturated fat 1.5 g
  trans fat 0.0 g
  polyunsaturated fat 0.0 g
  monounsaturated fat 1.5 g
cholesterol 64 mg

sodium 81 mg
carbohydrates 4 g
  fiber 0 g
  sugars 1 g
protein 26 g

dietary exchanges: 3 lean meat

anise-rubbed pork roast

Braising lets the pork cook to tender, juicy perfection and absorb all the flavors from the rub and the cooking liquid. Sweet and aromatic anise seed, which is used in the rub, is a member of the parsley family that provides the predominant flavor in black jelly beans. People in India often chew on the seeds after a meal to aid their digestion and sweeten their breath.

SERVES 8 | 3 ounces pork per serving

In a small bowl, stir together the thyme, oregano, anise seeds, and pepper. Sprinkle all over the pork. Using your fingertips, gently press the mixture so it adheres to the pork.

In a Dutch oven, heat the oil over medium-high heat, swirling to coat the bottom. Cook the pork for 30 minutes, turning to brown on all sides. Transfer to a plate.

Stir the broth and wine into the Dutch oven, scraping to dislodge any browned bits. Stir the onion, garlic, and parsley into the broth mixture. Place the pork back in the pot. Bring the broth mixture to a boil, still over medium-high heat. Reduce the heat to low. Cook, covered, for 2 hours, or until the pork is tender.

½ teaspoon dried thyme, crumbled

½ teaspoon dried oregano, crumbled

½ teaspoon anise seeds

⅛ teaspoon pepper

1 2-pound boneless pork loin roast, all visible fat discarded

1 teaspoon canola or corn oil

1¾ cups fat-free, low-sodium chicken broth

½ cup dry white wine (regular or nonalcoholic)

1 medium onion, chopped

2 medium garlic cloves, minced

1 tablespoon dried parsley, crumbled

¼ cup fat-free sour cream

Transfer the pork to a cutting board. Let stand for 15 to 20 minutes before slicing.

Meanwhile, increase the heat to medium high and bring the sauce to a boil. Boil until reduced by about half. Reduce the heat to low and let the sauce cool slightly. Spoon some of the sauce into the sour cream (this reduces curdling), then stir the sour cream mixture into the sauce. Cook for 1 minute, stirring constantly. Spoon over the sliced pork.

per serving

calories 194
total fat 9.0 g
  saturated fat 2.0 g
  trans fat 0.0 g
  polyunsaturated fat 1.0 g
  monounsaturated fat 2.5 g
cholesterol 66 mg

sodium 66 mg
carbohydrates 4 g
  fiber 1 g
  sugars 2 g
protein 22 g

dietary exchanges: 3 lean meat

moroccan-spiced lentils and vegetables

This hearty vegetarian stew is sure to satisfy, with meaty eggplant, sweet bell pepper, tender cabbage, and plump lentils. The warm blend of spices makes it perfect for a chilly evening.

SERVES 4 | 1½ cups per serving

In a large, heavy saucepan or Dutch oven, heat the oil over medium-high heat, swirling to coat the bottom. Cook the onion for about 3 minutes, or until soft, stirring frequently. Stir in the garlic. Cook for 30 seconds, stirring occasionally.

Stir in the eggplant, cabbage, and bell pepper. Cook for 5 to 6 minutes, or until the eggplant is lightly golden brown and the cabbage and bell pepper are tender, stirring frequently.

2   teaspoons olive oil

1   medium onion, chopped

2   medium garlic cloves, minced

1   small eggplant, diced

½   small red cabbage, thinly sliced

1   medium red bell pepper, chopped

1   cup dried lentils, sorted for stones and shriveled lentils, rinsed, and drained

1   teaspoon crushed coriander seeds (or ground coriander)

(continued)

Stir in the lentils, coriander seeds, cumin seeds, and anise seeds. Pour in the broth. Increase the heat to high and bring to a boil. Reduce the heat and simmer, covered, for 25 to 30 minutes, or until the lentils and vegetables are tender, stirring occasionally. Stir in the cilantro. Cook for 3 minutes, stirring occasionally. Serve with the lemon wedges.

1   teaspoon crushed cumin seeds (or ground cumin)

½   teaspoon crushed anise seeds

4   cups fat-free, low-sodium vegetable broth

½   cup fresh cilantro, coarsely chopped

1   small lemon, cut into 4 wedges

per serving

calories 264	sodium 49 mg
total fat 3.5 g	carbohydrates 46 g
saturated fat 0.5 g	fiber 18 g
trans fat 0.0 g	sugars 12 g
polyunsaturated fat 0.5 g	protein 17 g
monounsaturated fat 2.0 g	
cholesterol 0 mg	dietary exchanges: 2 starch, 3 vegetable, 1 lean meat

COOK'S TIP ON CRUSHING SPICES: Crushing your own spices and seeds adds more flavor than using the preground kind. The best tool for this is a mortar and pestle, but if you don't have one, you can crush the seeds between two spoons. Alternatively, spread them in a single layer on a cutting board and press them with the side of a chef's knife blade, or roll over them with a rolling pin.

korean-style tofu with mustard greens

Despite its exotic flavors, this entrée is easy to prepare and the ingredients are available in most grocery stores. Tofu loses its blandness when simmered with Asian seasonings, sharp daikon radish, and peppery mustard greens. Serve it on its own or over brown rice to soak up the broth.

SERVES 4 | 3 ounces tofu and ½ cup greens mixture per serving

. . . .

In a small bowl, whisk together the broth, soy sauce, oyster sauce, brown sugar, garlic, gingerroot, and sesame oil. Set aside.

In a large, heavy, deep skillet, heat the canola oil over medium-high heat, swirling to coat the bottom. Cook the greens and green onions for 3 to 4 minutes, or until the greens are wilted, stirring occasionally.

Arrange the radish slices in a single layer on top of the greens mixture. Arrange the tofu slices in a single layer on the radish slices.

- 1 cup fat-free, low-sodium vegetable broth
- 1 tablespoon soy sauce (lowest sodium available)
- 1 tablespoon oyster sauce (lowest sodium available)
- 1 tablespoon light brown sugar
- 2 medium garlic cloves, minced
- 1 teaspoon minced peeled gingerroot
- 1 teaspoon toasted sesame oil
- 2 teaspoons canola or corn oil

(continued)

Pour in enough of the broth mixture to come halfway up the tofu. Bring to a simmer, still over medium-high heat. Reduce the heat and simmer, covered, for 10 minutes (no stirring needed).

Using a slotted spoon, transfer the tofu and vegetables to shallow serving bowls. Ladle the broth over all. Sprinkle with the sesame seeds.

8   cups coarsely chopped mustard greens, stems and ribs discarded

8   medium green onions, thinly sliced

8   ounces daikon radish, peeled and cut into ¼-inch slices (about 1 small radish)

12 ounces light extra-firm tofu, drained, patted dry, and cut into 1-inch slices

2   teaspoons sesame seeds, dry-roasted (optional)

per serving

calories 181
total fat 6.0 g
  saturated fat 0.5 g
  trans fat 0.0 g
  polyunsaturated fat 2.0 g
  monounsaturated fat 3.0 g
cholesterol 0 mg

sodium 349 mg
carbohydrates 20 g
  fiber 8 g
  sugars 9 g
protein 12 g

dietary exchanges: ½ starch, 2 vegetable, 1 lean meat, ½ fat

COOK'S TIP ON DAIKON RADISH: This large Asian radish has a sweet, fresh flavor. Most range from 6 to 15 inches long with skin that is either white or black. If you have extra, use it raw in salads, roast daikon cubes with other root vegetables, or add some to your next stir-fry.

quinoa with kale, chickpeas, and feta

Tender greens mingle with fluffy quinoa, creamy chickpeas, and sharp feta in this main dish that's so full of flavors and textures that you're likely to discover something new in every bite.

SERVES 4 | ¾ cup kale mixture and ¾ cup quinoa per serving

Prepare the quinoa using the package directions, omitting the salt. Transfer to a medium bowl. Fluff with a fork. Set aside.

Meanwhile, in a large, heavy skillet, heat the oil over medium-high heat, swirling to coat the bottom. Cook the onion for 3 minutes, or until soft, stirring frequently. Stir in the garlic. Cook for 15 seconds, stirring constantly.

Stir in the chickpeas and broth. Bring to a boil, still over medium-high heat. Stir in the kale. Return to a boil. Reduce the heat and simmer, covered, for 8 minutes, or until the kale is softened, stirring occasionally. Remove from the heat. Stir in the salt.

Spoon the quinoa onto a serving platter or plates. Top with the chickpea mixture. Sprinkle with the feta.

- 1 cup uncooked quinoa, rinsed and drained
- 1 tablespoon olive oil
- ½ cup diced onion
- 2 medium garlic cloves, minced
- 1 15.5-ounce can no-salt-added chickpeas, rinsed and drained
- 1 cup fat-free, low-sodium vegetable broth
- 4 ounces chopped kale, any large stems discarded (about 4 cups tightly packed)
- ¼ teaspoon salt
- ⅓ cup crumbled fat-free feta cheese

per serving

calories 336
total fat 7.0 g
  saturated fat 1.0 g
  trans fat 0.0 g
  polyunsaturated fat 2.0 g
  monounsaturated fat 3.0 g
cholesterol 0 mg

sodium 396 mg
carbohydrates 53 g
  fiber 8 g
  sugars 4 g
protein 16 g

dietary exchanges: 3 starch, 1 vegetable, 1 lean meat

sweet-and-sour red cabbage

This traditional German and Austrian side dish pairs perfectly with pork. The slow braising makes the cabbage tender and sweet, and gives the flavors plenty of time to mellow and blend. Serve it hot or cold.

SERVES 8 | ½ cup per serving

In a large, heavy saucepan, heat the oil over medium-high heat, swirling to coat the bottom. Cook the onion for 3 minutes, or until soft, stirring frequently. Stir in the cabbage. Cook for 3 to 5 minutes, or until the cabbage is wilted, stirring frequently.

Stir in the remaining ingredients except the apples. Reduce the heat and simmer, covered, for 1 hour, stirring frequently.

Stir in the apples. Cook, covered, for 20 to 30 minutes, or until the apples are soft and the cabbage is very tender, stirring frequently.

- 1 tablespoon canola or corn oil
- 1 large onion, thinly sliced
- 1 1-pound red cabbage, cored and thinly sliced (about 8 cups)
- 1 cup 100% apple juice
- ¼ cup firmly packed brown sugar
- ¼ cup cider vinegar
- ½ teaspoon pepper (freshly ground preferred)
- ½ teaspoon ground cinnamon
- ¼ teaspoon ground cloves
- 2 large Granny Smith apples, peeled if desired and chopped

COOK'S TIP: This dish will taste even better the next day.

per serving

calories 110	sodium 20 mg
total fat 2.0 g	carbohydrates 23 g
saturated fat 0.0 g	fiber 2 g
trans fat 0.0 g	sugars 18 g
polyunsaturated fat 0.5 g	protein 1 g
monounsaturated fat 1.0 g	
cholesterol 0 mg	dietary exchanges: 1½ fruit, 1 vegetable, ½ fat

tender radishes with lemon and mint

Radishes are the often-overlooked heroes of the root family. Inexpensive and full of vitamin C, they become softer and sweeter when cooked, making them a delicious companion for any simple roasted pork or chicken entrée.

SERVES 4 | ½ cup per serving

In a medium, heavy saucepan, heat the oil over medium-low heat, swirling to coat the bottom. Cook the onion for 5 minutes, or until soft, stirring occasionally.

Stir in the radishes. Cook for 1 minute. Stir in the water, lemon juice, sugar, and salt. Increase the heat to high and bring to a boil. Reduce the heat and simmer, covered, for 4 minutes, or until the radishes are just tender-crisp. Remove from the heat.

Stir in the mint and lemon zest. Let stand for 10 minutes to serve warm or 25 to 30 minutes to serve at room temperature. Or cover and refrigerate for 1 hour to serve chilled.

1 teaspoon canola or corn oil

½ cup finely chopped red onion

2 cups radishes, trimmed and halved lengthwise

¼ cup water

1 teaspoon grated lemon zest

2 tablespoons fresh lemon juice

2 teaspoons sugar

⅛ teaspoon salt

2 tablespoons chopped fresh mint

COOK'S TIP: Leftover radishes make a tasty and unusual addition to any salad.

per serving

calories 39
total fat 1.5 g
  saturated fat 0.0 g
  trans fat 0.0 g
  polyunsaturated fat 0.5 g
  monounsaturated fat 1.0 g
cholesterol 0 mg

sodium 98 mg
carbohydrates 7 g
  fiber 2 g
  sugars 4 g
protein 1 g

dietary exchanges:
1 vegetable

eggs with smoked sausage, spinach, and tomatoes

This zesty breakfast dish also makes an excellent light lunch or dinner. The vegetables balance the smokiness of the sausage and the peppery hot sauce. *(See photo insert.)*

SERVES 4 | 1 egg and ½ cup sausage mixture per serving

In a large, heavy, nonstick skillet, heat ½ teaspoon oil over medium heat, swirling to coat the bottom. Cook the sausage for 5 minutes, or until beginning to brown lightly, stirring occasionally. Transfer to a small plate.

Meanwhile, crack the eggs into a bowl. Don't beat them. Reduce the heat to medium low. In the same skillet, heat the remaining 1 tablespoon oil, swirling to coat the bottom. Slide the eggs, one at a time, into the skillet. Cook for 1 minute. Gently pour the water into the skillet (not directly over the eggs). Sprinkle the eggs with the sausage, spinach, tomatoes, parsley, pepper, and hot-pepper sauce. Cook, covered, for 3 to 4 minutes, or until the egg whites are cooked.

½ teaspoon canola or corn oil and 1 tablespoon canola or corn oil, divided use

4 ounces low-fat smoked turkey sausage, casings discarded, diced

4 large eggs

¼ cup water

1 cup loosely packed spinach, coarsely chopped

1 cup grape tomatoes, quartered

2 tablespoons chopped fresh Italian (flat-leaf) parsley or finely chopped green onions

¼ teaspoon pepper

2 teaspoons mild Louisiana-style hot-pepper sauce

per serving

calories 168	sodium 362 mg
total fat 11.5 g	carbohydrates 5 g
saturated fat 3.0 g	fiber 1 g
trans fat 0.0 g	sugars 3 g
polyunsaturated fat 2.5 g	protein 11 g
monounsaturated fat 5.0 g	dietary exchanges:
cholesterol 201 mg	1 vegetable, 1½ lean meat, 1 fat

pomegranate pears

Fresh pears gently simmer in tangy-sweet pomegranate juice until they're mouthwateringly tender, then a hint of fresh orange zest and vanilla adds sophistication. Enjoy this guilt-free dessert warm, at room temperature, or chilled.

SERVES 4 | 1 pear half and 1 tablespoon sauce per serving

Place the pears with the cut side down in a medium, heavy skillet with a lid. Pour in the pomegranate juice. Sprinkle the sugar over the pears. Bring to a boil over medium-high heat. Reduce the heat and simmer, covered, for 20 minutes, or until the pears are tender, turning them over once halfway through. Transfer to plates or bowls.

Bring the pomegranate juice mixture to a boil over medium-high heat. Boil for 1 minute, or until reduced by half (to about ½ cup). Remove from the heat.

Stir in the orange zest and vanilla. Spoon the sauce over the pears. Serve the pears warm, let them cool for 30 minutes to serve at room temperature, or cover and refrigerate them for 1 hour to serve chilled.

2 **large firm Bosc or Bartlett pears (about 1 pound), peeled, halved, and cored**

½ **cup 100% pomegranate juice**

1 **tablespoon sugar**

1 **teaspoon grated orange zest**

1 **teaspoon vanilla extract**

COOK'S TIP: Be sure to use firm pears or your dessert will be mushy.

per serving

calories 100
total fat 0.0 g
　saturated fat 0.0 g
　trans fat 0.0 g
　polyunsaturated fat 0.0 g
　monounsaturated fat 0.0 g
cholesterol 0 mg

sodium 5 mg
carbohydrates 26 g
　fiber 4 g
　sugars 19 g
protein 1 g

dietary exchanges: 1½ fruit

stewing

If you like to cook one-dish meals, then stewing is an ideal technique for you. Fish, meat, poultry, or beans can easily be combined with vegetables in a pot to make dinner. Steakhouse Stew (page 150) and Grouper and Sausage Stew (page 143) are examples of recipes that show how easily this can be done. A tight-fitting cover on the stew pot minimizes evaporation, and the condensation formed inside creates a self-basting process to keep the food moist while locking in the nutrients.

Stewing is an ideal way to get dinner cooking while you're doing something else. It requires little attention while this gentle slow-cooking method simmers food in its own juices along with a liquid such as broth or wine. All you need is a heavy pot with a lid and healthy ingredients.

HERE'S HOW THIS TECHNIQUE WORKS*:

1. BROWN the meat or poultry (this step is skipped in seafood dishes to avoid overcooking). To do this, preheat the pot before browning the ingredients. Add the meat or poultry, then let it sit—without moving it—until the bottom is seared; if you turn the food before that, it will stick to the pot and the surface won't caramelize.

2. SAUTÉ the herbs and aromatics. Match the herbs and aromatics to the cooking time; a longer cooking time requires bigger pieces so they don't break down and disintegrate while cooking. Sauté them first with cooking spray or a bit of oil for the most flavor.

3. STIR in the vegetables, beans, and/or legumes.

4. ADD the liquid (to cover the food completely) and let the food simmer, covered, until it's tender.

*Sometimes the order of the steps varies

Tools & Equipment Needed: Pot with a tight-fitting lid (such as a Dutch oven or skillet with lid or saucepan with lid—the pot should be heavy to distribute the heat evenly and maintain an even temperature; it's also best to use a stainless steel or anodized aluminum or enameled cast-iron pan when cooking with acidic foods like tomatoes or citrus to avoid creating discolored foods and a metallic taste), kitchen timer

> **TO STEW:**
> To cook food covered with liquid and simmered slowly in a tightly covered pot, usually for a long period of time.

TIPS:

- Because stewing meat or poultry cooks the fat out into the sauce, begin a day ahead, if possible. Prepare the dish, then refrigerate it overnight. The extra time lets the flavors blend and causes the chilled fat to rise to the top and harden, making it easy to remove.

- Check the pot periodically to be sure that the liquid is still covering the food completely. If needed, add some additional liquid to keep the food covered.

- A constant simmer is not always easy to regulate, especially on a gas stovetop, so our recipes don't state at what temperature to simmer. Even at the lowest setting on some stovetops, the heat may be too intense, which will cause the liquid to boil.

STEWING

mediterranean fish stew

It doesn't take long to prep and cook this comforting but light stew, so it's a great choice for a quick summer dinner in which you can even use a fresh zucchini from your own garden or your weekend trip to the farmers' market. The stew's very mild fish flavor should appeal even to people who aren't usually seafood lovers.

SERVES 4 | heaping 1½ cups per serving

In a large, heavy saucepan, heat the oil over medium-high heat, swirling to coat the bottom. Cook the celery, carrot, onion, and garlic for 5 minutes, or until soft, stirring frequently.

Stir in the broth, tomatoes with liquid, tomato paste, thyme, salt, and pepper. Bring to a boil, still over medium-high heat. Reduce the heat and simmer, covered, for 8 to 10 minutes, or until the vegetables are very tender and the onion is very soft, with no crispness remaining.

Stir in the zucchini. Cook for 3 minutes, or until almost tender-crisp, stirring occasionally.

Stir in the fish. Cook for 2 to 3 minutes, or until it flakes easily when tested with a fork.

2 teaspoons olive oil

1 medium rib of celery, chopped

1 medium carrot, chopped

1 small onion, chopped

1 medium garlic clove, minced

2½ cups fat-free, low-sodium chicken broth

1 14.5-ounce can no-salt-added diced tomatoes, undrained

2 tablespoons no-salt-added tomato paste

½ teaspoon dried thyme, crumbled

⅛ teaspoon salt

⅛ teaspoon pepper

1 medium zucchini, chopped

12 ounces tilapia or other mild white fish fillets, rinsed, patted dry, and cut into 1-inch cubes

per serving
calories 164
total fat 4.0 g
  saturated fat 1.0 g
  trans fat 0.0 g
  polyunsaturated fat 0.5 g
  monounsaturated fat 2.0 g
cholesterol 43 mg

sodium 175 mg
carbohydrates 12 g
  fiber 3 g
  sugars 7 g
protein 21 g

dietary exchanges:
2 vegetable, 2½ lean meat

grouper and sausage stew

This slightly smoky stew features grouper, chickpeas, and turkey sausage. Leaving the fillets whole and ladling the stew on top makes for an elegant, modern presentation.

SERVES 4 | 1½ cups per serving

In a large, heavy saucepan or Dutch oven, heat the oil over medium-high heat, swirling to coat the bottom. Reduce the heat to medium. Cook the sausage for 3 to 5 minutes, or until lightly browned, stirring occasionally. Stir in the carrots and onion. Cook for about 3 minutes, stirring frequently. Stir in the garlic. Cook for 1 to 2 minutes, or until fragrant, stirring frequently.

Stir in the tomatoes with liquid, chickpeas, broth, and sherry. Bring to a boil. Gradually stir in the collard greens and pepper. Reduce the heat and simmer, covered, for 10 minutes, stirring frequently. Gently place the fish in the stew. Simmer, covered, for 5 minutes, or until the fish flakes easily when tested with a fork.

Using a spatula, carefully transfer the fish to shallow serving bowls. Ladle the collard greens mixture over the fish.

1	tablespoon olive oil
6	ounces low-fat sweet or hot Italian turkey or chicken sausage, casings discarded, cut into 1-inch slices
2	medium carrots, diced
1	medium onion, chopped
2	medium garlic cloves, minced
1	28-ounce can no-salt-added diced tomatoes, undrained
1	15.5-ounce can no-salt-added chickpeas, rinsed and drained
1	cup fat-free, low-sodium vegetable or chicken broth
½	cup sherry, dry red wine (regular or nonalcoholic), or fat-free, low-sodium vegetable broth
6	cups chopped collard greens, any large stems discarded
¼	teaspoon pepper (freshly ground preferred)
4	grouper or red snapper fillets (about 4 ounces each), rinsed and patted dry

per serving

calories 416	sodium 450 mg
total fat 9.0 g	carbohydrates 41 g
saturated fat 1.5 g	fiber 10 g
trans fat 0.0 g	sugars 12 g
polyunsaturated fat 2.0 g	protein 39 g
monounsaturated fat 4.0 g	dietary exchanges: 1½ starch,
cholesterol 75 mg	4 vegetable, 4 lean meat

tomatillo-chicken stew

Tomatillos (tohm-ah-TEE-ohs) add a fresh, lemonlike flavor to this Mexican stew, while masa harina, a corn flour best known for its use in tamales, thickens the dish. Peppers, corn, and cilantro round out this robust stew.

SERVES 6 | 1⅓ cups per serving

In a Dutch oven, heat the oil over medium-high heat, swirling to coat the bottom. Cook the chicken for 5 to 8 minutes, or until lightly browned, stirring occasionally. (Be sure to let the chicken sear before stirring.)

Reduce the heat to medium. Cook the onion for 3 to 4 minutes, or until beginning to soften, stirring frequently. Stir in the garlic. Cook for 30 seconds, stirring constantly. Stir in the Anaheim peppers and bell pepper. Cook for 3 minutes, or until beginning to soften, stirring frequently. Stir in the tomatillos, broth, and cumin. Increase the heat to high and bring to a boil, covered. Reduce the heat and simmer, partially covered, for 20 minutes, stirring occasionally.

- 2 teaspoons olive oil
- 1¼ pounds boneless, skinless chicken thighs, all visible fat discarded, cut into 1½-inch pieces
- 1 large onion, coarsely chopped
- 5 large garlic cloves, minced
- 2 medium Anaheim peppers, seeds and ribs discarded, chopped
- 1 large red bell pepper, chopped
- 12 ounces medium tomatillos, papery husks discarded, chopped
- 1½ cups fat-free, low-sodium chicken broth
- 1 tablespoon ground cumin
- 9 ounces frozen whole-kernel corn
- 3 tablespoons to ¼ cup masa harina
- ½ cup chopped fresh cilantro

Stir in the corn. Simmer, partially covered, for 10 minutes, or until the chicken is no longer pink in the center and the vegetables are tender.

Put the masa harina in a small bowl. Whisk in about ¼ cup of the broth from the stew to create a thick paste. Stir the masa harina mixture into the stew. Simmer for 5 minutes, or until the stew is slightly thickened. Stir in the cilantro. Serve the stew in shallow bowls.

per serving

calories 263	sodium 81 mg
total fat 10.0 g	carbohydrates 24 g
saturated fat 2.5 g	fiber 5 g
trans fat 0.0 g	sugars 8 g
polyunsaturated fat 2.5 g	protein 21 g
monounsaturated fat 4.0 g	
cholesterol 62 mg	dietary exchanges: 1 starch, 2 vegetable, 2½ lean meat

COOK'S TIP ON TOMATILLOS: Tomatillos look like small green tomatoes, but they have a tangy, slightly acidic taste. Choose hard-fleshed fruit. Discard the husks and wash the tomatillos well before using them. To store them, leave the husks on and refrigerate the tomatillos in a paper bag for up to one month.

COOK'S TIP: Masa harina is available in Hispanic specialty markets and in the Hispanic aisle of most supermarkets. If it's unavailable, you can substitute one finely chopped 6-inch corn tortilla or ¼ cup crushed baked unsalted corn tortilla chips. Stir the tortilla pieces or crushed chips right into the stew to thicken it.

chicken in tomato-wine sauce

White wine and the juice from tomatoes are the stars in the stewing liquid for this Italian-inspired dish. They infuse the chicken with flavor and moisture, and create a flavorful sauce. Serve over whole-grain couscous to soak up every drop.

SERVES 4 | 3 ounces chicken and scant 1½ cups sauce per serving

. . . .

In a large, heavy skillet or Dutch oven, heat the oil over medium heat, swirling to coat the bottom. Cook the onion and bell pepper for 3 to 5 minutes, or until beginning to soften, stirring occasionally. Stir in the mushrooms. Cook for 5 to 7 minutes, or until beginning to soften, stirring occasionally. Stir in the oregano, parsley, and garlic. Cook for 1 minute.

Place the chicken in the skillet. Stir in the tomatoes with liquid, water, wine, and tomato paste. Increase the heat to medium high and bring to a boil.

Reduce the heat and simmer, covered, for 30 to 35 minutes, or until the chicken is no longer pink in the center.

2	teaspoons canola or corn oil
1	medium onion, diced
1	medium green bell pepper, diced
8	ounces button mushrooms, sliced
2	teaspoons dried oregano, crumbled
2	teaspoons dried parsley, crumbled
2	medium garlic cloves, minced
4	boneless, skinless chicken breast halves (about 4 ounces each), all visible fat discarded
1	14.5-ounce can no-salt-added diced tomatoes, undrained
1¼	cups water
½	cup white wine (regular or nonalcoholic)
1	tablespoon tomato paste

per serving

calories 222
total fat 5.5 g
  saturated fat 1.0 g
  trans fat 0.0 g
  polyunsaturated fat 1.0 g
  monounsaturated fat 2.5 g
cholesterol 73 mg

sodium 155 mg
carbohydrates 13 g
  fiber 3 g
  sugars 8 g
protein 28 g

dietary exchanges:
3 vegetable, 3 lean meat

COOK'S TIP ON SIMMERING: A small bubble should break through the surface of the liquid every second or two. If more bubbles rise to the surface, then lower the heat or shift the pot to one side of the burner.

beef burgundy

This rich, hearty stew from France's Burgundy region is one of the country's most famous dishes.

SERVES 4 | 1 cup per serving

In a Dutch oven, cook the bacon over medium heat for 5 minutes, stirring occasionally. Transfer to a small plate lined with paper towels.

Increase the heat to medium high. In the same pot, cook half the beef for 5 to 7 minutes, or until browned, stirring occasionally. (Be sure to let the beef sear before stirring.) Transfer to a large plate. Repeat with the remaining beef.

Reduce the heat to medium. Cook the onion, garlic, and margarine for 5 minutes, stirring frequently. Stir in the flour. Stir in the bacon, beef, and the remaining ingredients except the thyme. Increase the heat to high and bring to a boil. Reduce the heat and simmer, covered, for 1½ hours, or until the beef is tender, stirring occasionally and adding more broth to barely cover the beef mixture if necessary. Just before serving, sprinkle with the thyme.

3	slices turkey bacon, chopped
1	pound boneless top round steak, all visible fat discarded, cut into ½-inch cubes
1	cup chopped onion
4	large garlic cloves, minced
1	tablespoon light tub margarine
2	tablespoons all-purpose flour
1½	cups dry red wine (regular or nonalcoholic)
1	cup coarsely chopped carrots
1	cup pearl onions, thawed if frozen
8	ounces chanterelle, shiitake (stems discarded), brown (cremini), or button mushrooms, or a combination (coarsely chopped if large)
1	cup fat-free, low-sodium beef broth, plus more if needed
½	cup water
¼	cup Cognac or brandy (optional)
1	tablespoon dark brown sugar
1	tablespoon no-salt-added tomato paste
1	teaspoon dried rosemary, crushed
1	tablespoon plus 1 teaspoon chopped fresh thyme

per serving

calories 322	sodium 224 mg
total fat 6.5 g	carbohydrates 26 g
saturated fat 1.5 g	fiber 3 g
trans fat 0.0 g	sugars 10 g
polyunsaturated fat 1.0 g	protein 32 g
monounsaturated fat 2.5 g	dietary exchanges: ½ starch,
cholesterol 71 mg	3 vegetable, 3 lean meat

STEWING

moroccan beef stew with fragrant couscous

Couscous is often served as a side dish with stewed or braised entrées. In this recipe, it's cooked in a steamer basket that's placed in the same pot with the beef and spices so the grain is delicately flavored while it steams. *(See photo insert.)*

SERVES 8 | 1 heaping cup per serving

In a large stockpot, heat the margarine and oil over medium-high heat, swirling to coat the bottom. Cook the beef for 5 minutes, or until browned, stirring occasionally. (Be sure to let the beef sear before stirring.)

Stir in the onion, pepper, ginger, turmeric, and saffron. Stir in enough water to cover the beef mixture by at least 2 inches. Bring to a simmer. Reduce the heat and simmer, covered, for 5 minutes.

Meanwhile, put the couscous in a large bowl. Slowly pour in the water, a little at a time, rubbing the couscous between your hands to remove all the lumps and to thoroughly moisten the couscous. (Don't get the couscous soaking wet.) Stir in the raisins and pine nuts.

Line a collapsible steamer basket with dampened cheesecloth or a clean, dampened dish towel. Spoon the couscous mixture into the cheesecloth lining; don't pack it. Place the steamer in the stockpot (the simmering beef mixture remains beneath the steamer). Cook, covered, for 1 hour, gently stirring the couscous

1½ teaspoons light tub margarine

1½ teaspoons olive oil

½ pound lean stew meat, all visible fat discarded, cut into 1-inch cubes

1 large onion, sliced

1 teaspoon pepper

½ teaspoon ground ginger

½ teaspoon ground turmeric

Pinch of saffron (optional)

8 ounces uncooked whole-wheat couscous

1 cup water

2 tablespoons raisins

2 tablespoons pine nuts, dry-roasted

3 medium carrots, quartered

2 medium potatoes, peeled and quartered

2 medium turnips, peeled and quartered

2 medium zucchini, sliced

½ 15.5-ounce can no-salt-added chickpeas, rinsed and drained

⅛ teaspoon salt

every 10 minutes (to keep it fluffy and help it cook evenly).

Carefully remove the steamer basket from the pot. Set aside.

Stir the carrots, potatoes, and turnips into the stew. Cook, covered, for 20 minutes. Stir in a little boiling water if the stew looks dry. Stir in the zucchini and chickpeas. Cook, covered, for 20 minutes. Stir in the salt.

Mound the couscous in the center of a large platter. Using a slotted spoon, remove the vegetables from the stew. Arrange them and the beef around the couscous. Serve the broth in a gravy boat on the side or drizzle it over the couscous.

per serving

calories 281
total fat 5.0 g
  saturated fat 1.0 g
  trans fat 0.0 g
  polyunsaturated fat 1.0 g
  monounsaturated fat 2.0 g
cholesterol 18 mg

sodium 109 mg
carbohydrates 48 g
  fiber 8 g
  sugars 7 g
protein 14 g

dietary exchanges:
2½ starch, 2 vegetable, 1 lean meat

steakhouse stew

A simple marinade and just a bit of turkey bacon add a big boost of flavor to this traditional beef stew.

SERVES 4 | 1½ cups per serving

. . . .

In a large shallow glass dish, stir together the beef, red onion, beer, garlic, and bay leaf. Cover and refrigerate for at least 3 hours, stirring occasionally.

Drain the beef, discarding the red onion, garlic, and bay leaf, and reserving the liquid.

Heat a large, heavy nonstick skillet over medium heat. Add the beef and bacon. Cook for 5 minutes, or until the beef is browned, stirring occasionally. Stir in the carrots, broth, thyme, tomato paste, paprika, pepper, and the reserved liquid from the marinade. If necessary, pour in enough water to cover the beef mixture. Bring to a boil. Boil for 5 minutes. Reduce the heat and simmer, covered, for 1½ hours.

Stir in the potatoes and pearl onions. Cook, covered, for 30 to 40 minutes.

Put the flour in a small bowl. Add the water, whisking to dissolve. Slowly stir the flour mixture into the stew. Cook for 5 minutes, or until thickened, stirring frequently.

- 1 pound boneless top sirloin steak, all visible fat discarded, cut into 1-inch cubes
- 1 large red onion, sliced into thin rings
- 1 cup light beer (regular or nonalcoholic)
- 2 medium garlic cloves, crushed
- 1 medium dried bay leaf
- 1 slice turkey bacon, minced
- 2 cups halved baby carrots
- 2 cups fat-free, low-sodium chicken broth
- 1 tablespoon chopped fresh thyme or 1 teaspoon dried thyme, crumbled
- 1 tablespoon no-salt-added tomato paste
- ½ teaspoon paprika
  Pepper to taste (freshly ground preferred)
- 6 small red potatoes, quartered
- 1 cup whole pearl onions, thawed if frozen
- 3 tablespoons all-purpose flour
- 3 to 4 tablespoons cold water

per serving

calories 307	sodium 159 mg
total fat 5.5 g	carbohydrates 29 g
saturated fat 2.0 g	fiber 3 g
trans fat 0.0 g	sugars 7 g
polyunsaturated fat 0.5 g	protein 30 g
monounsaturated fat 2.5 g	dietary exchanges: 1 starch,
cholesterol 63 mg	3 vegetable, 3 lean meat

egyptian ful

Beans of many kinds have been a dietary staple in Egypt since the pharaohs ruled. One favorite entrée is ful, or fava beans simmered to create a thick, savory stew. Start soaking the dried beans in the morning, and they'll be ready to cook for dinner. Serve the stew with warm whole-wheat pita bread and a salad of cucumbers and tomatoes.

SERVES 4 | 1 heaping cup per serving

In a medium, heavy saucepan, soak the beans for 8 hours in cold water to cover by at least 2 inches. Change the water several times, if possible. Rinse and drain the beans in a colander. Return them to the pan. Pour in fresh water to cover. Stir in the oil, cumin, and garlic. Simmer, covered, for 45 minutes, or until the beans are tender, stirring occasionally.

Stir in the parsley, lemon juice, and salt. Simmer, covered, for 30 minutes, or until some of the beans begin to break down, forming a creamy base for the rest.

2 cups dried fava beans or dark red kidney beans, sorted for stones and shriveled beans, rinsed, and drained

2 tablespoons olive oil

1 tablespoon ground cumin

3 medium garlic cloves, minced

1 small bunch Italian (flat-leaf) parsley, chopped

1 tablespoon fresh lemon juice

¼ teaspoon salt

COOK'S TIP: Leftovers are delicious when reheated. Ful (the pronunciation is halfway between "fool" and "full"), also called *ful medames*, is often served for breakfast, sometimes with a fried or boiled egg.

per serving

calories 330
total fat 8.5 g
  saturated fat 1.0 g
  trans fat 0.0 g
  polyunsaturated fat 1.0 g
  monounsaturated fat 5.0 g
cholesterol 0 mg

sodium 166 mg
carbohydrates 46 g
  fiber 19 g
  sugars 5 g
protein 20 g

dietary exchanges: 3 starch, 2 lean meat

meatless cassoulet

A typical French cassoulet, named after an earthenware pot called a *cassole,*
is a stew of white beans and meats. There are as many versions of this stew as
there are cooks who make it. This version preserves the superb, slow-simmered
flavor of the stew but omits the meat. Because this uses dried beans, be sure to
set aside time to cook or soak them.

SERVES 8 | 1 cup per serving

In a Dutch oven, stir together the Great
Northern beans, black beans, and water. Bring
to a boil over high heat. Reduce the heat and
simmer for 2 minutes, stirring occasionally.
Remove from the heat. Let stand, covered, for
1 hour. Rinse and drain the beans in a colander.
Dry the Dutch oven with paper towels.

Or, in a large bowl, stir together both types
of beans and the water. Let stand, covered, for
6 to 8 hours or overnight. After the beans have
soaked, rinse and drain them in a colander.

Lightly spray the Dutch oven with cooking
spray. Cook the carrots, celery, onion, bell
pepper, and garlic over medium heat for
20 minutes, or until the carrots, celery, and bell
pepper are tender and the onion is very soft,
stirring occasionally.

Stir in the beans and the remaining
ingredients. Increase the heat to high and

8 ounces dried Great Northern beans
   or other dried white beans, sorted
   for stones and shriveled beans,
   rinsed, and drained

8 ounces dried black beans, sorted for
   stones and shriveled beans, rinsed,
   and drained

6 cups water

   Cooking spray

1½ cups chopped carrots

1½ cups chopped celery

1 large onion, chopped

1 large green bell pepper, chopped

4 medium garlic cloves, crushed or
   minced

1¼ cups fat-free, low-sodium vegetable
   broth

1 8-ounce can no-salt-added tomato
   sauce

(continued)

bring to a boil. Reduce the heat and simmer, covered, for 2½ to 3 hours, or until the beans are tender, adding water if necessary and stirring occasionally. Discard the bay leaves before serving the stew.

½ cup dry white wine (regular or nonalcoholic)

¼ cup molasses

2 medium dried bay leaves

1½ teaspoons dried fennel seeds, crushed

½ to ¾ teaspoon crushed red pepper flakes

½ teaspoon salt

½ teaspoon dried thyme, crumbled

per serving

calories 244
total fat 1.0 g
  saturated fat 0.0 g
  trans fat 0.0 g
  polyunsaturated fat 0.5 g
  monounsaturated fat 0.0 g
cholesterol 0 mg

sodium 192 mg
carbohydrates 47 g
  fiber 13 g
  sugars 10 g
protein 13 g
dietary exchanges:
2½ starch, 2 vegetable, 1 lean meat

COOK'S TIP: Stewing is used throughout the world and is known by many different names: France's cassoulet, ratatouille, beef bourguignon, and bouillabaisse; Hungary's goulash; Louisiana's gumbo; the Southwest's chili con carne; Ethiopia's doro wat; and India's curries are all examples of stews.

porotos granados

This vegetarian Chilean stew makes a hearty meal in the fall, when fresh pumpkin is in season. The toasted pumpkin seed topping adds a nice crunch. If you're using butternut squash, toast the seeds as you would the pumpkin seeds, or buy raw pumpkin seeds and follow the directions in the recipe.

SERVES 4 | 1½ cups stew and 1 tablespoon pumpkin seeds per serving

Preheat the oven to 350°F.

Using a spoon, scoop out the pumpkin seeds. Rinse the seeds in a colander, discarding the strings. Pat the seeds dry with paper towels. Transfer them to a nonstick baking pan. Drizzle 1 teaspoon oil over the seeds. Sprinkle the seasoning blend over the seeds, stirring to combine. Bake for 30 minutes, or until golden brown, stirring every 10 minutes.

Meanwhile, cut the pumpkin into ¾-inch cubes.

In a large, heavy saucepan or a Dutch oven, heat the remaining 1 teaspoon oil over medium-high heat, swirling to coat the bottom. Cook the onion for 3 minutes, or until soft, stirring frequently.

Stir in the garlic. Cook for 30 seconds, stirring frequently. Stir in the remaining ingredients,

1	1-pound pie-style pumpkin, peeled and halved, or 3 cups cubed butternut squash
1	teaspoon olive oil and 1 teaspoon olive oil, divided use
1	teaspoon salt-free all-purpose seasoning blend
½	small onion, chopped
2	medium garlic cloves, minced
2	15.5-ounce cans no-salt-added navy beans, rinsed and drained
2	cups frozen whole-kernel corn
1	cup fat-free, low-sodium vegetable broth
1	teaspoon dried basil, crumbled
1	teaspoon paprika
¼	teaspoon salt
⅛	teaspoon pepper

including the pumpkin cubes. Bring to a simmer. Reduce the heat and simmer, covered, for 20 minutes, or until the pumpkin is tender. Ladle into serving bowls. Sprinkle each serving with 1 tablespoon pumpkin seeds.

COOK'S TIP: The remaining pumpkin seeds can be stored in an airtight container at room temperature for up to one week or frozen in an airtight freezer container for up to two months.

per serving

calories 362
total fat 6.5 g
  saturated fat 1.0 g
  trans fat 0.0 g
  polyunsaturated fat 2.0 g
  monounsaturated fat 3.0 g
cholesterol 0 mg

sodium 167 mg
carbohydrates 62 g
  fiber 12 g
  sugars 13 g
protein 18 g

dietary exchanges: 4 starch, 1 lean meat

garden-fresh ratatouille

This classic French dish usually includes eggplant, squash, and tomato stewed in olive oil with plenty of garlic and herbs. This version reduces the amount of oil and adds a bit of broth to bring out the flavors of the vegetables. Ratatouille can be served hot, cold, or at room temperature.

SERVES 4 | ½ cup per serving

In a large, heavy saucepan, heat the oil over medium-high heat, swirling to coat the bottom. Cook the eggplant for 5 to 6 minutes, or until light golden brown, stirring occasionally. Stir in the zucchini, bell pepper, onion, and garlic. Cook for 3 to 4 minutes, or until the bell pepper is tender-crisp and the onion is soft, stirring occasionally.

Stir in the tomato, broth, salt, and pepper. Bring to a simmer over medium-high heat. Reduce the heat and simmer, partially covered, for 10 to 15 minutes, or until the vegetables are tender, stirring occasionally.

Remove from the heat. Stir in the basil. Just before serving, garnish with the Parmesan.

1 teaspoon olive oil

½ small eggplant or 1 medium Japanese eggplant, chopped

1 medium zucchini, chopped

½ medium yellow bell pepper, chopped

½ small red onion, chopped

2 medium garlic cloves, minced

1 medium tomato, peeled and chopped

½ cup fat-free, low-sodium vegetable broth

⅛ teaspoon salt

⅛ teaspoon pepper (freshly ground preferred)

2 tablespoons chopped fresh basil

¼ cup shaved, shredded, or grated Parmesan cheese

per serving

calories 69	sodium 168 mg
total fat 3.0 g	carbohydrates 8 g
saturated fat 1.0 g	fiber 3 g
trans fat 0.0 g	sugars 4 g
polyunsaturated fat 0.5 g	protein 4 g
monounsaturated fat 1.5 g	dietary exchanges:
cholesterol 4 mg	2 vegetable, ½ fat

COOK'S TIP ON SHAVED PARMESAN: Most grocery stores sell chunks or wedges of Parmesan cheese. It usually has a stronger taste than the pre-grated kind, so a small amount adds big flavor. Use a vegetable peeler to shave off thin slices.

orange-kissed summer fruits

Take advantage of summer's bounty by quickly stewing your favorite combinations of fresh fruits in a sweet and spicy mix of apple juice, orange zest, and cinnamon. It's delicious eaten warm or chilled for breakfast, dessert, or even as a side dish.

SERVES 4 | ½ cup per serving

Peel and pit the fruit, cutting the larger fruit, such as peaches, into eighths and halving or quartering the smaller fruit, such as apricots and cherries.

In a medium, heavy saucepan, stir together the fruit and the remaining ingredients. Bring to a boil over medium-high heat. Reduce the heat and simmer for 10 to 15 minutes, or until the fruit is tender and the sauce has thickened, stirring frequently.

2 pounds peaches, nectarines, apricots, plums, or cherries, or a combination (about 4 cups)

½ cup 100% apple juice

Zest of 1 medium orange, cut into strips or grated

1 cinnamon stick (about 3 inches long)

1 tablespoon brown sugar

1 tablespoon orange-flavored liqueur, such as Grand Marnier (optional)

¼ teaspoon ground nutmeg (freshly grated preferred)

per serving

calories 115
total fat 0.5 g
  saturated fat 0.0 g
  trans fat 0.0 g
  polyunsaturated fat 0.0 g
  monounsaturated fat 0.0 g
cholesterol 0 mg

sodium 2 mg
carbohydrates 28 g
  fiber 4 g
  sugars 24 g
protein 2 g

dietary exchanges: 2 fruit

steaming

Steaming is one of the best ways for foods to retain their color and preserve their nutrients. By varying the steaming liquid and adding spices and aromatics, you can infuse steamed food with delicate flavor; for more intense flavor, add aromatics such as garlic and onion to the food itself or pair the food with a delicious sauce. Because steam transfers heat to food more efficiently than either boiling water or hot air, steaming is one of the quickest cooking techniques, making it ideal for the busy cook. Within minutes you can have a healthy meal or side dish on the table.

Steaming is ideal for vegetables. You can keep it simple by adding any fresh vegetable to a steamer basket, or you can spend a few extra minutes to make Walnut-Orange Broccoli (page 175) seasoned with citrus and thyme or Mixed Vegetables with Ginger (page 177) enhanced with garlic and lemon.

With steaming, you can incorporate more grains into your diet; this technique makes them light and fluffy. Try Peruvian Quinoa Salad (page 164) to see how simple it is. You can enrich your diet even further by adding necessary omega-3s with fish such as Salmon in Green Tea (page 166).

Most steaming is done by placing the food in a bamboo steamer or collapsible metal or silicone basket suspended over simmering liquid; the food is cooked by gentle hot vapor. Bamboo steamers, traditionally used in Asian cooking, are designed to fit in a wok, but they can also work in some larger saucepans. They can also be stacked on top of each other, so you can separately steam more than one food at a time. You can use the bamboo steamers to steam foods with different cooking times, removing the layers as each food is finished. Alternatively, collapsible or silicone steamers are compact, inexpensive, and easy to clean. They fit into a variety of pots, but they often can't hold as much food as can the bamboo steamers.

Food cooked *en papillote,* or enclosed in a packet of cooking parchment or aluminum foil and cooked in the oven, is also a form of steaming that uses the foods' own juices to cook. This method makes portion control and cleanup a snap, in addition to offering an attractive presentation, with each person getting his or her own packet—which can be personalized based on the diner's preferences.

Tools & Equipment Needed: Collapsible metal or silicone steamer basket, bamboo steamer, skillet, wok, or saucepan (with lid, if using a collapsible steamer basket), cooking parchment or aluminum foil, kitchen timer

TIPS:

- When steaming on the stovetop, make sure the food sits above the water and isn't submerged.

- Use thin, clear, or translucent liquids, such as water, broth, wine, or beer. Avoid cloudy liquids such as milk, which will curdle, and thick liquids such as tomato sauce, which can burn.

- If you need to steam something for more than 15 or 20 minutes, be sure to check the level of liquid occasionally. Have some extra liquid boiling in a separate pot or kettle and add the hot liquid if needed (be sure to add the liquid to the pot and not to the food).

- When cooking something *en papillote,* use cooking parchment rather than aluminum foil if you're working with highly acidic ingredients such as vinegar, tomatoes, tomato sauce, and citrus fruits, which will react to the foil.

- The lid of a bamboo steamer will absorb excess moisture, rather than dripping it back onto the food when the lid is lifted (which can dilute the flavor).

- When steaming tofu, score the surface so that the flavors will penetrate the tofu better.

- Vegetables should fit in a single layer in the steamer basket to avoid some becoming overcooked while others are undercooked.

- Most vegetables should be steamed just until tender-crisp. To test, insert the tip of a paring knife into the thickest part; if the knife meets a little resistance, then the vegetables are steamed properly.

- Steamed foods should be served immediately after cooking because they can become rubbery and dry as they cool.

- A constant simmer is not always easy to regulate, especially on a gas stovetop, so our recipes don't state at what temperature to simmer. Even at the lowest setting on some stovetops, the heat may be too intense, which will cause the liquid to boil. When simmering, a small bubble should break through the surface of the liquid every second or two. If more bubbles rise to the surface, then lower the heat or shift the pot to one side of the burner.

thai-style chicken potstickers

Lemongrass and cilantro give these little packages a hint of Thai flavor. The simple dipping sauce, made with serrano pepper, provides an added spark for these already-dynamite bites. This recipe doubles easily if you want to serve these potstickers as an appetizer at your next gathering.

SERVES 8 | 3 potstickers per serving

In a large bowl, using your hands or a spoon, combine the filling ingredients.

In a small bowl, whisk together the egg white and 1 tablespoon water.

Arrange the wonton wrappers in a single layer on a large baking sheet. Line a separate large baking sheet with cooking parchment.

Put the large bowl, baking sheet with the wonton wrappers, small bowl, and baking sheet with cooking parchment in a row, assembly-line fashion.

Place a scant tablespoon of filling in the center of each wrapper. Brush the egg white mixture around the edges of one wrapper. Gather the corners and pinch them together at the top, making sure all the edges are sealed. Place the potsticker on the baking sheet with the cooking parchment (the parchment will keep the potstickers from sticking to the baking sheet while they stand). Repeat with the remaining wrappers, arranging so the potstickers don't touch.

In a large nonstick skillet, heat 1½ teaspoons oil over medium-high heat, swirling to coat

FILLING

- 8 ounces ground skinless chicken breast
- ¼ cup minced water chestnuts, drained
- 2 tablespoons very finely minced lemongrass
- 2 tablespoons minced green onions (green part only)
- 2 tablespoons minced fresh cilantro
- 1 tablespoon soy sauce (lowest sodium available)
- 1 teaspoon sugar
- 1 teaspoon grated peeled gingerroot
- 1 medium garlic clove, minced
- ¼ teaspoon crushed red pepper flakes

———————

- 1 large egg white
- 1 tablespoon water, ½ cup water, and ½ cup water, divided use
- 24 wonton wrappers, thawed if frozen
- 1½ teaspoons canola or corn oil and 1½ teaspoons canola or corn oil, divided use

(continued)

the bottom. Place half the potstickers in the skillet so they don't touch. Cook for 2 minutes, or until the bottoms are browned. Pour ½ cup water into the skillet. Steam the potstickers, covered, for about 3 minutes, or until the chicken is no longer pink in the center when you cut a potsticker in half. Using a spatula, transfer to a warm serving platter. Repeat with the remaining 1½ teaspoons oil, potstickers, and ½ cup water.

Meanwhile, in a small microwaveable bowl, stir together the sauce ingredients. Microwave on 100 percent power (high) for 30 seconds. Serve the sauce with the potstickers.

per serving

calories 130	sodium 106 mg
total fat 3.0 g	carbohydrates 16 g
saturated fat 0.5 g	fiber 1 g
trans fat 0.0 g	sugars 1 g
polyunsaturated fat 1.0 g	protein 9 g
monounsaturated fat 1.5 g	
cholesterol 20 mg	dietary exchanges: 1 starch, 1 lean meat

SAUCE

- ⅓ cup plain rice vinegar
- 2 tablespoons matchstick-size strips of peeled gingerroot
- 1 small fresh serrano pepper, thinly sliced (see Cook's Tip on page 45)

COOK'S TIP ON LEMONGRASS: Frequently used in Southeast Asian cuisines, lemongrass adds a lemonlike flavor to foods. Lemongrass should have a pale to medium green stalk and a pale yellow to almost white root end. Discard the bulb and outer leaves and use only the bottom 3 to 5 inches of the inner stalk. Lemongrass can be found in Asian markets and in the produce section of many grocery stores.

peruvian quinoa salad

In this vegetarian entrée salad, a bright cilantro-lime dressing lightly coats a colorful blend of Peruvian staples including quinoa, beans, corn, bell peppers, and tomatoes. Steaming the quinoa makes the grains light and fluffy and is well worth the extra time.

SERVES 4 | 1½ cups per serving

. . . .

In a small bowl, whisk together the dressing ingredients. Cover and refrigerate.

In a large saucepan, bring 1 cup water to a boil over high heat. Stir in the quinoa. Cook for 10 minutes, or until the quinoa is partially cooked. Drain in a fine-mesh sieve. Rinse with cold water to cool. Drain well. Transfer the quinoa to a collapsible steamer basket.

In the same large pan, bring 1 inch of water to a boil over medium heat. Place the steamer basket in the pan. Make sure the water doesn't

DRESSING

¼ cup fresh lime juice

3 tablespoons fresh orange juice

3 tablespoons chopped fresh cilantro

1½ tablespoons olive oil (extra virgin preferred)

1 teaspoon ground coriander

1 teaspoon honey

1 medium garlic clove, minced

¼ teaspoon pepper

(continued)

touch the bottom of the steamer. Cover the basket with a clean, folded dish towel. Cook the quinoa, covered, for 10 minutes, or until tender. Remove from the heat. Fluff with a fork.

Transfer the quinoa to a large serving bowl. Stir in the remaining salad ingredients except the eggs. Pour the dressing over the salad, tossing to coat. Garnish with the eggs. Serve immediately or cover and refrigerate for about 2 hours to serve chilled.

per serving

calories 357
total fat 10.5 g
  saturated fat 1.5 g
  trans fat 0.0 g
  polyunsaturated fat 2.0 g
  monounsaturated fat 5.0 g
cholesterol 93 mg

sodium 83 mg
carbohydrates 56 g
  fiber 12 g
  sugars 11 g
protein 14 g

dietary exchanges: 3 starch, 2 vegetable, 1 lean meat, 1 fat

SALAD

- 1 cup water
- ½ cup uncooked quinoa, rinsed and drained
- 1 15.5-ounce can no-salt-added Great Northern beans, rinsed and drained
- 9 ounces frozen whole-kernel corn, thawed
- 1 medium tomato, chopped
- ¾ cup thinly sliced assorted mini bell peppers (about 4)
- 1 small onion, halved and thinly sliced
- ⅓ cup chopped fresh cilantro
- 2 large hard-boiled eggs, each cut into 4 wedges

COOK'S TIP: If you prefer, you can substitute no-salt-added black beans or Peruvian beans, also known as peruano beans or Mexican yellow beans, for the Great Northern beans.

COOK'S TIP ON QUINOA: Partially cooking the quinoa in boiling water and then steaming it keeps the grain from becoming mushy. Quinoa is fully cooked when it is tender and a tiny curled white thread emerges from the grain.

salmon in green tea

Rich salmon gently steams to perfection on a bed of thinly sliced fresh lime. Green tea infused with black peppercorns is the steaming liquid. A sweetly piquant sauce of green onions, soy, honey, and more lime finishes the dish. Pair this with a whole grain such as brown rice or quinoa and Lemony Green Beans with Almonds (page 176) to complete your meal.

SERVES 4 | 3 ounces fish and 2 tablespoons sauce per serving

Put the tea bags and peppercorns in a medium glass bowl. Pour in 4 cups hot water. Steep, covered, for 5 to 6 minutes.

Meanwhile, line a large bamboo or collapsible steamer basket with the lime slices, overlapping them until they completely cover the bottom. Place the fish fillets on the lime slices, spacing them at least 1 inch apart.

Into a skillet or wok large enough to hold the steamer, pour the tea mixture to a depth of about 2 inches. If needed, pour in some or all of the remaining 1 cup water. Bring to a simmer over medium heat.

6 **single-serving bags of green tea**

1 **tablespoon black peppercorns (optional)**

4 **cups hot water and 1 cup hot water (if needed), divided use**

5 **medium limes, thinly sliced**

4 **salmon fillets with skin (about 5 ounces each), rinsed and patted dry**

(continued)

Put the steamer in the skillet. Make sure the liquid doesn't touch the bottom of the steamer. If using a bamboo steamer, cover it with the lid. If using a collapsible steamer basket, tightly cover the skillet. Simmer for 5 to 7 minutes, or until the fish is cooked to the desired doneness.

Meanwhile, in a small saucepan, heat the oil over medium-high heat, swirling to coat the bottom. Cook the garlic and red pepper flakes for 1 to 2 minutes, or until fragrant, stirring constantly. Stir in the wine and broth. Bring to a boil. Boil for 2 to 3 minutes, stirring constantly. Stir in the lime juice, honey, and soy sauce. Reduce the heat and simmer for 3 to 5 minutes, or until thickened, stirring frequently. Stir in the green onions.

Transfer the fish to plates. Drizzle with the sauce.

SAUCE

- 1 teaspoon canola or corn oil
- 1 small garlic clove, finely minced
- ¼ teaspoon crushed red pepper flakes (optional)
- ¼ cup Riesling or other medium-sweet white wine (regular or nonalcoholic) or ¼ cup 100% apple juice
- ¼ cup fat-free, low-sodium chicken or vegetable broth
- 1 to 2 tablespoons fresh lime juice
- 1 tablespoon honey
- ½ teaspoon soy sauce (lowest sodium available)
- 1 medium green onion (dark and light green parts only), thinly sliced diagonally

per serving

calories 187
total fat 6.5 g
  saturated fat 1.0 g
  trans fat 0.0 g
  polyunsaturated fat 1.5 g
  monounsaturated fat 2.5 g
cholesterol 53 mg

sodium 117 mg
carbohydrates 6 g
  fiber 0 g
  sugars 5 g
protein 24 g

dietary exchanges: ½ other carbohydrate, 3 lean meat

tilapia packets with artichokes

Wrapping food in cooking parchment and cooking the packets in the oven makes for mess-free steaming and preserves all those luscious juices.

SERVES 4 | 3 ounces fish and ⅔ cup artichoke mixture per serving

. . . .

Preheat the oven to 425°F.

Cut eight 12-inch-square pieces of cooking parchment. Lightly spray one side of each square with cooking spray. Place 2 lemon slices in the center of the sprayed side of four of the squares. Place the fish on the lemon slices. Sprinkle the oregano and red pepper flakes over the fish. Top with the artichokes and tomatoes. Place one of the remaining squares with the sprayed side down over each serving. Fold the edges of both parchment pieces together to seal the packets securely. Transfer to a large baking sheet.

Bake the packets for 12 minutes. Using the tines of a fork, carefully open a packet away from you. If the fish flakes easily when tested with the fork, carefully open the remaining packets and serve. If the fish isn't cooked enough, reclose the open packet and continue baking all the packets for about 2 minutes.

Just before serving, drizzle the fish and vegetables with the oil. Sprinkle with the feta.

Cooking spray

- 2 medium lemons, each cut into 4 slices
- 4 tilapia fillets (about 4 ounces each), rinsed and patted dry
- 1 teaspoon dried oregano, crumbled
- ⅛ teaspoon crushed red pepper flakes
- 1 14-ounce can quartered artichoke hearts, drained and coarsely chopped
- 1 cup grape tomatoes, quartered
- 1 tablespoon olive oil (extra virgin preferred)
- ⅓ cup crumbled fat-free feta cheese

per serving

calories 188
total fat 5.5 g
  saturated fat 1.0 g
  trans fat 0.0 g
  polyunsaturated fat 1.0 g
  monounsaturated fat 3.0 g
cholesterol 57 mg

sodium 445 mg
carbohydrates 8 g
  fiber 2 g
  sugars 3 g
protein 28 g

dietary exchanges:
2 vegetable, 3 lean meat

mussels cooked in wine

Coastal Mediterranean peoples have gleaned shellfish from the sea for eons. Exposed on the rocks at low tide, mussels were easy pickings—a succulent morsel for the wealthy and a reliable meal for the poor. This simple dish presents the delicate flavor of mussels at their best. With whole-grain bread to sop up the broth and a leafy dark green salad, it makes a light but nourishing meal.

SERVES 6 | 3 ounces mussels per serving

. . . .

In a large stockpot, melt the margarine over medium heat, swirling to coat the bottom. Cook the shallots and garlic for 5 minutes, or until softened, stirring occasionally. Stir in the wine, bay leaf, thyme, and pepper. Increase the heat to high and bring to a boil. Stir in the mussels. Reduce the heat to low and simmer, covered, for 5 to 10 minutes, or until the shells open. Remove from the heat. Discard the bay leaf.

Using a slotted spoon, transfer the mussels to a serving bowl. Discard any that haven't opened. Spoon some of the cooking liquid over the mussels. Serve immediately.

2 tablespoons light tub margarine

3 medium shallots, chopped

1 medium garlic clove, minced

1 cup dry white wine (regular or nonalcoholic) or ¾ cup water plus 3 tablespoons fresh lemon juice

1 medium dried bay leaf

½ teaspoon dried thyme, crumbled

½ teaspoon pepper

1½ pounds fresh debearded and rinsed medium mussels

per serving

calories 119	sodium 316 mg
total fat 3.5 g	carbohydrates 5 g
saturated fat 0.5 g	fiber 0 g
trans fat 0.0 g	sugars 0 g
polyunsaturated fat 1.0 g	protein 12 g
monounsaturated fat 1.5 g	
cholesterol 28 mg	dietary exchanges: ½ other carbohydrate, 2 lean meat

stuffed napa cabbage rolls with orange-ginger sauce

Napa cabbage leaves enclose a moist and tender Asian-spiced chicken filling. The light and airy rolls are delectable when dipped in a pungent sauce.

SERVES 4 | 2 rolls and 1 tablespoon sauce per serving

Line the bottom of a large bamboo steamer with the orange slices, overlapping them until they completely cover the bottom. Set aside.

Microwave the cabbage on 100 percent power (high) for 3 minutes, or until softened.

Meanwhile, in a large bowl, crumble the chicken. Add the rice, egg, parsley, shallot, minced gingerroot, and pepper. Using your hands or a spoon, combine the ingredients.

Put the cabbage leaves on a flat surface with the stem end toward you. Pat dry if needed. Place ¼ cup of the chicken mixture on each leaf toward the base of the leaf. Fold the edges of the leaves to the center so they slightly overlap. Trying to keep the cabbage rolls fairly tight, roll up from the stem end.

1 medium orange, thinly sliced

8 large napa cabbage leaves

1 pound ground skinless chicken breast

½ cup cooked brown rice

1 large egg, lightly beaten

2 tablespoons minced fresh parsley

1 tablespoon minced shallot

1 tablespoon finely minced peeled gingerroot

¼ teaspoon pepper (freshly ground preferred)

2 cups fat-free, low-sodium chicken broth or water

(continued)

Transfer the rolls with the seam side down to the steamer. Tightly cover the steamer.

Into a large skillet or a wok that's large enough to hold the steamer snugly, pour the broth to a depth of about 2 inches. Bring to a boil over high heat. Reduce the heat to a simmer. Place the steamer in the skillet. Make sure the broth doesn't touch the bottom of the steamer. Simmer for 10 to 12 minutes, or until the chicken registers 165°F on an instant-read thermometer. Transfer the rolls to plates.

Meanwhile, in a medium saucepan, heat the oil over medium-high heat, swirling to coat the bottom. Cook the green onions and grated gingerroot for 1 to 2 minutes, or until fragrant, stirring frequently. Stir in the remaining ingredients. Bring to a boil, still over medium-high heat. Reduce the heat and simmer for 5 to 8 minutes, or until the sauce begins to thicken, stirring frequently.

Just before serving, drizzle the cabbage rolls with the sauce.

SAUCE

- 2 teaspoons canola or corn oil
- 4 or 5 medium green onions, thinly sliced (½ cup)
- 2 tablespoons grated peeled gingerroot
- 1 cup fat-free, low-sodium chicken broth
- 2 tablespoons grated orange zest
- ⅓ cup fresh orange juice
- 1 teaspoon soy sauce (lowest sodium available)

per serving

calories 232
total fat 7.0 g
  saturated fat 1.5 g
  trans fat 0.0 g
  polyunsaturated fat 1.5 g
  monounsaturated fat 3.0 g
cholesterol 119 mg

sodium 208 mg
carbohydrates 13 g
  fiber 3 g
  sugars 4 g
protein 28 g

dietary exchanges: ½ starch, 1 vegetable, 3 lean meat

tofu in green onion broth

When it's steamed, tofu becomes soft and puffy rather than chewy. This simple preparation is complemented by the tangy lemon and subtle onion flavors of the broth.

SERVES 4 | 1 slice tofu and 3 tablespoons sauce per serving

Put the tofu on a cutting board lined with four layers of paper towels. Cover with four layers of paper towels. Place a large, heavy baking dish on top. Let stand for 30 minutes so the tofu releases its excess moisture, replacing the paper towels if necessary.

Line the bottom of a large bamboo steamer with the lemon slices, overlapping them until they completely cover the bottom. Place the tofu on the lemon slices. Cover tightly with the steamer lid. Set aside.

In a medium saucepan, heat the oil over medium-high heat, swirling to coat the bottom. Cook the green onions, shallot, and garlic for 1 to 2 minutes, or until fragrant. Stir in the wine. Cook for 1 to 2 minutes (no stirring needed). Stir in 2 cups broth, the parsley, and honey. Bring to a boil. Reduce the heat and simmer for 5 to 8 minutes, or until slightly thickened.

16 ounces light extra-firm tofu, drained, patted dry, and cut into 4 slices

4 to 5 medium lemons, thinly sliced

1 tablespoon canola or corn oil

4 or 5 medium green onions, sliced (½ cup)

1 large shallot, minced

2 medium garlic cloves, minced

¼ cup dry white wine (regular or nonalcoholic)

2 cups fat-free, low-sodium vegetable broth plus 1 cup fat-free, low-sodium vegetable broth (if needed)

¼ cup chopped fresh parsley

2 tablespoons honey

In a food processor or blender (vent the blender lid), process the broth mixture until smooth.

Pour the broth mixture into a skillet or wok large enough to hold the steamer. Bring to a simmer over medium heat.

Put the steamer in the skillet. Make sure the liquid doesn't touch the bottom of the steamer. Simmer for 7 to 10 minutes, or until the tofu is warm and puffy. Carefully transfer the steamer to a rimmed baking sheet. Carefully remove the lid away from you (to prevent steam burns).

Increase the heat to medium high. Bring the broth mixture to a boil. Reduce the heat and simmer for 5 minutes, or until the mixture is reduced by about half (to ¾ cup).

Transfer the tofu to plates or shallow bowls. Spoon the broth mixture over the tofu.

per serving

calories 179	sodium 97 mg
total fat 6.5 g	carbohydrates 17 g
saturated fat 0.5 g	fiber 3 g
trans fat 0.0 g	sugars 10 g
polyunsaturated fat 2.0 g	protein 12 g
monounsaturated fat 4.0 g	dietary exchanges: ½ starch,
cholesterol 0 mg	½ other carbohydrate,
	1½ lean meat

beer-scented chicken with veggies

If you like beer-can grilled chicken, you will love this recipe. Light beer is part of the steaming liquid and imbues the chicken and vegetables with flavor while they cook.

SERVES 4 | 3 ounces chicken and ½ cup vegetables per serving

. . . .

In a large saucepan fitted with a collapsible steamer basket, stir together the beer and water. Make sure the liquid doesn't touch the bottom of the steamer. Bring to a simmer over medium-high heat.

Meanwhile, in a small bowl, stir together the parsley, dillweed, salt, and pepper. Sprinkle over both sides of the chicken.

Arrange the chicken in a single layer in the steamer basket. Arrange the vegetables around the chicken. Steam, covered, for 11 to 12 minutes, or until the chicken is no longer pink in the center and the vegetables are tender. Remove from the heat. Carefully uncover the pan away from you (to prevent steam burns).

12 **ounces light beer (regular or nonalcoholic)**

1 **cup water**

½ **cup chopped fresh parsley**

1 **teaspoon dried dillweed, crumbled**

¼ **teaspoon salt**

¼ **teaspoon pepper**

4 **boneless, skinless chicken breast halves (about 4 ounces each), flattened to ½-inch thickness**

1 **medium yellow summer squash, cut crosswise into ½-inch slices**

1 **medium carrot, sliced crosswise**

½ **cup broccoli florets**

1 **medium Italian plum (Roma) tomato, thinly sliced**

per serving

calories 155	sodium 300 mg
total fat 3.0 g	carbohydrates 5 g
saturated fat 0.5 g	fiber 2 g
trans fat 0.0 g	sugars 3 g
polyunsaturated fat 0.5 g	protein 26 g
monounsaturated fat 1.0 g	dietary exchanges:
cholesterol 73 mg	1 vegetable, 3 lean meat

COOK'S TIP: For a fancier presentation, "roll-cut" the carrot. Start by cutting through the carrot at a 45-degree angle at one end. Roll the carrot a quarter turn. Make another 45-degree cut. Repeat the process until the carrot is completely cut into wedge-shaped pieces.

walnut-orange broccoli

This recipe is all about fresh ingredients—broccoli, orange juice and zest, and thyme—plus some crunch from dry-roasted walnuts.

SERVES 4 | ½ cup per serving

Fill a large saucepan with water to a depth of 1 inch. Place a collapsible steamer basket in the pan. Make sure the water doesn't touch the bottom of the steamer. Bring the water to a boil over high heat. Put the broccoli in the steamer. Steam, covered, for 5 to 6 minutes, or until tender-crisp. Remove from the heat. Carefully uncover the pan away from you (to prevent steam burns). Drain the broccoli well in a colander.

Meanwhile, in a medium bowl, whisk together the remaining ingredients except the walnuts.

Using tongs or a slotted spoon, transfer the broccoli to the bowl. Add the walnuts, stirring to coat.

- 8 ounces broccoli florets
- ½ teaspoon grated orange zest
- 2 tablespoons fresh orange juice
- 2 teaspoons olive oil
- 1 teaspoon fresh thyme
- ⅛ teaspoon salt
- ¼ cup chopped walnuts, dry-roasted

per serving

calories 91	sodium 92 mg
total fat 7.5 g	carbohydrates 6 g
saturated fat 1.0 g	fiber 2 g
trans fat 0.0 g	sugars 2 g
polyunsaturated fat 3.5 g	protein 3 g
monounsaturated fat 2.5 g	dietary exchanges:
cholesterol 0 mg	1 vegetable, 1½ fat

lemony green beans with almonds

The lively taste of lemon and a pop of fresh parsley add the perfect accents to fresh green beans.

SERVES 4 | ½ cup per serving

. . . .

Fill a large saucepan with water to a depth of 1 inch. Place a collapsible steamer basket in the pan. Make sure the water doesn't touch the bottom of the steamer. Bring the water to a boil over high heat. Put the green beans in the steamer. Steam, covered, for 3 to 5 minutes, or until tender-crisp. Remove from the heat. Carefully uncover the pan away from you (to prevent steam burns). Drain the green beans well in a colander.

Using tongs, transfer the green beans to a serving bowl. Sprinkle with the remaining ingredients, stirring gently to coat. Serve immediately for the best texture.

8	ounces green beans, trimmed, cut into 1½- to 2-inch pieces (about 2 cups)
2	tablespoons sliced almonds, dry-roasted
1	tablespoon minced fresh parsley
½	teaspoon grated lemon zest
1	teaspoon fresh lemon juice
⅛	teaspoon pepper

COOK'S TIP ON DRY-ROASTING NUTS IN A SKILLET: Dry-roasting nuts brings out their flavor. Put the nuts in a single layer in an ungreased skillet. Dry-roast over medium heat for about 4 minutes, or until just fragrant, stirring frequently and watching carefully so they don't burn. Remove the skillet from the heat to stop the cooking process.

per serving

calories 35	sodium 4 mg
total fat 1.5 g	carbohydrates 5 g
saturated fat 0.0 g	fiber 2 g
trans fat 0.0 g	sugars 2 g
polyunsaturated fat 0.5 g	protein 2 g
monounsaturated fat 1.0 g	dietary exchanges:
cholesterol 0 mg	1 vegetable, ½ fat

mixed vegetables with ginger

Using lemon juice as the steaming liquid imparts a light, citrusy flavor to this simple vegetable dish. Feel free to substitute whatever vegetables you have on hand.

SERVES 4 | ½ cup per serving

. . . .

Pour the lemon juice into a large saucepan. Add water to bring the liquid to a depth of 1 inch. Place a collapsible steamer basket in the pan. Make sure the liquid doesn't touch the bottom of the steamer. Bring the liquid to a boil over high heat. In the steamer, layer, in order, the carrots, cauliflower, peas, garlic, and gingerroot. Steam, covered, for 5 to 7 minutes, or until the vegetables are tender-crisp. Remove from the heat. Carefully uncover the pan away from you (to prevent steam burns). Drain the vegetables well in a colander, discarding the cooking liquid.

¼ cup fresh lemon juice

1 cup sliced carrots

2 cups cauliflower florets

1 cup sugar snap peas, trimmed

2 medium garlic cloves, halved

1 1½-inch piece peeled gingerroot, cut into matchstick-size strips

per serving

calories 39
total fat 0.0 g
  saturated fat 0.0 g
  trans fat 0.0 g
  polyunsaturated fat 0.0 g
  monounsaturated fat 0.0 g
cholesterol 0 mg

sodium 40 mg
carbohydrates 8 g
  fiber 3 g
  sugars 4 g
protein 2 g

dietary exchanges:
2 vegetable

thai sweet rice with mango

This dessert is popular in Thai restaurants, and for good reason. Be sure to buy sweet rice (also called sticky rice), as the regular kind won't work.

SERVES 4 | heaping ⅓ cup rice and ¼ cup mango per serving

. . . .

Put the rice in a medium bowl. Pour in enough water to cover the rice by at least 1 inch. Let stand, covered, for 8 to 12 hours.

After the rice has soaked, cut a circle of cooking parchment to fit inside a bamboo or collapsible steamer basket. Using a fork, pierce the paper several times. Place the paper in the steamer.

In a saucepan or wok large enough to hold the steamer, add water to a depth of 2 inches. Place the steamer in the pan. Make sure the water doesn't touch the bottom of the steamer. Bring to a simmer over medium heat.

Meanwhile, drain the rice, discarding the soaking water. Transfer the rice to the steamer. Reduce the heat and simmer, covered, for 45 minutes, or until the rice is tender (no stirring needed). Check the water level occasionally, adding more if needed.

In a medium bowl, stir together the coconut milk, brown sugar, and salt until the brown sugar is dissolved. Stir in the rice. Garnish with the mango and mint sprigs.

- ¾ cup uncooked Thai-style sweet rice
- ⅓ cup lite coconut milk or ¼ cup fat-free milk and ¼ teaspoon coconut extract
- 1 tablespoon light brown sugar
- ¼ teaspoon salt
- 1 medium mango, thinly sliced
- 4 sprigs of fresh mint

COOK'S TIP: Thai-style sweet rice is sometimes called sticky or glutinous rice because of the consistency. As with other rice, it's gluten-free. It's sold in Asian markets and in the Asian section of some grocery stores.

per serving

calories 211
total fat 1.5 g
  saturated fat 1.0 g
  trans fat 0.0 g
  polyunsaturated fat 0.0 g
  monounsaturated fat 0.0 g
cholesterol 0 mg

sodium 156 mg
carbohydrates 47 g
  fiber 2 g
  sugars 15 g
protein 3 g

dietary exchanges: 2 starch, 1 fruit

poaching

Poaching is a simple way to prepare meals, especially delicate foods like fish and eggs. Poaching brings water or a flavorful poaching liquid, such as wine, broth, fruit juice, or tea, to a boil and then gently simmers the food until done, which helps retain the food's shape and moisture. Although the liquid does come to a boil at first, poaching shouldn't be confused with cooking by boiling. Poached food is cooked more slowly, and the liquid often becomes a tasty base for a sauce, which means you retain all the food's vitamins and minerals.

Tired of the same old chicken dishes? Poaching is a great cooking method for infusing chicken breasts with tons of flavor while keeping them moist and tender. Try Lemon Chicken with Dill Sauce (page 190). Need to add more fruit to your diet? Try poaching it, as in Vanilla-Infused Pears (page 198), in which the fruit simmers in white wine made fragrant with orange zest, cinnamon, and vanilla.

Another benefit for busy home cooks is that poaching is fast and doesn't require much hands-on time, as the food is moved very little in the pan. You don't need much more than a pot with a lid and healthy ingredients to put a nutritious poached meal on the table.

HERE'S HOW THIS TECHNIQUE WORKS:

1. USE a pan that is just large enough to contain the food you want to cook but deep enough to add the amount of liquid needed. Add

herbs, aromatics, and spices, such as garlic, onions, cinnamon sticks, fresh ginger, citrus peels, bay leaves, cardamom pods, peppercorns, or whole cloves.

2.   Next, barely SUBMERGE the food in the simmering liquid, and cook it with a cover. Larger foods, such as whole fish, should be added to the pan in the beginning and heated along with the liquid. Smaller foods, such as fish fillets, eggs, and chicken breasts, should be added after the liquid is hot.

3.   After the food is cooked, REMOVE it from the pan (a slotted spoon or spatula works best). Serve it with the broth or reduce the remaining liquid (decrease the volume by boiling the liquid rapidly) to make a flavorful sauce.

Tools & Equipment Needed: Skillet or Dutch oven with lid, saucepan with lid, slotted spoon or spatula, kitchen timer

TO POACH:
To cook food gently immersed in simmering liquid.

TIPS:

• Keep a close eye on the poaching liquid, which should never reach a boil after the food has been added. It's a good idea to keep the lid ajar (especially if you don't have glass pot lids) so you can watch that the liquid isn't boiling. If you don't have a lid, use a round piece of cooking parchment cut to fit the pot. The parchment will trap some steam but let enough out so the water doesn't boil.

• Although you can use water as the liquid, you can also use 100 percent fruit juice, tea, wine, or fat-free, low-sodium broth to infuse the food with flavor. An acid, such as vinegar, wine, or lemon juice, can be added to the poaching liquid to help firm up the proteins in the food.

- It's key to use uniform-size pieces so that everything cooks evenly at the same time.

- A constant simmer is not always easy to regulate, especially on a gas stovetop, so our recipes don't state at what temperature to simmer. Even at the lowest setting on some stovetops, the heat may be too intense, which will cause the liquid to boil. When simmering, a small bubble should break through the surface of the liquid every second or two. If more bubbles rise to the surface, then lower the heat or use a burner plate, sometimes called a simmer plate, to diffuse the heat.

cod in green curry broth

The lively flavors of Thailand permeate this rich-tasting entrée, which contains Thai curry paste and a liberal dose of lime. Serve it with a green vegetable such as baby bok choy and brown rice or brown rice noodles.

SERVES 4 | 3 ounces fish and 1 cup broth per serving

. . . .

In a medium bowl, whisk together 4 cups broth, the lime zest, lime juice, and curry paste.

In a large skillet, heat the oil over medium-high heat, swirling to coat the bottom. Cook the shallots and garlic for 2 to 3 minutes, or until soft, stirring frequently. Stir in the broth mixture. Reduce the heat to medium. Cook, covered, until just boiling.

Gently place the fish in the broth mixture. If necessary, pour in enough of the remaining 1 cup broth to barely cover the fish. Reduce the heat and simmer, partially covered, for 7 minutes, or until the fish flakes easily when tested with a fork.

Transfer the fish to serving bowls. Ladle the broth over the fish. Sprinkle with the green onions and cilantro. Serve with the lime wedges.

4 cups fat-free, low-sodium chicken broth and 1 cup fat-free, low-sodium chicken broth (if needed), divided use

1 tablespoon grated lime zest

3 tablespoons fresh lime juice

1 tablespoon Thai green curry paste

1 tablespoon canola or corn oil

2 medium shallots, minced

1 medium garlic clove, minced

4 cod fillets (about 4 ounces each), rinsed and patted dry

2 medium green onions, thinly sliced diagonally

1 tablespoon minced fresh cilantro or ¼ cup basil chiffonade (Thai basil preferred)

1 medium lime, cut into 4 wedges

per serving

calories 146	sodium 208 mg
total fat 4.0 g	carbohydrates 5 g
saturated fat 0.5 g	fiber 1 g
trans fat 0.0 g	sugars 1 g
polyunsaturated fat 1.0 g	protein 21 g
monounsaturated fat 2.5 g	dietary exchanges: ½ other
cholesterol 43 mg	carbohydrate, 3 lean meat

green tea halibut with baby spinach

Adding green tea to the poaching liquid enhances the Asian flavors that infuse this dish. Topping the raw spinach with the hot fish and the tea mixture cooks it just enough, right in the bowl.

SERVES 4 | 3 ounces fish, 1 cup spinach, and ½ cup broth per serving

In a shallow saucepan, stir together the water, soy sauce, gingerroot, sesame oil, garlic, and pepper. Add the tea bag, letting the tag hang over the side of the pan. Bring to a simmer over medium-high heat. Reduce the heat and simmer for 5 minutes, or until the tea bag has steeped. Discard the tea bag. Increase the heat to medium. Cook, covered, until just boiling.

Gently place the fish in the tea mixture. If necessary, pour in enough hot water to barely cover the fish. Reduce the heat and simmer, partially covered, for 10 to 11 minutes, or until the fish flakes easily when tested with a fork.

Put the spinach in serving bowls. Place the fish on the spinach. Sprinkle with the green onions. Ladle the broth over all. Sprinkle with the sesame seeds.

2 cups water

1 tablespoon soy sauce (lowest sodium available)

1 teaspoon minced peeled gingerroot

1 teaspoon toasted sesame oil

1 medium garlic clove, minced

⅛ teaspoon pepper

1 single-serving bag of green tea (with a tag preferred)

4 halibut fillets (about 4 ounces each), about 1 inch thick, rinsed and patted dry

4 cups loosely packed baby spinach

2 medium green onions, thinly sliced

2 teaspoons sesame seeds, dry-roasted

per serving

calories 161
total fat 5.0 g
  saturated fat 0.5 g
  trans fat 0.0 g
  polyunsaturated fat 2.0 g
  monounsaturated fat 1.5 g
cholesterol 36 mg

sodium 189 mg
carbohydrates 3 g
  fiber 1 g
  sugars 1 g
protein 25 g

dietary exchanges: 3 lean meat

pineapple and ginger mahi mahi

A versatile and mildly flavored fish known by its Hawaiian name, mahi mahi is a natural with the tropical Asian flavors of pineapple and ginger. Serve this with brown rice or soba noodles to soak up the fruity broth.

SERVES 4 | 3 ounces fish and 1 cup pineapple mixture per serving

. . . .

In a large skillet, heat the oil over medium-high heat, swirling to coat the bottom. Cook the carrots, bell pepper, and garlic for 2 to 3 minutes, or until the carrots and bell pepper are tender-crisp, stirring frequently. Stir in 2 cups broth and the gingerroot. Reduce the heat to medium. Cook, covered, until just boiling.

Stir in the pineapple. Gently place the fish in the broth mixture. If necessary, pour in enough of the remaining 1 cup broth to barely cover the fish. Reduce the heat and simmer, partially covered, for 5 to 7 minutes, or until the fish flakes easily when tested with a fork.

Transfer the fish to serving bowls. Ladle the broth mixture over the fish. Sprinkle with the cilantro and green onions.

1 tablespoon canola or corn oil

2 medium carrots, thinly sliced diagonally

1 medium red bell pepper, thinly sliced

2 medium garlic cloves, minced

2 cups fat-free, low-sodium chicken broth and 1 cup fat-free, low-sodium chicken broth (if needed), divided use

1 tablespoon grated peeled gingerroot

4 cups chopped pineapple (1-inch pieces)

4 mahi mahi fillets (about 4 ounces each), rinsed and patted dry

¼ cup chopped fresh cilantro

3 medium green onions, thinly sliced diagonally (green parts only)

per serving

calories 252	sodium 177 mg
total fat 4.5 g	carbohydrates 29 g
saturated fat 0.5 g	fiber 5 g
trans fat 0.0 g	sugars 21 g
polyunsaturated fat 1.5 g	protein 24 g
monounsaturated fat 2.5 g	dietary exchanges: 1½ fruit,
cholesterol 83 mg	1 vegetable, 3 lean meat

salmon with lemon-watercress sauce

Traditionally served cold, this showy salmon dish is equally inviting when warm.

SERVES 4 | 3 ounces fish and 2 tablespoons sauce per serving

In a small bowl, stir together the yogurt, mayonnaise, watercress, green onions, lemon zest, and pepper. Cover and refrigerate.

Put the celery, onion, carrot, lemon slices, bay leaf, and peppercorns in a large skillet. Pour in the broth and wine. Cook, covered, over medium-high heat until just boiling.

Gently place the fish in the broth mixture. If necessary, pour in enough hot water to barely cover the fish. Reduce the heat and simmer, partially covered, for 8 to 12 minutes, or until the fish is the desired doneness. Using a slotted spatula, transfer the fish to a plate. Pat the fish dry with paper towels. Discard the liquid.

Serve the fish warm or wrap it in plastic wrap or aluminum foil and refrigerate for 3 to 24 hours to serve chilled. Just before serving, cut the fish into four pieces. Sprinkle with the paprika. Serve the sauce on the side.

¼ cup fat-free plain Greek yogurt

¼ cup light mayonnaise

2 tablespoons finely chopped watercress or parsley

1 tablespoon thinly sliced green onions or chives

1 tablespoon grated lemon zest

Pinch of pepper (white preferred)

2 medium ribs of celery, sliced

1 medium onion, sliced

1 medium carrot, sliced

2 slices lemon, about ¼ inch thick

1 medium dried bay leaf

3 black peppercorns

1¾ cups fat-free, low-sodium chicken broth

1 cup dry white wine (regular or nonalcoholic)

1 1-pound skinless salmon fillet, about 1 inch thick, rinsed and patted dry

¼ teaspoon paprika

per serving

calories 216
total fat 8.5 g
  saturated fat 1.0 g
  trans fat 0.0 g
  polyunsaturated fat 3.5 g
  monounsaturated fat 2.5 g
cholesterol 58 mg

sodium 236 mg
carbohydrates 3 g
  fiber 0 g
  sugars 1 g
protein 26 g

dietary exchanges: 3 lean meat

COOK'S TIP: If you prefer, you can substitute redfish, sea bass, or monkfish fillets for the salmon.

honeyed salmon with spiced honeydew salsa

The beauty of poaching fish is that the fish stays moist and delicate. Honey and lime juice give this poaching liquid a sweet-and-sour taste.

SERVES 4 | 3 ounces fish and ⅓ cup salsa per serving

. . . .

In a medium bowl, stir together 1½ tablespoons honey, 1 teaspoon lime juice, and the red pepper flakes. Gently stir in the remaining salsa ingredients, including the lime zest. Set aside.

In a medium skillet, stir together the water and the remaining ¼ cup green onions, 3 tablespoons lime juice, and 2 tablespoons honey. Cook, covered, over medium-high heat until just boiling.

Gently place the fish in the poaching liquid. If necessary, pour in enough hot water to barely cover the fish. Reduce the heat and simmer, partially covered, for 6 to 8 minutes, or until the fish is the desired doneness. Using a slotted spatula, transfer to serving plates. Discard the poaching liquid. Serve the fish with the salsa.

SALSA

- 1½ tablespoons honey
- 1 teaspoon grated lime zest
- 1 teaspoon fresh lime juice
- ⅛ to ¼ teaspoon crushed red pepper flakes
- 1 cup chopped honeydew melon
- ⅓ cup finely chopped red bell pepper
- ¼ cup sliced green onions
- 1 tablespoon chopped fresh cilantro

- 2 cups water
- ¼ cup sliced green onions (white and light green parts)
- 3 tablespoons fresh lime juice
- 2 tablespoons honey
- 4 salmon fillets (about 4 ounces each), rinsed and patted dry

per serving

calories 194	sodium 98 mg
total fat 5.0 g	carbohydrates 12 g
saturated fat 1.0 g	fiber 1 g
trans fat 0.0 g	sugars 11 g
polyunsaturated fat 1.0 g	protein 24 g
monounsaturated fat 1.5 g	dietary exchanges: ½ fruit,
cholesterol 53 mg	½ other carbohydrate, 3 lean meat

citrus tea tilapia

This sweet and savory fish dish gets a triple dose of citrus from fresh orange zest and juice, as well as citrus-flavored tea. Serve with steamed veggies, such as Walnut-Orange Broccoli (page 175).

SERVES 4 | 3 ounces fish and 2 tablespoons sauce per serving

Put the tea bags in a 4-cup glass measuring cup. Pour in 3 cups hot water. Steep, covered, for 4 to 5 minutes. Discard the tea bags. Stir in the brown sugar.

In a large skillet, heat the oil over medium-high heat, swirling to coat the bottom. Cook the shallots and garlic for 2 to 3 minutes, or until soft, stirring frequently. Stir in the tea mixture, orange zest, orange juice, and pepper. Reduce the heat to medium. Cook, covered, until just boiling.

Gently place the fish in the tea mixture. If necessary, pour in enough of the 1 cup hot water to barely cover the fish. Reduce the heat and simmer, partially covered, for 4 to 5 minutes, or until the fish flakes easily when tested with a fork.

4 single-serving bags of citrus tea

3 cups hot water, 1 cup hot water (if needed), and 1 tablespoon water, divided use

1 tablespoon light or dark brown sugar

1 tablespoon canola or corn oil

2 medium shallots, chopped

2 medium garlic cloves, minced

2 tablespoons grated orange zest

⅓ to ½ cup fresh orange juice

¼ teaspoon pepper (freshly ground preferred)

4 tilapia fillets (about 4 ounces each), rinsed and patted dry

1 tablespoon cornstarch

1 tablespoon minced fresh parsley

1 medium lemon, cut into 4 wedges

Without turning off the heat, transfer the fish to plates. Cover the fish loosely with aluminum foil to keep warm.

Put the cornstarch in a small bowl. Add the remaining 1 tablespoon water, stirring to dissolve. Gradually add to the sauce, whisking until it begins to thicken. Bring just to a boil. Reduce the heat and simmer for 3 to 5 minutes, whisking frequently.

Spoon the sauce over the fish. Sprinkle with the parsley. Serve with the lemon wedges.

COOK'S TIP: Flounder, red snapper, or other types of flaky white fish may be substituted for the tilapia.

per serving

calories 181
total fat 5.5 g
  saturated fat 1.0 g
  trans fat 0.0 g
  polyunsaturated fat 1.5 g
  monounsaturated fat 3.0 g
cholesterol 57 mg

sodium 69 mg
carbohydrates 10 g
  fiber 1 g
  sugars 5 g
protein 23 g

dietary exchanges: ½ other carbohydrate, 3 lean meat

lemon chicken with dill sauce

Whether you are a novice or an experienced cook, you'll love the simplicity of this vibrantly flavored dish. Serve it with brown rice or farro, along with your favorite vegetable. Or serve the moist and tender chicken over a salad of dark, leafy greens.

SERVES 4 | 3 ounces chicken and 2 tablespoons sauce per serving

. . . .

In a large, shallow saucepan, stir together the broth, wine, lemon slices, dill seeds, oregano, and pepper. Bring to a boil over high heat. Reduce the heat and simmer, covered, for 5 minutes.

Place the chicken in the broth mixture. If necessary, add enough hot water to barely cover the chicken. Increase the heat to medium high and return to a simmer. Reduce the heat and simmer, partially covered, for 8 minutes, or until the chicken is no longer pink in the center.

1½ cups fat-free, low-sodium chicken broth

½ cup dry white wine (regular or nonalcoholic)

1 small lemon, thinly sliced

1 teaspoon dill seeds

1 teaspoon dried oregano, crumbled

⅛ teaspoon pepper (freshly ground preferred)

4 boneless, skinless chicken breast halves (about 4 ounces each), all visible fat discarded, flattened to ¾-inch thickness

(continued)

Meanwhile, in a small bowl, whisk together the sauce ingredients.

Using a slotted spoon or spatula, transfer the cooked chicken to a cutting board. Discard the poaching liquid. Cut the chicken diagonally across the grain into thick slices. Transfer to plates. Spoon the sauce over the chicken. Garnish with the remaining lemon slices and sprigs of dillweed.

SAUCE

½ cup fat-free plain Greek yogurt

2 teaspoons chopped fresh dillweed

½ teaspoon grated lemon zest

1 teaspoon fresh lemon juice

⅛ teaspoon pepper (freshly ground preferred)

---

1 medium lemon, thinly sliced

4 sprigs of fresh dillweed (stems trimmed to the feathery tops)

COOK'S TIP: The sauce can be prepared up to three days in advance. Cover and refrigerate it until needed.

per serving

calories 149
total fat 3.0 g
  saturated fat 0.5 g
  trans fat 0.0 g
  polyunsaturated fat 0.5 g
  monounsaturated fat 1.0 g
cholesterol 73 mg

sodium 165 mg
carbohydrates 1 g
  fiber 0 g
  sugars 1 g
protein 27 g

dietary exchanges: 3½ lean meat

chicken and vegetables with thyme-scented broth

A poached chicken breast served with tender vegetables is the height of simplicity, letting the fresh ingredients shine through. Serve this in a bowl, like a soup or stew, to enjoy all the comforting, fragrant broth.

SERVES 4 | 3 ounces chicken and 1 cup vegetables and broth per serving

In a large saucepan, heat the oil over medium-high heat, swirling to coat the bottom. Cook the leeks and celery for 3 to 5 minutes, or until soft, stirring frequently.

Stir in 4 cups broth, the carrots, potato, and thyme. Increase the heat to high and bring to a boil. Reduce the heat and simmer, covered, for 5 minutes. Place the chicken in the broth mixture. If necessary, pour in enough of the remaining 1 cup broth to barely cover the chicken. Increase the heat to medium high and return to a simmer. Reduce the heat and simmer, partially covered, for 4 to 5 minutes (the chicken won't be done at this point). Using a slotted spoon, discard the thyme.

1 tablespoon olive oil

2 medium leeks, thinly sliced (white parts only)

2 medium ribs of celery, thinly sliced diagonally

4 cups fat-free, low-sodium chicken broth and 1 cup fat-free, low-sodium chicken broth (if needed), divided use

2 small carrots, thinly sliced diagonally

1 medium red potato, quartered and thinly sliced

3 sprigs of fresh thyme

(continued)

Add the kale. Cook for 3 minutes, or until the kale is just tender and the chicken is no longer pink in the center.

Using a slotted spoon or spatula, transfer the chicken to a cutting board. Cut diagonally across the grain into thick slices. Transfer to bowls. Ladle the vegetables and broth over the chicken. Sprinkle with the pepper.

4   boneless, skinless chicken breast halves (about 4 ounces each), all visible fat discarded

8   ounces chopped kale, tough stems discarded

¼   teaspoon pepper (freshly ground preferred)

per serving

calories 278
total fat 7.0 g
  saturated fat 1.0 g
  trans fat 0.0 g
  polyunsaturated fat 1.0 g
  monounsaturated fat 3.5 g
cholesterol 73 mg

sodium 280 mg
carbohydrates 23 g
  fiber 4 g
  sugars 4 g
protein 31 g

dietary exchanges: ½ starch, 3 vegetable, 3 lean meat

COOK'S TIP ON LEEKS: To prepare leeks, cut off and discard the roots on the white bulb. Cut off the tougher dark green leaves. If you wish, you can save these to make stock. Halve the leek lengthwise. Then cut the halves crosswise into thin slices. Transfer the slices to a small colander. Rinse them well under cold water. Drain them well. If necessary, repeat the process to clean off all the sandy grit.

cheesy open-face egg sandwiches

Perfectly poached eggs are easy to prepare, making them an ideal breakfast for those in a hurry. Here they top crisp toasted whole-grain English muffin halves, while a cheesy béchamel sauce ties the dish together. The eggs and sauce are equally tasty when served over steamed or sautéed spinach.

SERVES 4 | 1 sandwich per serving

In a small bowl, whisk together the milk, flour, oil, pepper, nutmeg, and cayenne. In a small saucepan, bring the mixture to a simmer over medium-high heat. Simmer for 1 to 2 minutes, or until thickened, whisking frequently. Remove from the heat.

Add the Cheddar, stirring until melted. Cover to keep warm. Set aside.

In a shallow saucepan, bring the water and vinegar to just below the boiling point (140°F to 180°F on an instant-read thermometer); tiny bubbles may form at the bottom of the pan, but they won't break the surface of the water. Place a double layer of paper towels on a large plate.

Using a clean medium-size whisk, quickly and gently stir the water to create a swirl in the

½ cup fat-free milk

2 teaspoons all-purpose flour

½ teaspoon olive oil

⅛ teaspoon pepper (freshly ground preferred)

⅛ teaspoon ground nutmeg

⅛ teaspoon cayenne (optional)

⅓ cup shredded low-fat Cheddar cheese

3 cups water

1 teaspoon white vinegar

4 large eggs, cracked into separate small bowls or cups

2 whole-grain English muffins (lowest sodium available), halved and toasted

center of the pan. Carefully slip one of the eggs into the swirl. Using a spoon, gently stir the water around the egg for 10 seconds to help the egg white wrap around the yolk. Cook for 2 to 4 minutes, or until the white is completely set and the yolk is the desired doneness. Using a slotted spoon, transfer the egg to the paper towel. Repeat with the remaining eggs.

Just before serving, put the English muffin halves on plates with the cut sides up. Top each muffin half with an egg. Spoon the sauce over the eggs.

COOK'S TIP: For added visual appeal and flavor, top each sandwich with a pinch of freshly ground pepper, paprika, or chopped fresh herbs (chives, thyme, oregano, basil, and rosemary are great choices).

per serving

calories 176	sodium 263 mg
total fat 7.0 g	carbohydrates 17 g
saturated fat 2.0 g	fiber 2 g
trans fat 0.0 g	sugars 5 g
polyunsaturated fat 1.5 g	protein 13 g
monounsaturated fat 2.5 g	dietary exchanges: 1 starch,
cholesterol 189 mg	1½ lean meat

cardamom-orange plums

Aromatic cardamom gives these poached plums a distinctive spicy-sweet flavor. Serve the fruit warm or chilled, alone or with a scoop of fat-free frozen vanilla yogurt.

SERVES 4 | 2 plum halves per serving

In a medium saucepan, stir together 2½ cups orange juice, the liqueur, sugar, cardamom, and orange zest. Bring to a simmer over medium heat, stirring until the sugar is dissolved.

Gently place the plums in the orange juice mixture. If necessary, pour in enough of the remaining 1 cup orange juice to barely cover the plums. Increase the heat to high and bring to a simmer. Reduce the heat and simmer for 5 to 7 minutes, or until the plums are just tender when pierced with the tip of a sharp knife, stirring frequently.

1 teaspoon grated orange zest

2½ cups fresh orange juice and 1 cup fresh orange juice (if needed)

½ cup orange liqueur, such as Grand Marnier (optional)

1 tablespoon sugar

1 tablespoon crushed cardamom pods (about 3 to 4 pods)

4 medium plums, halved

Using a slotted spoon, transfer the plums to dessert dishes.

Increase the heat to high and bring the orange juice mixture to a boil. Boil for 10 to 12 minutes, or until reduced by half (to about 1½ cups), stirring constantly. Using a fine-mesh sieve, strain the sauce, discarding the solids. Spoon the sauce over the plums.

per serving

calories 141	sodium 2 mg
total fat 0.5 g	carbohydrates 33 g
saturated fat 0.0 g	fiber 1 g
trans fat 0.0 g	sugars 28 g
polyunsaturated fat 0.0 g	protein 2 g
monounsaturated fat 0.0 g	
cholesterol 0 mg	dietary exchanges: 2 fruit

COOK'S TIP: Used in equal parts, a combination of cinnamon and cloves or cinnamon and nutmeg can substitute for cardamom. In this recipe, use 1 cinnamon stick (about 3 inches long) and ¼ teaspoon whole cloves instead of the cardamom pods.

COOK'S TIP ON CARDAMOM: Cardamom pods are popular in Scandinavian, Indian, and Greek cooking. They have a short shelf life and should be stored in an airtight container in the freezer. Ground cardamom loses its potency very quickly, so choose the pods whenever possible.

vanilla-infused pears

Vanilla and pears make a heavenly pair, especially when the fruit is gently simmered and served with a thick sauce made from the cinnamon-scented poaching liquid. Serve warm or chilled.

SERVES 4 | 1 pear half and 2 tablespoons sauce per serving

. . . .

In a medium saucepan, whisk together all the ingredients except the pears. Bring to a boil over medium-high heat. Boil for 5 minutes, or until the sugar is dissolved, stirring frequently.

Gently place the pears in the wine mixture. If necessary, pour in enough hot water to barely cover the pears. Reduce the heat and simmer, partially covered, for 10 to 15 minutes, or until the tip of a sharp knife inserted into a pear comes out easily.

Using a slotted spoon, transfer the pears to plates. Discard the cinnamon stick and orange zest from the sauce.

Simmer the sauce for 12 to 15 minutes, or until reduced by half (to about ½ cup), stirring constantly. Spoon over the pears.

1 cup Riesling or other medium-sweet white wine (regular or nonalcoholic)

½ cup water

2½ tablespoons sugar

1 cinnamon stick (about 3 inches long)

Zest of ½ medium orange, cut into strips

1 teaspoon vanilla extract

2 medium firm Bosc or Bartlett pears, peeled, halved, and cored

COOK'S TIP: For a deeper flavor, let the pears cool in the poaching liquid. Cover and refrigerate overnight. Serve chilled, or remove from the refrigerator and let stand for about 1 hour to serve at room temperature.

per serving

calories 108
total fat 0.0 g
  saturated fat 0.0 g
  trans fat 0.0 g
  polyunsaturated fat 0.0 g
  monounsaturated fat 0.0 g
cholesterol 0 mg

sodium 2 mg
carbohydrates 23 g
  fiber 3 g
  sugars 17 g
protein 0 g

dietary exchanges: 1 fruit, ½ other carbohydrate

broiling

The speed and simplicity of broiling—and the fact that ovens come equipped with a built-in broiler—make it a convenient and simple way to prepare healthy meals. What is broiling? Think of it as upside-down grilling, with the food on the bottom and the flame or heating element on top. Just about anything that you can grill can be broiled. You can broil many nutritious foods, including seafood, vegetables, and even fruit, such as in Brazilian Halibut (page 204), Broiled Foiled Tomatoes (page 218), and Grapefruit with Crunchy Ginger (page 219).

The high heat of broiling creates a crisp, browned crust on fish, meat, and poultry and a moist, tender interior while allowing excess saturated fat to drip away into the broiler pan. The intense, direct heat cooks food fast and caramelizes it, giving it a distinctive flavor.

Tools & Equipment Needed: Broiler pan and rack, broiler-safe baking sheets, ovenproof skillet, oven mitts and pot holders, oven thermometer, instant-read thermometer, kitchen timer

TIPS:

- In electric ovens, the broiler is always at the top. In gas ovens, broilers can be either at the top or in a separate drawer under the oven. If you have a toaster oven, you most likely have a broiler there, too.

- Position food under the heating element for best results, rotating it as necessary to evenly cook the food's surface.

TO BROIL:

To cook food directly under a heat source in an electric or gas oven.

- Remember that if a recipe specifies a distance from the heat, it means the number of inches from the heating element to the top of the food you are broiling, not to the top of the broiler rack. As a rule of thumb, food should be placed about 4 inches from the heating element to avoid burning.

- Most ovens come with a broiler pan and rack, but if you don't have a broiler pan, then you can use any all-metal pan.

- To make cleanup easier, line the broiler pan with aluminum foil.

- Trim and discard all visible fat from poultry and meats before broiling; this will both cut down on saturated fat and help prevent flare-ups.

- Use lower-sodium marinades and glazes as well as salt-free rubs to add flavor.

- To avoid both overcooking and undercooking meat and poultry, use a meat thermometer to check doneness. Remove the meat or poultry from the oven before inserting the instant-read thermometer. Insert the thermometer into the center, or thickest part, of the meat, making sure the thermometer doesn't touch bone or fat.

- See broiling safety tips on page 280.

warm caesar salad with tofu "croutons"

Briefly broiling the lettuce gives this salad a warm, toasty flavor and a softer texture. Crisp, seasoned tofu stands in for traditional croutons in a surprising but delicious way. To turn this into an entrée, just add lean leftover chicken or turkey, cooked without salt.

SERVES 4 | 1 cup per serving

Preheat the broiler. Lightly spray a broiler pan and rack with cooking spray.

Arrange the tofu in a single layer on the broiler rack. Lightly spray the top of the cubes with cooking spray. Sprinkle ½ teaspoon seasoning blend over the tofu. Broil about 4 inches from the heat for 5 to 10 minutes, or until golden brown (watch carefully so the tofu doesn't burn). Remove from the oven. Gently stir the tofu. Lightly spray with cooking spray. Sprinkle with the remaining ½ teaspoon seasoning blend. Broil for 5 to 10 minutes, or until golden brown (watch carefully so the tofu doesn't burn). Transfer to a plate. Set aside.

Meanwhile, in a large bowl, whisk together the dressing ingredients. Set aside.

Olive oil cooking spray

4 ounces light extra-firm tofu, drained, patted dry, and cut into ½-inch cubes

½ teaspoon salt-free all-purpose seasoning blend and ½ teaspoon salt-free all-purpose seasoning blend, divided use

DRESSING

2 tablespoons white wine vinegar

1 tablespoon olive oil

1 tablespoon Dijon mustard (lowest sodium available)

1 teaspoon soy sauce (lowest sodium available)

1 teaspoon fresh lemon juice

1 medium garlic clove, minced

(continued)

Put the romaine with the cut sides up on the broiler pan. Lightly spray with cooking spray. Broil about 6 inches from the heat for 1 to 2 minutes on each side, or until golden brown. Transfer to a cutting board. Chop into bite-size pieces.

Add the romaine, Parmesan, and pepper to the dressing, tossing to coat. Sprinkle with the tofu.

1   medium head of romaine, halved lengthwise

2   tablespoons shredded or grated Parmesan cheese

⅛   to ¼ teaspoon pepper (freshly ground preferred)

COOK'S TIP: Putting the dressing in the bowl first and then adding the salad not only saves on cleanup, it also distributes the dressing more evenly when the salad is tossed, allowing you to use less.

per serving

calories 81
total fat 5.0 g
  saturated fat 1.0 g
  trans fat 0.0 g
  polyunsaturated fat 0.5 g
  monounsaturated fat 2.5 g
cholesterol 2 mg

sodium 189 mg
carbohydrates 6 g
  fiber 3 g
  sugars 2 g
protein 5 g
dietary exchanges:
1 vegetable, ½ lean meat, ½ fat

brazilian halibut

Firm, meaty halibut stands up well to the rich, earthy flavor of coffee, while lemon juice adds a light freshness.

SERVES 4 | 3 ounces fish per serving

Put the coffee granules in a shallow baking dish. Add the lemon juice, stirring to dissolve. Stir in the margarine and onion powder. Transfer 2 teaspoons of the marinade to a small bowl. Set aside. Add the fish to the marinade in the baking dish, turning to coat. Cover and refrigerate for 30 minutes, turning once halfway through.

Preheat the broiler. Lightly spray the broiler pan and rack with cooking spray.

Drain the fish, discarding the marinade. Broil about 4 inches from the heat for 4 to 5 minutes. Remove from the oven.

Carefully turn over the fish. Brush the top with the reserved marinade. Broil for 4 to 5 minutes, or until the fish flakes easily when tested with a fork. Just before serving, sprinkle with the parsley.

1½ teaspoons instant coffee granules

1 tablespoon fresh lemon juice

2 tablespoons light tub margarine, melted

½ teaspoon onion powder

1 1-pound halibut or other firm fish steak, rinsed and patted dry

Cooking spray

1½ teaspoons chopped fresh parsley

per serving

calories 108
total fat 2.0 g
  saturated fat 0.5 g
  trans fat 0.0 g
  polyunsaturated fat 0.5 g
  monounsaturated fat 1.0 g
cholesterol 56 mg

sodium 89 mg
carbohydrates 0 g
  fiber 0 g
  sugars 0 g
protein 21 g

dietary exchanges: 3 lean meat

portobello-tuna melts

A deli classic goes classy in these sophisticated tuna melts. Creamy tuna salad is spiked with green onions, shallot, and carrots, then piled onto meaty portobello mushroom caps and topped with two kinds of cheese.

SERVES 4 | 1 stuffed mushroom per serving

. . . .

Preheat the broiler. Line a large, heavy-duty rimmed baking sheet with aluminum foil. Lightly spray the foil with cooking spray.

In a small bowl, using a fork, stir together the tuna, carrot, green onions, and shallot. Stir in the mayonnaise and ¼ teaspoon pepper.

Arrange the mushroom caps in a single layer on the baking sheet with the stem sides up. Sprinkle the remaining ¼ teaspoon pepper over the mushrooms. Broil about 6 inches from the heat for 5 to 8 minutes, or until they begin to soften. Remove from the oven.

Fill the mushrooms with the tuna mixture. Sprinkle with the Parmesan. Top with the Cheddar. Broil about 6 inches from the heat for 2 to 4 minutes, or until the cheeses are melted and lightly browned and the tuna mixture is hot.

Cooking spray

2   4.5-ounce cans very low sodium solid albacore tuna, packed in water, drained and flaked

⅓   cup shredded carrot

2   to 3 medium green onions, sliced

1   large shallot, minced

¼   cup light mayonnaise

¼   teaspoon pepper and ¼ teaspoon pepper, divided use

4   4-inch portobello mushroom caps

¼   cup shredded or grated Parmesan cheese

½   cup shredded low-fat Cheddar cheese

per serving

calories 174	sodium 352 mg
total fat 7.0 g	carbohydrates 7 g
saturated fat 2.0 g	fiber 2 g
trans fat 0.0 g	sugars 2 g
polyunsaturated fat 2.5 g	protein 23 g
monounsaturated fat 1.5 g	dietary exchanges:
cholesterol 39 mg	1 vegetable, 3 lean meat

sweet and tangy scallops

Infused with the warmth of curry powder, a honey-mustard sauce highlights the sweetness of scallops in this entrée that's simple to make but loaded with complex flavor.

SERVES 4 | 2 ounces scallops per serving

Preheat the broiler. Lightly spray a broiler pan with cooking spray.

In a small bowl, whisk together the honey, mustard, curry powder, and lemon juice.

Arrange the scallops in a single layer in the pan. Brush with the honey mixture. Broil about 4 inches from the heat for 5 to 8 minutes, or until browned. Serve with the lemon wedges.

Cooking spray

2 tablespoons honey

2 tablespoons yellow mustard (lowest sodium available)

½ teaspoon curry powder

½ teaspoon fresh lemon juice

12 ounces sea scallops, rinsed and patted dry

1 medium lemon, cut into 4 wedges

per serving

calories 97
total fat 1.0 g
  saturated fat 0.0 g
  trans fat 0.0 g
  polyunsaturated fat 0.0 g
  monounsaturated fat 0.5 g
cholesterol 20 mg

sodium 419 mg
carbohydrates 12 g
  fiber 0 g
  sugars 9 g
protein 11 g

dietary exchanges: 1 other carbohydrate, 2 lean meat

chicken and green onion kebabs

The kebabs in this recipe are reminiscent of the grilled kebabs known as yakitori that are sold on the streets of Japan, from carts that function very much like those that sell hot dogs in New York City.

SERVES 6 | 2 skewers per serving

. . . .

In a shallow glass dish, whisk together the marinade ingredients. Add the chicken and green onions, turning to coat. Cover and refrigerate for 30 minutes, turning occasionally.

Meanwhile, soak twelve 8-inch wooden skewers in cold water for at least 10 minutes to keep them from charring, or use metal skewers.

Drain the chicken and green onions, discarding the marinade. Alternate threading the chicken cubes and green onion pieces onto the skewers.

Preheat the broiler. Lightly spray a broiler pan with cooking spray. Arrange the skewers in a single layer in the pan. Broil about 4 inches from the heat for 3 minutes on each side, or until the chicken is no longer pink in the center.

MARINADE

¼ cup soy sauce (lowest sodium available)

1½ tablespoons sugar or honey

1 teaspoon canola or corn oil

1 teaspoon minced peeled gingerroot

1 medium garlic clove, minced

———

1½ pounds boneless, skinless chicken breasts, all visible fat discarded, cut into 24 1-inch cubes

1 medium bunch of green onions (green part only), cut crosswise into 24 1-inch pieces

Cooking spray

per serving

calories 146	sodium 397 mg
total fat 3.0 g	carbohydrates 3 g
saturated fat 0.5 g	fiber 1 g
trans fat 0.0 g	sugars 2 g
polyunsaturated fat 0.5 g	protein 25 g
monounsaturated fat 1.0 g	
cholesterol 73 mg	dietary exchanges: 3 lean meat

COOK'S TIP ON SOY SAUCE: Be sure to check the milligrams of sodium per serving on the nutrition facts panel before you purchase soy sauce. Surprisingly, some brands of regular soy sauce may contain less sodium than some brands that are labeled "light" soy sauce.

sweet and spicy drumsticks

For a change from chicken breasts, try drumsticks that have been marinated in fresh lime juice and a bit of soy sauce. Broiling caramelizes the sugars, and a spicy honey-mustard sauce adds the final touch.

SERVES 4 | 2 drumsticks and 1 scant tablespoon sauce per serving

In a medium shallow glass baking dish, whisk together the lime juice, soy sauce, and oil. Add the chicken, turning to coat. Cover and refrigerate for 1 to 24 hours, turning occasionally.

Preheat the broiler. Lightly spray a broiler pan and rack with cooking spray.

Drain the chicken, discarding the marinade. Broil the chicken about 4 inches from the heat for 20 to 25 minutes, or until no longer pink in the center, turning occasionally.

Meanwhile, in a small bowl, whisk together the sauce ingredients. Just before serving, drizzle the sauce over the chicken.

2 tablespoons fresh lime juice

1 tablespoon soy sauce (lowest sodium available)

1½ teaspoons canola or corn oil

8 chicken drumsticks (about 5 ounces each), skin and all visible fat discarded

Cooking spray

SAUCE

2 tablespoons honey

1 tablespoon yellow mustard (lowest sodium available)

1 teaspoon fresh lime juice

1 teaspoon hot chile sauce (sriracha preferred)

per serving

calories 231	sodium 318 mg
total fat 7.0 g	carbohydrates 10 g
saturated fat 2.0 g	fiber 0 g
trans fat 0.0 g	sugars 9 g
polyunsaturated fat 1.5 g	protein 31 g
monounsaturated fat 2.5 g	
cholesterol 168 mg	dietary exchanges: ½ other carbohydrate, 4 lean meat

COOK'S TIP ON REMOVING POULTRY SKIN: To remove poultry skin easily, grip the skin with paper towels. The towels keep your fingers from slipping while you're pulling.

porcupine meatballs

The grains of rice stick out of the meatballs like porcupine quills! Lighten up this kid-pleasing favorite by using ground turkey breast and brown rice.

SERVES 4 | 4 meatballs per serving

Preheat the broiler. Lightly spray the broiler pan and rack with cooking spray.

Prepare the rice using the package directions, omitting the salt and margarine.

In a large bowl, using a spoon or your hands, combine the rice, turkey, onion, Italian seasoning, oil, and pepper. Shape into 16 meatballs. Transfer them to the broiler rack.

Broil about 6 inches from the heat for 6 to 8 minutes, turning occasionally until browned evenly on all sides (the meatballs won't be done at this point). In a medium saucepan, stir together the tomato sauce, bell pepper, and chili powder. Bring to a boil over medium-high heat. Gently stir in the meatballs. Reduce the heat and simmer, covered, for 20 minutes, gently stirring occasionally.

Cooking spray

½ cup uncooked instant brown rice

1 pound ground skinless turkey breast

¼ cup chopped onion

1 teaspoon dried Italian seasoning, crumbled

1 teaspoon canola or corn oil

¼ teaspoon pepper

2 cups no-salt-added tomato sauce

½ cup chopped green bell pepper

½ teaspoon chili powder

COOK'S TIP ON SHAPING MEATBALLS: To help make your meatballs uniform in size and shape, use a small ice cream scoop or the large end of a melon baller to scoop out the ground turkey mixture. Use your free hand to round the tops.

per serving

calories 223	sodium 78 mg
total fat 2.5 g	carbohydrates 19 g
saturated fat 0.5 g	fiber 3 g
trans fat 0.0 g	sugars 6 g
polyunsaturated fat 1.0 g	protein 31 g
monounsaturated fat 1.0 g	
cholesterol 70 mg	

dietary exchanges: ½ starch, 2 vegetable, 3 lean meat

sirloin steak with creamy horseradish sauce

The zing of horseradish and Dijon mustard is a perfect foil for succulent sirloin steak that's been marinating for 24 hours in a mouthwatering mix of balsamic vinegar and Worcestershire sauce. That same blend flavors the tomatoes that broil alongside the beef.

SERVES 4 | 3 ounces beef, 1 tomato half, and 2 tablespoons sauce per serving

In a large, shallow glass baking dish, whisk together the Worcestershire sauce, vinegar, garlic powder, and pepper. Set aside 1 tablespoon of the marinade. Cover and refrigerate the reserved marinade. Add the beef to the marinade in the baking dish, turning to coat. Cover and refrigerate for about 24 hours, turning occasionally.

Preheat the broiler. Lightly spray a broiler pan and rack with cooking spray.

Stir ¼ teaspoon salt into the reserved marinade.

1 tablespoon Worcestershire sauce (lowest sodium available)

1 tablespoon balsamic vinegar

½ teaspoon garlic powder

½ teaspoon pepper

1 1-pound boneless sirloin steak, all visible fat discarded

Cooking spray

¼ teaspoon salt

2 medium tomatoes, halved crosswise

(continued)

Drain the beef, discarding the marinade in the baking dish. Broil the beef and tomatoes with the cut side up about 4 inches from the heat for 3 minutes. Turn over the beef. Brush the beef and tomatoes with the reserved marinade. Broil for 3 to 5 minutes, or until the beef is the desired doneness. Transfer the tomatoes to plates. Transfer the beef to a cutting board. Let stand for 3 minutes before thinly slicing diagonally across the grain.

Meanwhile, in a small bowl, whisk together the sauce ingredients. Serve with the beef and tomatoes.

SAUCE

½ cup fat-free sour cream

2 tablespoons grated peeled horseradish

2 tablespoons water

1 tablespoon olive oil (extra virgin preferred)

2 teaspoons coarse-grain Dijon mustard (lowest sodium available)

⅛ teaspoon salt

per serving

calories 235
total fat 8.0 g
  saturated fat 2.5 g
  trans fat 0.0 g
  polyunsaturated fat 0.5 g
  monounsaturated fat 4.5 g
cholesterol 65 mg

sodium 383 mg
carbohydrates 10 g
  fiber 1 g
  sugars 5 g
protein 29 g

dietary exchanges: ½ other carbohydrate, 3 lean meat

BROILING

lettuce-wrap sliders

The beefy flavor of these Asian-spiced burgers contrasts well with the sweet-hot garnish of shredded carrots and Thai chili sauce.

SERVES 6 | 2 sliders per serving

. . . .

Preheat the broiler. Lightly spray a broiler pan and rack with cooking spray.

Crumble the beef into a large bowl. Add the water chestnuts, soy sauce, garlic, and gingerroot. Using your hands or a spoon, combine the ingredients. Shape into twelve ½-inch balls (about 1½ teaspoons each). Flatten into patties.

Broil the patties about 4 inches from the heat for 3 minutes, or until browned. Turn over the patties. Broil for 2 to 3 minutes, or until they register 160°F on an instant-read thermometer.

Place the lettuce on a flat surface. Place a patty in the center of each leaf. Spoon the chili sauce onto each patty. Sprinkle with the carrots. Fold the sides of the lettuce over the patties. Secure with a wooden toothpick, if desired.

Cooking spray

1 pound extra-lean ground beef

1 8-ounce can water chestnuts, drained and chopped

2 tablespoons soy sauce (lowest sodium available)

2 medium garlic cloves, minced

1 teaspoon grated peeled gingerroot

12 Bibb lettuce leaves

¼ cup Thai sweet chili sauce (lowest sodium available)

2 medium carrots, shredded (about ¾ cup)

per serving

calories 151
total fat 4.0 g
  saturated fat 1.5 g
  trans fat 0.0 g
  polyunsaturated fat 0.5 g
  monounsaturated fat 1.5 g
cholesterol 42 mg

sodium 341 mg
carbohydrates 12 g
  fiber 2 g
  sugars 7 g
protein 17 g

dietary exchanges:
1 vegetable, ½ other carbohydrate, 2 lean meat

portobello pizzas

This recipe is perfect for a meatless Monday or as a healthy substitute on pizza night.

SERVES 4 | 1 pizza per serving

. . . .

Preheat the broiler. Lightly spray the broiler pan with cooking spray.

Lightly spray both sides of the mushrooms with cooking spray. Sprinkle the seasoning blend over both sides. Broil about 6 inches from the heat for 1 to 2 minutes on each side, or until golden brown. Remove from the oven.

Meanwhile, in a small bowl, stir together the beans and vinegar.

In each mushroom cap, layer as follows: 1 tablespoon tomato sauce, 1 tablespoon basil, ¼ cup bean mixture, and ¼ cup roasted peppers. Sprinkle with the mozzarella and Parmesan. Broil about 6 inches from the heat for 1 to 2 minutes, or until the filling is heated through and the cheeses are melted and light golden brown.

Olive oil cooking spray

4 medium portobello mushrooms

1 teaspoon salt-free all-purpose seasoning blend

1 cup canned no-salt-added cannellini beans, rinsed and drained

1 tablespoon balsamic vinegar

¼ cup no-salt-added tomato sauce

¼ cup loosely packed fresh basil

1 cup roasted red bell peppers, drained if bottled, thinly sliced

1 cup shredded low-fat mozzarella cheese

¼ cup shredded or grated Parmesan cheese

per serving

calories 153
total fat 4.5 g
   saturated fat 2.0 g
   trans fat 0.0 g
   polyunsaturated fat 0.0 g
   monounsaturated fat 1.5 g
cholesterol 14 mg

sodium 341 mg
carbohydrates 15 g
   fiber 4 g
   sugars 3 g
protein 13 g

dietary exchanges: ½ starch, 1 vegetable, 1½ lean meat

browned tofu with bok choy

Broiled tofu takes on bright Asian flavors when it's infused with a mixture of citrus and soy, then served with a crisp vegetable and a sauce that adds just a little bit of sweet and heat.

SERVES 4 | 1 slice tofu and ½ cup bok choy per serving

Put the tofu on a cutting board lined with four layers of paper towels. Cover with four layers of paper towels. Place a large, heavy baking dish on top. Let stand for 30 minutes so the tofu releases its excess moisture, replacing the paper towels if necessary.

In a 13 x 9 x 2-inch glass baking dish, whisk together the orange juice, soy sauce, brown sugar, sesame oil, 1 teaspoon canola oil, gingerroot, chili sauce, and garlic. Place the tofu slices in the dish. Let stand for 20 minutes, turning once halfway through.

Preheat the broiler. Line a heavy-duty rimmed baking sheet with aluminum foil. Lightly spray the foil with cooking spray.

Drain the tofu, reserving the marinade. Using a slotted spatula, transfer the tofu to the baking

16 ounces light firm tofu, drained, patted dry, and cut into 4 slices

½ cup fresh orange juice

1 tablespoon soy sauce (lowest sodium available)

1 tablespoon light or dark brown sugar

1 teaspoon toasted sesame oil

1 teaspoon canola or corn oil and 2 teaspoons canola or corn oil, divided use

1 teaspoon grated peeled gingerroot

1 teaspoon Thai sweet red chili sauce

1 medium garlic clove, finely minced

Cooking spray

1½ pounds baby bok choy, heads halved lengthwise

sheet. Broil about 4 inches from the heat for 8 to 10 minutes on each side, or until a deep golden brown. Transfer to plates. Cover to keep warm.

Put the bok choy on the baking sheet. Drizzle with the remaining 2 teaspoons canola oil, turning to coat. Broil about 6 inches from the heat for 6 minutes on each side, or until the leaves are slightly charred and the stems are tender-crisp. Serve with the tofu. Spoon the reserved marinade over all.

per serving

calories 158	sodium 265 mg
total fat 7.0 g	carbohydrates 13 g
saturated fat 0.5 g	fiber 3 g
trans fat 0.0 g	sugars 9 g
polyunsaturated fat 3.0 g	protein 13 g
monounsaturated fat 3.0 g	
cholesterol 0 mg	

dietary exchanges:
1 vegetable, ½ other carbohydrate, 1½ lean meat, ½ fat

BROILING BONUS: *Bok choy isn't the only vegetable that tastes grilled or roasted when it's broiled. To "quick-roast" vegetables, use big chunks of hardy vegetables such as broccoli, cauliflower, bell peppers, onion, mushrooms, eggplant, or zucchini. Toss with a small amount of olive or grapeseed oil or lightly spray with olive oil spray, then sprinkle with salt-free lemon pepper or another salt-free seasoning mix. Spread the vegetables in a single layer on a large baking sheet. Broil until the desired doneness, turning every 5 minutes. Add the cooked vegetables to your favorite pasta dish, use them to top pizza, tuck them into sandwiches, or let them cool and toss them with salad greens.*

swiss chard and swiss cheese frittata

Eaten hot or cold, a frittata is a quick, versatile entrée for a hectic day. You can try other herbs and cheeses for variety. Use whatever greens or leftover vegetables you have on hand instead of the Swiss chard. Serve with whole-grain toast for breakfast or a side of roasted potatoes for dinner.

SERVES 4 | 1 wedge per serving

. . . .

Preheat the broiler.

In a medium mixing bowl, using an electric mixer on high speed, beat the egg whites until soft peaks form. Set aside.

In a small ovenproof skillet, heat the oil over medium-high heat, swirling to coat the bottom. Cook the shallots for 2 minutes, or until soft, stirring frequently. Stir in the chard in batches, adding more as each batch wilts. Cook for 5 to 7 minutes, or until the liquid has evaporated, stirring constantly. Remove from the heat. Sprinkle with the Swiss cheese.

In a small bowl, whisk together the egg yolks, thyme, parsley, nutmeg, and pepper. Fold the

2 large eggs, separated

2 teaspoons olive oil

2 medium shallots, minced

1 pound chopped Swiss chard, tough stems discarded, or 1 pound baby spinach

⅔ cup shredded low-fat Swiss cheese

1 teaspoon chopped fresh thyme or ¼ teaspoon dried thyme, crumbled

1 teaspoon minced fresh parsley (optional)

¼ teaspoon ground nutmeg (freshly grated preferred)

¼ teaspoon pepper (freshly ground preferred)

mixture into the egg whites, blending until no yellow streaks remain.

Spread the egg mixture over the Swiss cheese, smoothing the top. Broil about 4 inches from the heat for 5 to 6 minutes, or until the frittata is set and just firm (the frittata doesn't jiggle when the skillet is gently shaken). Cut into 4 wedges.

per serving

calories 115	sodium 325 mg
total fat 6.0 g	carbohydrates 7 g
saturated fat 2.0 g	fiber 2 g
trans fat 0.0 g	sugars 2 g
polyunsaturated fat 1.0 g	protein 11 g
monounsaturated fat 3.0 g	dietary exchanges:
cholesterol 99 mg	1 vegetable, 1 lean meat, ½ fat

COOK'S TIP ON OVENPROOFING A SKILLET: You can ovenproof a skillet by wrapping the handle with aluminum foil.

COOK'S TIP ON EGG WHITES: Even a single drop of egg yolk will prevent egg whites from forming peaks when beaten, so separate eggs very carefully. Also, before beating the egg whites, make sure they are cold and the bowl and beaters are well chilled. The coldness will improve the stability and volume of the beaten whites.

broiled foiled tomatoes

This side dish is a favorite, especially in summer when tomatoes are at their peak. We solve the problem of overbrowned topping by turning off the broiler and covering the tomatoes with aluminum foil.

SERVES 4 | 1 tomato half per serving

Preheat the broiler. Lightly spray the broiler pan and rack with cooking spray.

In a small bowl, whisk together the basil, oil, mustard, and vinegar. Spoon onto the cut side of the tomatoes.

In a separate small bowl, stir together the panko and Parmesan. Sprinkle over the tomatoes.

Broil the tomatoes about 4 inches from the heat for 1 minute, or until the topping is golden brown, watching carefully so it doesn't burn. Turn off the broiler. Cover the tomatoes with aluminum foil. Let stand beneath the broiler for 8 minutes, or until the tomatoes are tender when pierced with a fork. Remove from the oven. Let stand for 10 minutes before serving.

Cooking spray

2 teaspoons dried basil, crumbled

2 teaspoons olive oil (extra virgin preferred)

1½ teaspoons coarse-grain Dijon mustard (lowest sodium available)

1 teaspoon cider vinegar

2 large tomatoes, halved crosswise

2 tablespoons whole-wheat panko (Japanese-style bread crumbs)

2 tablespoons shredded or grated Parmesan cheese

per serving

calories 58
total fat 3.5 g
  saturated fat 1.0 g
  trans fat 0.0 g
  polyunsaturated fat 0.5 g
  monounsaturated fat 2.0 g
cholesterol 2 mg

sodium 89 mg
carbohydrates 6 g
  fiber 1 g
  sugars 3 g
protein 2 g
dietary exchanges:
1 vegetable, ½ fat

grapefruit with crunchy ginger

Honey and crystallized ginger form a crisp, spicy-sweet crust similar to the kind found on crème brûlée, taming the tartness of grapefruit in this modern take on an old standby. This dessert also makes an excellent addition to breakfast or brunch.

SERVES 4 | 1 grapefruit half per serving

Preheat the broiler. Line a baking sheet with aluminum foil.

In a small bowl, stir together the ginger, cinnamon, and nutmeg.

Cut a thin slice from the bottom of each grapefruit half to keep it steady. Transfer them all to the baking sheet. Drizzle the honey over the cut side of each half. Using the back of a spoon, spread the honey. Sprinkle the ginger mixture over the honey.

Broil the grapefruit about 4 inches from the heat for 5 to 7 minutes, or until golden brown. Watch carefully so they don't burn. Remove from the oven. Let cool slightly before serving.

2   **tablespoons finely minced crystallized ginger (about 3 to 4 pieces)**

¼   **teaspoon ground cinnamon**

⅛   **teaspoon ground nutmeg (freshly grated preferred)**

2   **medium grapefruit, halved crosswise**

1   **tablespoon plus 1 teaspoon honey**

COOK'S TIP ON GRAPEFRUIT: Grapefruit can interact with a number of medications, including many heart medicines. Be sure to check with your doctor or pharmacist if you take any medication, and substitute two large navel oranges in this recipe, if necessary.

BROILING BONUS: *Other fruits are also delicious when caramelized by the broiler. Try broiling pineapple rings, mango slices, or peach halves, then cutting them up and adding them to a salsa or a side dish.*

per serving

calories 87	sodium 0 mg
total fat 0.0 g	carbohydrates 23 g
saturated fat 0.0 g	fiber 2 g
trans fat 0.0 g	sugars 18 g
polyunsaturated fat 0.0 g	protein 1 g
monounsaturated fat 0.0 g	dietary exchanges: 1 fruit,
cholesterol 0 mg	½ other carbohydrate

roasting

Roasting preserves the nutrients in food while enhancing the flavors and textures. For vegetables and fruits, this cooking method brings out their natural sugars, concentrating and intensifying their flavors and giving them a sweeter taste. For seafood, poultry, and meat, the high heat dries the exterior of the food, creating a crunchy, caramelized texture while leaving the inside moist and succulent.

Roasting is simply done in the oven under high heat. This method uses the dry heat of an oven to cook food, which is left uncovered so that it won't steam. When we think of roasting, turkey and meats come to mind because roasting is indeed best for tender foods and larger cuts of meat, poultry, and fish, such as whole chickens or turkeys, pork or beef tenderloin, whole fish, or thick fish fillets. Try family comfort dishes such as Herb-Roasted Chicken (page 232) and Pork Roast with Vegetables (page 240). You'll also find recipes that will help you push past the familiar including Roasted Melon Soup and Balsamic Drizzle (page 224) and Beet and Farro Salad with Goat Cheese (page 226).

Tools & Equipment Needed: Roasting pan and rack, rimmed baking sheet, oven mitts and pot holders, oven thermometer, instant-read thermometer, basting brush, kitchen timer

TO ROAST:
To cook food in the oven in a shallow uncovered pan at temperatures usually higher than baking.

- Because roasting requires the oven to use high heat, be sure your oven is clean to minimize smoking. Vent the area well, opening windows and using your kitchen exhaust fan as necessary.

- Since the temperatures of most ovens are not calibrated exactly, check the accuracy of yours with an oven thermometer and either have the oven recalibrated if it's way off or adjust the roasting temperature accordingly.

- Take the time to preheat the oven; starting with a hot oven will help the food brown properly. Food cooks unevenly, and more slowly, when started in a cold oven.

- If using a disposable aluminum roasting pan, be sure it's sturdy enough to support the weight of the food.

- To roast vegetables, cut them to a uniform size and spread them in a single layer on a rimmed baking sheet to ensure proper browning.

- If you don't have a roasting rack, you can place a bed of thickly sliced vegetables such as onions or potatoes on the bottom of the pan and set the meat or poultry on top.

- For whole birds, discard as much fat as you can before roasting, but leave the skin on until the poultry is cooked. Discard the skin before serving.

- If you're roasting a whole bird, put it in the oven legs first. The back of the oven is the hottest part, and dark meat takes longer to cook.

- To avoid both overcooking and undercooking meat and poultry, use an instant-read meat thermometer to check doneness. Remove the meat or poultry from the oven before inserting the thermometer, and insert it into the center, or thickest part, of the meat, making sure the thermometer doesn't touch bone or fat.

- Check the internal temperature of roasted poultry or meat after about three-fourths of the total suggested cooking time, then every 5 to 10 minutes after that to avoid overcooking.

- Let meat or poultry stand at room temperature for about 5 to 10 minutes when it comes out of the oven to finish the cooking process and allow the muscle fibers to relax, making the meat more tender and helping it to retain its juices. Open the oven door only when necessary. Every time the door is opened, heat escapes and the temperature of the oven is lowered, adding to the cooking time. When you do open the door, protect yourself from the escaping heat, which can burn.

roasted melon soup and balsamic drizzle

This twist on fruit soup combines the sweetness of cantaloupe with savory onion and broth. Roasting the melon concentrates its summery flavor. Drizzled with a mellow balsamic glaze, the sunset-orange soup is a showstopper.

SERVES 4 | 1 cup per serving

Preheat the oven to 425°F. Lightly spray a large rimmed baking sheet with cooking spray. Arrange the cantaloupe in a single layer on the baking sheet. Roast for 20 to 25 minutes, or until the edges begin to brown. Remove from the oven. Let stand until cool.

Meanwhile, in a medium nonstick skillet, heat the oil over medium-high heat, swirling to coat the bottom. Cook the onion for about 5 minutes, or until lightly browned, stirring frequently. Stir in the gingerroot, cumin, cinnamon, and cayenne. Cook for 30 seconds, or until fragrant, stirring constantly.

In a food processor or blender, process the cantaloupe and any accumulated juices for

Cooking spray

6 cups cubed cantaloupe (from about 1 medium)

2 teaspoons olive oil

¾ cup chopped sweet onion, such as Vidalia, Maui, or Oso Sweet

1 teaspoon minced peeled gingerroot

¼ teaspoon ground cumin

¼ teaspoon ground cinnamon

Dash of cayenne

1 cup fat-free, low-sodium chicken or vegetable broth

½ cup fat-free half-and-half

¼ cup balsamic vinegar

1 minute, or until smooth. Add the broth and onion mixture. Process until smooth. Pour in the half-and-half. Process for 30 seconds to 1 minute, or until blended. Serve at room temperature or cover and refrigerate for 2 hours to serve chilled.

Just before serving, in a small saucepan, bring the vinegar to a boil over medium-high heat. Cook for 30 seconds to 1 minute, or until the vinegar is syrupy and reduced by almost half (to about 2 tablespoons). Drizzle the soup with the vinegar.

COOK'S TIP: You've seen roasted pumpkin and sunflower seeds, but did you know you can also roast melon seeds? Rinse and dry the seeds from a cantaloupe, honeydew melon, or watermelon. Lightly spray with olive oil cooking spray. Spread the seeds on a baking sheet and roast at 325°F for about 15 minutes, or until browned.

per serving

calories 151	sodium 89 mg
total fat 3.0 g	carbohydrates 30 g
saturated fat 0.5 g	fiber 3 g
trans fat 0.0 g	sugars 24 g
polyunsaturated fat 0.5 g	protein 5 g
monounsaturated fat 1.5 g	dietary exchanges: 1½ fruit,
cholesterol 0 mg	½ fat-free milk

beet and farro salad with goat cheese

Sometimes known as the mother of all grains, farro is an ancient variety of wheat grown in the Mediterranean. With its high protein and fiber content, this nutty grain pairs beautifully with sweet roasted beets and tangy goat cheese for a filling salad.

SERVES 4 | 1 cup per serving

. . . .

Preheat the oven to 400°F.

Trim the greens and roots from the beets. Refrigerate the greens.

Put the beets on a large piece of aluminum foil. Fold the foil over the beets. Crimp the edges to seal the packet. Roast for 45 minutes, or until the beets are tender when pierced with a fork. Remove from the oven. Set aside to cool.

Meanwhile, in a medium saucepan, heat 2 teaspoons oil over medium-high heat, swirling to coat the bottom. Cook the shallot for 1 to 2 minutes, stirring constantly. Pour in the water. Increase the heat to high and bring to a boil. Stir in the farro. Reduce the heat and simmer for 15 minutes, or until the farro is

1½ pounds beets with greens

2 teaspoons olive oil and 2 tablespoons olive oil (extra virgin preferred), divided use

1 large shallot, minced

3 cups water

¾ cup uncooked farro, rinsed and drained

¼ teaspoon pepper (freshly ground preferred)

¼ cup plus 1 tablespoon fresh lemon juice

2 tablespoons honey

1 small garlic clove, finely minced

2 ounces soft goat cheese, crumbled

tender. Drain well in a fine-mesh sieve. Transfer the farro mixture to a large bowl. Fluff with a fork. Stir in the pepper. Set aside to cool.

Gently peel off the beet skins. Cut the beets into 1-inch pieces. Stir into the farro mixture.

Thinly slice the beet greens. Stir into the farro mixture.

In a small bowl, whisk together the lemon juice, honey, garlic, and the remaining 2 tablespoons oil. Drizzle over the salad, tossing to coat. Transfer to serving plates. Sprinkle with the goat cheese.

per serving

calories 353	sodium 256 mg
total fat 12.5 g	carbohydrates 51 g
saturated fat 3.5 g	fiber 7 g
trans fat 0.0 g	sugars 19 g
polyunsaturated fat 1.0 g	protein 11 g
monounsaturated fat 7.5 g	dietary exchanges: 2 starch,
cholesterol 7 mg	3 vegetable, ½ other carbo-
	hydrate, ½ lean meat, 2 fat

COOK'S TIP: To prepare this dish one day in advance, cook the farro and beets as directed. Cover and refrigerate separately, so the beets don't stain the farro. Just before serving, prepare the dressing and assemble the salad.

ROASTING BONUS: *Roasting grains, such as farro, quinoa, bulgur, or rice, before cooking them brings out their natural nutty flavor and shortens their cooking times. Preheat the oven to 350 °F. Spread the grains on a baking sheet in a single layer. Roast for 10 to 30 minutes (smaller grains like quinoa and fine-grain bulgur will take less time than larger grains such as rice and farro), or until fragrant and beginning to lightly brown, stirring every 2 to 5 minutes. Store the cooled grains in an airtight container in the pantry or refrigerator for up to one month.*

oven-fried catfish over seared spinach

Roasting breaded foods on a preheated baking sheet gives them a crisp crust, which is how this cornmeal-coated catfish gets so crunchy. The preheated sheet also roasts vegetables and fish quickly. The fish is done in a flash using this method, and the accompanying spinach can be ready in two minutes.

SERVES 4 | 3 ounces fish and ½ cup spinach per serving

. . . .

Put a large, heavy-duty rimmed baking sheet on the middle oven rack. Preheat the oven to 425°F.

Put the flour in a medium shallow dish. Pour the buttermilk into a separate medium shallow dish. In a third medium shallow dish, stir together the cornmeal, paprika, garlic powder, and oregano. Carefully remove the baking sheet from the oven. Drizzle with the oil.

Set the dishes and baking sheet in a row, assembly-line fashion. Sprinkle the pepper and salt over the fish. Dip the fish in the flour, then in the buttermilk, and finally in the cornmeal mixture, turning to coat at each step and gently shaking off any excess. Using

⅓	cup all-purpose flour
½	cup low-fat buttermilk
½	cup cornmeal
2	teaspoons paprika
1	teaspoon garlic powder
1	teaspoon dried oregano, crumbled (Greek preferred)
2	teaspoons olive oil
4	catfish or tilapia fillets (about 4 ounces each), rinsed and patted dry
¼	teaspoon pepper
⅛	teaspoon salt
8	cups loosely packed baby spinach
1	tablespoon chopped fresh dillweed

your fingertips, gently press the coating so it adheres to the fish. Place the fish on the preheated baking sheet.

Roast for 8 to 10 minutes, or until the fish flakes easily when tested with a fork. Transfer the fish to a large plate. Cover to keep warm.

Put the spinach on the baking sheet. Sprinkle the dillweed over the spinach. Roast for 1 to 2 minutes, or until the spinach is barely wilted. Transfer to plates. Serve the fish on the spinach.

per serving

calories 232	sodium 193 mg
total fat 6.5 g	carbohydrates 21 g
saturated fat 1.5 g	fiber 3 g
trans fat 0.0 g	sugars 2 g
polyunsaturated fat 1.5 g	protein 23 g
monounsaturated fat 3.0 g	
cholesterol 67 mg	dietary exchanges: 1½ starch, 3 lean meat

COOK'S TIP: To avoid warping your baking sheet, use a heavy-duty baking sheet, such as the professional-style rimmed sheet pans that are widely available where baking pans are sold.

ROASTING BONUS: *Don't limit yourself to cornmeal, bread crumbs, or panko when you want crisp-coated fish, chicken, or vegetables. Many other foods are delicious once processed into crumbs. Try root vegetable chips or air-popped popcorn processed into crumbs, dry-roasted uncooked oatmeal, quinoa flakes, or quinoa that has been cooked using the package directions and then baked at 375°F for 15 to 25 minutes, or until crisp.*

salmon with creamy chipotle-orange sauce

A spicy chipotle sauce with notes of sweet-tart citrus turns succulent salmon into something spectacular. Roasting keeps the fish tender and moist.

SERVES 4 | 3 ounces fish and 2 tablespoons sauce per serving

Preheat the oven to 400°F. Line a large, heavy-duty baking sheet with aluminum foil. Lightly spray the foil with cooking spray.

Put the fish on the baking sheet with the skin side down.

In a small bowl, whisk together the lime juice, oil, and ½ teaspoon adobo sauce. Brush the mixture over the top of the fish. Roast for 20 minutes, or until the desired doneness.

Meanwhile, in a food processor or blender, process the orange juice, cornstarch, chipotle pepper, sugar, salt, and the remaining ¼ to

Cooking spray

4   salmon fillets with skin (about 5 ounces each), rinsed and patted dry

1   tablespoon fresh lime juice

1   teaspoon canola or corn oil

½   teaspoon adobo sauce and ¼ to ½ teaspoon adobo sauce (from chipotle peppers canned in adobo sauce), divided use

½   teaspoon grated orange zest

⅔   cup fresh orange juice

2   teaspoons cornstarch

(continued)

½ teaspoon adobo sauce until smooth. Pour into a small saucepan. Bring to a boil over medium-high heat. Boil for 2 minutes, or until thickened and reduced by half (to about ⅓ cup). Remove from the heat.

Let stand for 3 minutes, or until slightly cooled.

Whisk in the half-and-half and orange zest. Spoon the sauce onto plates. Place the fish on the sauce. Sprinkle with the cilantro. Serve with the lime wedges.

½ **medium chipotle pepper (from chipotle peppers canned in adobo sauce), minced**

½ **teaspoon sugar**

⅛ **teaspoon salt**

¼ **cup fat-free half-and-half**

¼ **cup chopped fresh cilantro**

1 **medium lime, cut into 4 wedges**

per serving

calories 199	sodium 223 mg
total fat 6.5 g	carbohydrates 9 g
saturated fat 1.0 g	fiber 0 g
trans fat 0.0 g	sugars 5 g
polyunsaturated fat 1.5 g	protein 25 g
monounsaturated fat 2.5 g	dietary exchanges: ½ fruit,
cholesterol 53 mg	3 lean meat

herb-roasted chicken

No chapter on roasting would be complete without a classic roast chicken recipe. Plan for five to six hours of marinating time to allow the seasonings to permeate the meat and give it the maximum flavor. Leave the skin on the chicken while it roasts to keep the meat extra moist, but be sure to remove it before serving. For an easy side dish, try Asparagus with Dijon Vinaigrette (page 242). Just pop the asparagus in the oven when the chicken is almost done.

SERVES 6 | *3 ounces chicken per serving*

In a small bowl, stir together the thyme, basil, salt, and pepper. Rub the mixture over the outside of the chicken and in the chicken cavity. Put the onions, lemon, bay leaf, and garlic in the cavity. Using kitchen twine, tie the legs together. Cover and refrigerate for 5 to 6 hours.

Preheat the oven to 425°F.

Place the chicken with the breast side up on a rack in a nonstick roasting pan. Pour the wine and margarine over the chicken. Transfer to the oven with the legs facing the back of the oven. Roast for 1 hour to 1 hour 15 minutes, or until the chicken registers 165°F on an instant-read thermometer, basting once halfway through. The chicken should be golden brown and

1½ teaspoons dried thyme, crumbled

½ teaspoon dried basil, crumbled

½ teaspoon salt

½ teaspoon pepper (freshly ground preferred), or to taste

1 2½- to 3-pound chicken, all visible fat, neck, and giblets discarded

2 medium onions, halved

1 medium lemon, cut into wedges

1 large dried bay leaf

2 medium garlic cloves, coarsely chopped

½ cup dry white wine (regular or nonalcoholic)

2 tablespoons light tub margarine, melted

its juices should run clear when the thigh is pierced with the tip of a sharp knife. Remove from the oven. Let stand, loosely covered, for 5 minutes.

Transfer the chicken to a serving platter. Discard the twine. Discard the onions, lemon, bay leaf, and garlic. Discard the skin before carving the chicken.

To make gravy, skim and discard the fat from the cooking liquid in the roasting pan. Pour the remaining liquid into a small saucepan. Bring to a boil over medium-high heat. Boil for 5 minutes, stirring occasionally. Serve with the chicken.

per serving

calories 139
total fat 4.5 g
  saturated fat 0.5 g
  trans fat 0.0 g
  polyunsaturated fat 1.0 g
  monounsaturated fat 1.5 g
cholesterol 69 mg

sodium 304 mg
carbohydrates 1 g
  fiber 0 g
  sugars 0 g
protein 22 g

dietary exchanges: 3 lean meat

chicken with artichokes and tomatoes

A simple roast chicken can be served at any time, for any occasion. This one highlights the warm, sunny flavors of Greece. It's roasted with artichoke hearts, tomatoes, shallots, olives, and garlic, all bathed in fresh lemon juice.

SERVES 6 | 3 ounces chicken and ⅓ cup vegetables per serving

Preheat the oven to 350°F.

Put the olives in a large roasting pan. Using the back of a spoon, slightly crush them. Stir the artichokes, shallots, tomatoes, and garlic into the olives. Pour the lemon juice and oil over the artichoke mixture, stirring to coat. Sprinkle with the rosemary, thyme, salt, and ¼ teaspoon pepper. Pour in the broth. Bake, covered, for 20 minutes.

Meanwhile, sprinkle the remaining ¼ teaspoon pepper over the outside of the chicken and rub it into the chicken cavity. Using kitchen twine, tie the legs together.

Increase the oven temperature to 425°F. Remove the pan from the oven. Place the chicken in the pan. Transfer to the oven with the chicken's legs facing the back of the oven. Roast, covered, for 25 minutes, basting occasionally with the pan juices (add a little water if necessary).

Roast the chicken, uncovered, for 40 minutes to 1 hour, or until it registers 165°F on an instant-read thermometer. The skin should be

- ¼ cup kalamata olives, rinsed and drained
- 9 ounces frozen artichoke hearts, thawed and drained
- 8 large shallots, halved
- 6 medium Italian plum (Roma) tomatoes, quartered
- 1 medium garlic bulb, cloves separated
- 3 tablespoons fresh lemon juice
- 2 teaspoons olive oil
- 2 tablespoons chopped fresh rosemary or 2 teaspoons dried rosemary, crushed
- 2 tablespoons chopped fresh thyme or 2 teaspoons dried thyme, crumbled
- ¼ teaspoon salt
- ¼ teaspoon pepper and ¼ teaspoon pepper (or to taste), divided use
- 1 cup fat-free, low-sodium chicken broth
- 1 2½- to 3-pound chicken, all visible fat, neck, and giblets discarded

golden brown and crisp, and the juices should run clear when the thigh is pierced with a sharp knife. Remove from the oven. Let stand, loosely covered, for 5 minutes.

Transfer the chicken to a serving platter. Discard the twine. Using a slotted spoon, transfer 8 of the garlic cloves to a food processor or blender. Transfer the artichokes, shallots, tomatoes, olives, and the remaining garlic to the platter, arranging the vegetables around the chicken. Cover to keep warm. Discard the skin before carving the chicken.

To prepare the sauce, skim and discard the fat from the cooking liquid in the roasting pan. Add the defatted liquid to the garlic in the food processor or blender. Process until smooth, diluting with a little water if necessary. Serve with the chicken.

per serving

calories 209	sodium 332 mg
total fat 6.5 g	carbohydrates 13 g
saturated fat 1.0 g	fiber 4 g
trans fat 0.0 g	sugars 3 g
polyunsaturated fat 1.0 g	protein 24 g
monounsaturated fat 3.5 g	dietary exchanges:
cholesterol 69 mg	3 vegetable, 3 lean meat

lemon-garlic turkey tenderloin

The turkey roasts atop a "rack" of fresh carrots in the pan, basting those carrots with rich juices and giving them a deep, meaty flavor.

SERVES 4 | 3 ounces turkey and 2 carrots per serving

. . . .

Preheat the oven to 400°F. Lightly spray a shallow roasting pan with cooking spray.

Arrange the carrots in a single layer in the pan. Arrange the turkey on the carrots. Brush the oil over the turkey and any carrots that aren't under the turkey. In a small bowl, stir together the lemon zest and garlic. Sprinkle over both sides of the turkey. Sprinkle the pepper and salt over the turkey and carrots.

Roast for 30 minutes. Turn over the carrots (they'll be browned on the bottom).

Roast for 10 to 15 minutes, or until the turkey registers 165°F on an instant-read thermometer and the carrots are tender. Remove from the oven. Transfer the turkey to a cutting board. Let stand, loosely covered, for 5 minutes before slicing. Serve the carrots with the turkey.

Cooking spray

8 medium carrots, 1 inch of greens left on if the carrots are young

1 1-pound turkey tenderloin, all visible fat discarded

2 teaspoons olive oil

2 teaspoons grated lemon zest

3 medium garlic cloves, minced

¼ teaspoon pepper

⅛ teaspoon salt

per serving

calories 209
total fat 3.5 g
  saturated fat 0.5 g
  trans fat 0.0 g
  polyunsaturated fat 0.5 g
  monounsaturated fat 2.0 g
cholesterol 70 mg

sodium 228 mg
carbohydrates 15 g
  fiber 4 g
  sugars 7 g
protein 29 g

dietary exchanges:
3 vegetable, 3 lean meat

savory beef tenderloin

A rub of garlic and a touch of thyme are all that's needed to accent the robust flavor of beef tenderloin. While the beef is resting, you can make Asparagus with Dijon Vinaigrette (page 242) and have everything on the table at once.

SERVES 4 | 3 ounces beef per serving

Preheat the oven to 425°F.

Using kitchen twine, tie the beef in three or four places to help it keep its shape during roasting.

Rub the garlic all over the beef. Sprinkle with the pepper. Put the beef in a nonstick roasting pan. Arrange the thyme on the beef. Drizzle with the oil. Place the onion and carrots around the beef.

Roast for 30 to 40 minutes, or until the beef is the desired doneness. Remove from the oven. Sprinkle with the salt. Let stand, loosely covered, for 10 minutes. Discard the twine. Thinly slice the beef diagonally across the grain. Serve with the onion and carrots.

1 1-pound beef tenderloin, all visible fat discarded

3 medium garlic cloves, crushed

¼ teaspoon pepper (freshly ground preferred), or to taste

4 or 5 sprigs of fresh thyme or 1 teaspoon dried thyme, crumbled

1 tablespoon olive oil

1 medium onion, sliced

2 medium carrots, thinly sliced

¼ teaspoon salt

per serving

calories 209
total fat 8.5 g
  saturated fat 3.0 g
  trans fat 0.0 g
  polyunsaturated fat 0.5 g
  monounsaturated fat 5.0 g
cholesterol 53 mg

sodium 222 mg
carbohydrates 7 g
  fiber 2 g
  sugars 4 g
protein 25 g

dietary exchanges:
1 vegetable, 3 lean meat

basil pork tenderloin with black bean salsa

Fresh basil and tomatoes flavor both the pork and the hearty salsa in this tempting entrée. Slice any leftover pork into strips and layer them inside corn tortillas with the salsa to make tasty tacos.

SERVES 4 | 3 ounces pork and ½ cup salsa per serving

For the marinade, put 2 tablespoons tomato in a medium glass baking dish. Using the back of a wooden spoon, gently press on the pieces to bruise them and release some of their juice. Stir in the remaining marinade ingredients.

Add the pork, turning to coat. Cover and refrigerate for 30 minutes, turning once halfway through.

Meanwhile, preheat the oven to 425°F. Lightly spray a roasting pan and rack with cooking spray.

MARINADE

2 tablespoons chopped, seeded tomato

2 tablespoons minced fresh basil

1 tablespoon fresh lime juice

2 medium garlic cloves, minced

¼ teaspoon pepper

⅛ teaspoon salt

1 1-pound pork tenderloin, all visible fat discarded

Cooking spray

(continued)

Drain the pork, discarding the marinade. Transfer the pork to the rack, tucking the ends under if they are thin. Roast for 20 to 25 minutes, or until the pork registers 145°F on an instant-read thermometer. Transfer to a cutting board. Let stand for 3 minutes before cutting crosswise into slices.

Meanwhile, in a medium bowl, stir together the salsa ingredients. Let stand at room temperature for 5 minutes so the flavors blend. Serve with the pork.

SALSA

1 15.5-ounce can no-salt-added black beans, rinsed and drained

½ cup chopped, seeded tomato

1 medium green onion, sliced

2 tablespoons minced fresh basil

1 tablespoon minced fresh cilantro

1 tablespoon fresh lime juice

1 medium garlic clove, minced

⅛ teaspoon salt

per serving

calories 219
total fat 3.0 g
  saturated fat 1.0 g
  trans fat 0.0 g
  polyunsaturated fat 0.5 g
  monounsaturated fat 1.0 g
cholesterol 60 mg

sodium 195 mg
carbohydrates 19 g
  fiber 5 g
  sugars 4 g
protein 28 g

dietary exchanges: 1 starch, 3½ lean meat

COOK'S TIP ON TESTING DONENESS OF MEAT: To avoid both overcooking and undercooking your meat, use a meat thermometer to check doneness. Remove the meat from the oven before inserting the instant-read thermometer. Insert the thermometer into the center, or thickest part, of the meat, making sure the thermometer doesn't touch bone or fat.

pork roast with vegetables

Once you get this easy-to-assemble dinner in the oven, you can relax.

SERVES 4 | 3 ounces pork and ½ cup vegetables per serving

. . . .

Preheat the oven to 425°F. Lightly spray a 13 x 9 x 2-inch baking dish with cooking spray.

Brush the apple juice concentrate all over the pork. In a small bowl, stir together the brown sugar, garlic powder, oregano, thyme, paprika, and pepper. Set aside 1 teaspoon of the mixture. Sprinkle the remaining mixture all over the pork. Transfer the pork to the pan.

In a medium bowl, stir together the potatoes, carrots, cauliflower, zucchini, onion, and reserved 1 teaspoon brown sugar mixture. Place around the pork. Lightly spray the pork and vegetables with cooking spray.

Roast for 35 to 40 minutes or until the pork registers 145°F on an instant-read thermometer. Remove from the oven. Let stand, loosely covered, for 3 minutes before cutting the pork crosswise into slices. Serve with the vegetables.

Cooking spray

- 1 tablespoon frozen 100% apple juice concentrate, thawed
- 1 1-pound boneless center-cut pork loin roast, all visible fat discarded
- 1½ teaspoons light brown sugar
- 1½ teaspoons garlic powder
- 1½ teaspoons dried oregano, crumbled
- 1½ teaspoons dried thyme, crumbled
- 1½ teaspoons paprika
- ½ teaspoon pepper
- 2 small red potatoes, cut into ½-inch cubes
- ½ cup baby carrots
- ½ cup bite-size pieces of cauliflower florets
- ½ small zucchini, cut into ½-inch cubes
- ¼ small red onion, cut into ½-inch pieces

per serving

calories 210	sodium 76 mg
total fat 6.0 g	carbohydrates 14 g
saturated fat 2.0 g	fiber 2 g
trans fat 0.0 g	sugars 6 g
polyunsaturated fat 1.0 g	protein 24 g
monounsaturated fat 2.5 g	
cholesterol 60 mg	dietary exchanges: ½ starch, 1 vegetable, 3 lean meat

chickpeas with zucchini, peppers, and onion

This colorful entrée—with green zucchini, red and orange bell peppers, cherry tomatoes, and snow-white feta cheese—can be served warm or at room temperature. Roasting brings out the sweetness of the vegetables and adds richness to the flavor of the chickpeas.

SERVES 4 | 1½ cups per serving

Preheat the oven to 425°F.

In a large bowl, stir together the zucchini, bell peppers, onion, rosemary, and garlic. Add the oil, stirring to coat. Arrange in a single layer on a large, heavy-duty rimmed baking sheet. Roast for 20 minutes. Stir.

Top with the chickpeas and tomatoes. Roast for 10 to 15 minutes, or until the zucchini and bell peppers are tender, the onion is soft, and the chickpeas are lightly browned. Just before serving, sprinkle with the feta.

- 2 medium zucchini, halved lengthwise, cut into 1½-inch pieces
- 1 large red bell pepper, cut into 1½-inch pieces
- 1 large orange bell pepper, cut into 1½-inch pieces
- 1 small red onion, cut into 1-inch wedges
- 1½ tablespoons chopped fresh rosemary
- 3 large garlic cloves, minced
- 2 teaspoons olive oil (extra virgin preferred)
- 1 15.5-ounce can no-salt-added chickpeas, rinsed and drained
- 1½ cups cherry tomatoes
- ½ cup crumbled low-fat feta cheese (about 2 ounces)

per serving

calories 235
total fat 6.0 g
  saturated fat 2.0 g
  trans fat 0.0 g
  polyunsaturated fat 0.5 g
  monounsaturated fat 2.0 g
cholesterol 7 mg

sodium 293 mg
carbohydrates 35 g
  fiber 8 g
  sugars 10 g
protein 12 g

dietary exchanges: 1½ starch, 3 vegetable, 1 lean meat

COOK'S TIP ON ROSEMARY: To chop rosemary easily, put the leaves in a small cup or bowl. Using scissors or kitchen shears, snip the sprigs into small pieces.

asparagus with dijon vinaigrette

This easy side dish goes nicely with Herb-Roasted Chicken (page 232). Start preparing the ingredients when the chicken goes in the oven and then both dishes can finish together, so that dinner will be ready by the time you set the table. Don't use frozen asparagus for this recipe. It won't hold up well and will become mushy.

SERVES 4 | 6 spears per serving

Preheat the oven to 425°F.

Arrange the asparagus in a single layer on a large, heavy-duty baking sheet. Lightly spray the asparagus with cooking spray. Roast for 12 to 15 minutes, or until tender-crisp and lightly browned.

Meanwhile, in a small bowl, whisk together the remaining ingredients.

Serve this side dish hot, at room temperature, or chilled. Just before serving, drizzle with the vinaigrette.

24 medium asparagus spears, trimmed
Cooking spray
¼ teaspoon grated lemon zest
1 tablespoon fresh lemon juice
1 tablespoon fat-free, low-sodium chicken broth
¾ teaspoon Dijon mustard (lowest sodium available)
½ teaspoon olive oil (extra virgin preferred)
Pepper to taste

per serving

calories 31
total fat 0.5 g
  saturated fat 0.0 g
  trans fat 0.0 g
  polyunsaturated fat 0.0 g
  monounsaturated fat 0.5 g
cholesterol 0 mg

sodium 20 mg
carbohydrates 5 g
  fiber 3 g
  sugars 3 g
protein 3 g
dietary exchanges:
1 vegetable

toasted cauliflower and garlic

Nutmeg adds a bit of sweetness while red pepper flakes bring spice to cauliflower, transforming this ordinary vegetable into a memorable side dish.

SERVES 4 | ¾ cup per serving

. . . .

Preheat the oven to 500°F. Line a large, heavy-duty baking sheet with aluminum foil.

Arrange the cauliflower, onion, and garlic in a single layer on the baking sheet. Drizzle 1 tablespoon oil over all. Roast for 12 minutes. Stir. Roast for 3 minutes, or until the cauliflower and onion are tender-crisp and the garlic is soft. Remove from the oven.

Drizzle with the remaining 1 tablespoon oil. Sprinkle with the remaining ingredients. Don't stir. Fold the edges of the foil to the center to cover the vegetables and garlic completely. Fold together to tightly seal. Let stand for 5 minutes so the flavors blend and the vegetables release some of their juices.

1 **pound 1-inch cauliflower florets (from 1 medium head of cauliflower)**

1½ **cups chopped onion**

8 **medium garlic cloves**

1 **tablespoon canola or corn oil and 1 tablespoon canola or corn oil, divided use**

1½ **teaspoons sugar**

¼ **teaspoon ground nutmeg**

¼ **teaspoon crushed red pepper flakes**

⅛ **teaspoon salt**

COOK'S TIP: Be sure to cut all the florets about the same size.

ROASTING BONUS: *If you enjoy the garlic in this recipe but would also like to try it with other foods, roast a whole bulb (or more than one) at once: Preheat the oven to 400°F. Place a large garlic bulb on aluminum foil. Slice off and discard the top of the garlic. Drizzle the bulb with ½ teaspoon olive oil. Top with a sprig of thyme or rosemary. Fold the foil up to enclose the garlic and seal the edges. Roast for 45 minutes, or until soft.*

per serving

calories 128	sodium 111 mg
total fat 7.0 g	carbohydrates 15 g
saturated fat 1.0 g	fiber 3 g
trans fat 0.0 g	sugars 6 g
polyunsaturated fat 1.0 g	protein 3 g
monounsaturated fat 5.0 g	
cholesterol 0 mg	dietary exchanges:
	3 vegetable, 1½ fat

lemony herbed potatoes

Traditional Italian seasonings get a sunny boost from lemon pepper to give these potatoes a Mediterranean flair. They pair well with nearly any baked or roasted entrée, but are especially good with Lemon-Garlic Turkey Tenderloin (page 236).

SERVES 4 | 4 potatoes per serving

Preheat the oven to 400°F.

Put the potatoes on a heavy-duty nonstick rimmed baking sheet. Lightly spray them with cooking spray.

Roast for 30 minutes, or until tender when pierced with a fork.

Remove the baking sheet from the oven. Drizzle the potatoes with the oil, stirring to coat. Sprinkle the remaining ingredients over the potatoes, stirring to coat.

16 small red potatoes (about 1 pound), patted very dry with paper towels

Cooking spray

2 teaspoons olive oil (extra virgin preferred)

2 tablespoons chopped fresh parsley

½ teaspoon dried oregano, crumbled

½ teaspoon salt-free lemon pepper

¼ teaspoon salt

COOK'S TIP: If you can't easily find 1-ounce potatoes, you can use eight 2-ounce potatoes instead. Just halve them crosswise.

per serving

calories 101
total fat 2.5 g
  saturated fat 0.5 g
  trans fat 0.0 g
  polyunsaturated fat 0.5 g
  monounsaturated fat 1.5 g
cholesterol 0 mg

sodium 167 mg
carbohydrates 18 g
  fiber 2 g
  sugars 2 g
protein 2 g

dietary exchanges: 1 starch

root vegetable medley

Typically served in winter, this dish features earthy flavors that go well with anything from Thanksgiving turkey to steaks on the grill. You can also substitute other root vegetables, such as beets, carrots, or rutabagas.

SERVES 10 | ½ cup per serving

. . . .

Preheat the oven to 400°F. Line a large, heavy-duty rimmed baking sheet with aluminum foil.

Put the turnips, radishes, onions, parsnips, and garlic in a large bowl. Drizzle with the oil. Sprinkle the salt and pepper over the vegetables and garlic, stirring to coat well. Arrange the vegetables and garlic in a single layer on the baking sheet.

Roast for 30 minutes, or until tender and beginning to brown, stirring occasionally. Remove the baking sheet from the oven. Sprinkle the oregano over all.

Roast for 10 minutes. Just before serving, sprinkle with the parsley.

3 small turnips, peeled and cut into eighths

12 radishes, trimmed and quartered

12 pearl onions, peeled

2 medium parsnips, peeled and cut crosswise into 1-inch slices

12 medium garlic cloves

1½ tablespoons olive oil

⅛ teaspoon salt

Pepper to taste

1½ teaspoons dried oregano, crumbled

2 tablespoons chopped fresh parsley

per serving

calories 50
total fat 2.0 g
  saturated fat 0.5 g
  trans fat 0.0 g
  polyunsaturated fat 0.5 g
  monounsaturated fat 1.5 g
cholesterol 0 mg

sodium 47 mg
carbohydrates 8 g
  fiber 2 g
  sugars 2 g
protein 1 g

dietary exchanges: ½ starch

honeyed strawberries with almonds

This dessert creates its own rich, delicately sweet sauce as the honey-drizzled strawberries cook. The sliced almonds roast with the berries during the last few minutes to deepen their flavor. Enjoy this nutty fruit delight alone, over fat-free yogurt, or over whole-grain waffles for breakfast or brunch.

SERVES 4 | ½ cup per serving

Preheat the oven to 400°F. Line a large, heavy-duty rimmed baking sheet with aluminum foil.

Arrange the strawberries in a single layer on the baking sheet. Lightly spray with cooking spray. Roast for 13 to 15 minutes, or until tender and just beginning to darken slightly. Drizzle with the honey. Roast for 8 minutes.

Reduce the heat to 350°F. Sprinkle the almonds over and around the strawberries. Bake for 2 to 3 minutes, or until the almonds are golden. Watch carefully so the almonds and honey don't burn. Transfer the baking sheet to a cooling rack. Let stand for 10 minutes before serving.

3 cups hulled strawberries, patted dry
  Cooking spray
2 tablespoons plus 2 teaspoons honey
¼ cup sliced almonds

COOK'S TIP ON STRAWBERRIES: Don't have a strawberry huller? Use a regular drinking straw instead. Just start at the bottom of the berry and push the straw straight through the center to the stem.

ROASTING BONUS: *If you enjoy roasted nuts like the almonds in this recipe, try dry-roasting a larger amount to have on hand. Preheat the oven to 350°F. Spread the nuts (chopped or whole) on a baking sheet in a single layer. Roast for 10 to 15 minutes, or until fragrant, stirring occasionally (watch carefully so they don't burn). Store the cooled nuts in an airtight container in the freezer for up to one year.*

per serving

calories 110
total fat 3.0 g
  saturated fat 0.0 g
  trans fat 0.0 g
  polyunsaturated fat 1.0 g
  monounsaturated fat 2.0 g
cholesterol 0 mg

sodium 2 mg
carbohydrates 21 g
  fiber 3 g
  sugars 17 g
protein 2 g

dietary exchanges: ½ fruit, 1 other carbohydrate, ½ fat

baking

Baking is one of the most familiar cooking techniques to most home cooks. It's as simple as turning on the oven and allowing the dry heat to cook the food. This method keeps food moist and flavorful without needing to add any unhealthy saturated fat. Baking usually requires limited hands-on time or attention; there's no need to turn foods over, stir them frequently, or keep an eye on the dish. You combine ingredients, put them in a baking vessel, place it in the oven, set the timer, and let the food cook while you go on to do something else until dinner is ready.

When you think about baking, what foods come to mind—bread, cookies, and casseroles? The gentle heat of the oven not only melds flavors but can also provide crisp textures, making almost any food taste scrumptious, including fish, poultry, vegetables, and tofu. Similar to roasting, baking usually involves lower temperatures and smaller pieces of meat, such as the chicken breasts used in Mediterranean Chicken with Mushrooms and Artichokes (page 254), or fish fillets, such as Salmon with Honey-Balsamic Glaze (page 251). Baking can also turn large vegetables, such as whole or halved squash, into tender, succulent edible bowls with fabulous fillings, such as Acorn Squash Stuffed with Cranberry-Studded Quinoa (page 267). It can mimic the crisp exteriors of fried foods, as in Cheesy Kale Chips (page 265) or Sweet Potato Fries with Curry Dipping Sauce (page 266). And, of course, it's perfect for classic family favorites such as Mini Meat Loaves (page 257) and Spinach Lasagna (page 262).

Tools & Equipment Needed: Oven thermometer, instant-read thermometer, oven mitts and pot holders, glass baking dishes, metal baking pans, baking sheets (rimmed and unrimmed), loaf pan, muffin pans, wire rack, kitchen timer

TIPS:

- Since the temperatures of most ovens are not calibrated exactly, check the accuracy of yours with an oven thermometer and either have the oven recalibrated if it's way off or adjust the baking temperature accordingly.

- Be sure to preheat the oven; it's worth the wait. If you get impatient and put food into the oven before it has reached the proper temperature, you're likely to end up with unevenly cooked food that hasn't browned properly. Food also cooks faster if it's started at the correct temperature. And some foods, like those made with yeast, baking soda, or baking powder, won't rise properly if they're put in a cold oven because those ingredients react immediately to heat.

- To preheat the oven more quickly, use the broiler setting for a few minutes before switching to the required oven temperature.

- It's best to leave the oven door closed as much as possible. Opening it lets out the heat and lowers the temperature in the oven, which can result in uneven cooking and longer cooking times.

- Use a meat thermometer to check the doneness of meat and poultry. Remove the food from the oven before inserting the instant-read thermometer. Insert the thermometer into the center, or thickest part, of the meat, making sure the thermometer doesn't touch bone or fat.

BAKING

lemon-basil halibut with linguine

Tender chunks of halibut nestle in nutty whole-grain linguine along with crisp broccoli and sweet roasted red bell pepper, while a creamy sauce coats each bite of this delectable casserole.

SERVES 4 | 1½ cups per serving

. . . .

Prepare the pasta using the package directions, omitting the salt. Drain well in a colander.

Preheat the oven to 350°F. Lightly spray an 11 x 7 x 2-inch glass baking dish with cooking spray.

In the baking dish, stir together the pasta, broccoli, roasted peppers, and basil. Arrange the fish in a single layer on the pasta mixture.

In a small bowl, whisk together the remaining ingredients except the Parmesan. Pour over the fish and pasta mixture. Bake, covered, for 25 minutes, or until the fish flakes easily when tested with a fork. Sprinkle with the Parmesan.

- 4 **ounces dried whole-grain linguine**
  Cooking spray
- 2 **cups broccoli florets, blanched**
- 1 **cup roasted red bell peppers, drained if bottled, coarsely chopped**
- ½ **cup loosely packed fresh basil, coarsely chopped**
- 1 **pound halibut fillets, rinsed, patted dry, and cut into ¾-inch pieces**
- 1 **cup fat-free half-and-half**
- 1½ **tablespoons all-purpose flour**
- 1 **teaspoon garlic powder**
- 1 **teaspoon grated lemon zest**
- ¼ **teaspoon salt**
- ⅛ **teaspoon pepper**
- 2 **tablespoons shredded or grated Parmesan cheese**

per serving

calories 289	sodium 371 mg
total fat 3.0 g	carbohydrates 36 g
saturated fat 1.0 g	fiber 5 g
trans fat 0.0 g	sugars 6 g
polyunsaturated fat 0.5 g	protein 31 g
monounsaturated fat 1.0 g	
cholesterol 57 mg	dietary exchanges: 2 starch, 1 vegetable, 3½ lean meat

COOK'S TIP ON BLANCHING: To blanch broccoli or other vegetables, fill a saucepan three-quarters full of water. Bring to a boil over high heat. Boil the broccoli for 1 to 2 minutes, or until lightly cooked. Drain the broccoli and briefly submerge it in ice water to stop the cooking process.

salmon with honey-balsamic glaze

Use simple ingredients likely to be found in your kitchen to create a sweet and savory glaze for salmon. Sesame seeds add texture to this entrée that's sure to become a family favorite. When the fish is cooked, put Easy Peach Crisp (page 271) in the oven to have a warm, delicious dessert after dinner is done.

SERVES 4 | 3 ounces fish per serving

. . . .

Preheat the oven to 375°F. Lightly spray a shallow baking dish with cooking spray.

In a small bowl, whisk together the mayonnaise and vinegar until smooth. Whisk in the remaining ingredients except the fish.

Put the fish in the baking dish. Lightly spread the mayonnaise mixture over the top and sides of the fish.

Bake for 15 to 20 minutes, or until the fish is cooked to the desired doneness.

Cooking spray

1½ tablespoons light mayonnaise

1½ tablespoons balsamic vinegar

1 tablespoon honey

1½ teaspoons sesame seeds

¾ teaspoon dried oregano, crumbled

¾ teaspoon olive oil

1 medium garlic clove, minced

4 salmon fillets (about 4 ounces each), rinsed and patted dry

per serving

calories 204
total fat 8.5 g
  saturated fat 1.5 g
  trans fat 0.0 g
  polyunsaturated fat 1.5 g
  monounsaturated fat 2.5 g
cholesterol 55 mg

sodium 125 mg
carbohydrates 7 g
  fiber 0 g
  sugars 6 g
protein 24 g

dietary exchanges: ½ other carbohydrate, 3 lean meat

tilapia with pumpkin seed crust and pineapple-avocado salsa

Pumpkin seeds give a crisp crunch and nutty flavor to this fish dish, while creamy avocado adds richness to the spicy-sweet fruit salsa that accompanies it.

SERVES 4 | 3 ounces fish and ⅓ cup salsa per serving

Preheat the oven to 400°F.

Put the flour in a medium shallow dish. In a separate medium shallow dish, whisk the egg whites until foamy. In a third medium shallow dish, stir together the pumpkin seeds, panko, and paprika. Dip the fish in the flour, then in the egg whites, and finally in the pumpkin seed mixture, turning to coat at each step and gently shaking off any excess. Using your fingertips, gently press the mixture so it adheres to the fish. Place the fish on a baking sheet.

Reduce the oven temperature to 375°F. Bake the fish for 12 to 15 minutes, or until it flakes easily when tested with a fork.

Meanwhile, in a small bowl, gently stir together the salsa ingredients. Serve the fish topped with the salsa.

FISH

- ¼ cup all-purpose flour
- 2 large egg whites
- ¼ cup finely chopped unsalted shelled pumpkin seeds, dry-roasted (about 2 ounces)
- ¼ cup whole-wheat panko (Japanese-style bread crumbs)
- 1 teaspoon paprika
- 4 tilapia fillets (about 4 ounces each), rinsed and patted dry

SALSA

- 1 8-ounce can pineapple tidbits in their own juice, drained
- 1 medium avocado, chopped
- ¼ cup finely chopped red onion
- ¼ cup chopped fresh cilantro
- 2 tablespoons finely chopped fresh jalapeño, seeds and ribs discarded (see Cook's Tip on page 45)
- 1 to 2 tablespoons fresh lime juice

per serving

calories 331
total fat 13.5 g
  saturated fat 2.5 g
  trans fat 0.0 g
  polyunsaturated fat 3.0 g
  monounsaturated fat 7.0 g
cholesterol 57 mg

sodium 99 mg
carbohydrates 25 g
  fiber 6 g
  sugars 8 g
protein 30 g

dietary exchanges: 1 starch, ½ fruit, 1 vegetable, 3½ lean meat

basil chicken

Baking the chicken with its skin on helps keep the meat moist and tender. The skin also presses the basil, paprika, and lemon tightly against the meat so it can soak up their flavors.

SERVES 4 | 3 ounces chicken per serving

. . . .

Preheat the oven to 375°F. Lightly spray a 9-inch glass baking dish with cooking spray.

In a small bowl, stir together the paprika and pepper.

Gently pull back the skin from one piece of chicken, leaving it attached at one end and being careful not to tear it. Sprinkle one-fourth of the lemon juice and one-fourth of the paprika mixture over the exposed meat. Arrange 2 basil leaves on top. Pull the skin back into place, covering the basil leaves. Transfer to the baking dish with the skin side up. Repeat with the remaining chicken.

Bake for 30 minutes, or until the chicken is no longer pink in the center. Discard the skin. Just before serving, sprinkle the chicken with the salt.

Cooking spray

½ teaspoon paprika

¼ teaspoon pepper

4 bone-in chicken breast halves with skin, all visible fat discarded

2 to 3 tablespoons fresh lemon juice

8 medium fresh basil leaves

¼ teaspoon salt

per serving

calories 138
total fat 3.0 g
  saturated fat 0.5 g
  trans fat 0.0 g
  polyunsaturated fat 0.5 g
  monounsaturated fat 1.0 g
cholesterol 76 mg

sodium 283 mg
carbohydrates 1 g
  fiber 0 g
  sugars 0 g
protein 25 g

dietary exchanges: 3 lean meat

mediterranean chicken with mushrooms and artichokes

Juicy chicken is baked to perfection with tender mushrooms, tangy artichoke hearts, and sweet tomatoes to create the warm flavors of the Mediterranean. Serve over brown rice or whole-grain orzo.

SERVES 4 | 3 ounces chicken per serving

Preheat the oven to 350°F.

Put the flour in a medium shallow dish. Dip the chicken in the flour, turning to coat and gently shaking off any excess. Transfer to a large plate.

In a large nonstick skillet, heat the oil over medium-high heat, swirling to coat the bottom. Cook the chicken for 2 minutes on each side, or until lightly browned. Transfer to an 11 x 7 x 2-inch baking dish. Place the mushrooms and artichokes around the chicken.

In a small bowl, stir together the tomatoes, garlic, oregano, and pepper. Pour over the chicken, mushrooms, and artichokes. Bake for 25 minutes. Remove from the oven and stir in the sherry. Bake for 5 minutes, or until the chicken is no longer pink in the center.

½ cup all-purpose flour

4 boneless, skinless chicken breast halves (about 4 ounces each), all visible fat discarded

2 tablespoons olive oil

8 ounces sliced button mushrooms

1 6-ounce jar marinated artichoke hearts, drained

2 cups chopped tomatoes

2 medium garlic cloves, minced

½ teaspoon dried oregano, crumbled

½ teaspoon pepper (freshly ground preferred), or to taste

½ cup dry sherry or fat-free, low-sodium chicken broth

per serving

calories 324
total fat 13.5 g
  saturated fat 1.5 g
  trans fat 0.0 g
  polyunsaturated fat 2.5 g
  monounsaturated fat 7.0 g
cholesterol 73 mg

sodium 263 mg
carbohydrates 21 g
  fiber 4 g
  sugars 4 g
protein 28 g

dietary exchanges: 1 starch, 2 vegetable, 3 lean meat, ½ fat

manicotti-style chicken roll-ups

In this fresh take on a classic dish, we replace the traditional pasta tubes with chicken breasts that have been flattened to roll around a creamy, herbed filling.

SERVES 4 | 1 roll-up per serving

Preheat the oven to 350°F.

In a small bowl, stir together the oregano, basil, marjoram, and pepper. In a small saucepan, stir together the water, tomato paste, garlic, and 1½ teaspoons of the oregano mixture. Bring to a boil. Reduce the heat and simmer for 10 minutes, stirring occasionally.

Place the chicken on a flat surface. In a separate small bowl, stir together the ricotta and the remaining oregano mixture. Spoon onto the center of each chicken breast. Roll up jelly-roll style.

Spread half the tomato paste mixture in an 11 x 7 x 2-inch baking dish. Place the roll-ups on the tomato paste mixture. Spoon the remaining mixture over the chicken. Sprinkle with the mozzarella. Bake for 45 minutes, or until the chicken is no longer pink in the center.

¾ **teaspoon dried oregano, crumbled**

¾ **teaspoon dried basil, crumbled**

½ **teaspoon dried marjoram, crumbled**

¼ **teaspoon pepper (freshly ground preferred), or to taste**

1 **cup water**

1 **6-ounce can no-salt-added tomato paste**

1 **medium garlic clove, minced**

4 **boneless, skinless chicken breast halves (about 4 ounces each), all visible fat discarded, flattened to ¼-inch thickness**

4 **ounces fat-free ricotta cheese**

2 **ounces shredded or grated low-fat mozzarella cheese**

COOK'S TIP ON FLATTENING CHICKEN BREASTS: Put a chicken breast with the smooth side up between two pieces of plastic wrap. With the smooth side of a meat mallet or a heavy pan, flatten the chicken to the desired thickness. Be careful not to tear the meat.

per serving

calories 216	sodium 314 mg
total fat 4.5 g	carbohydrates 10 g
saturated fat 1.0 g	fiber 2 g
trans fat 0.0 g	sugars 6 g
polyunsaturated fat 0.5 g	protein 33 g
monounsaturated fat 1.5 g	dietary exchanges:
cholesterol 80 mg	2 vegetable, 4 lean meat

layered mexican casserole

A spritz of fresh lime juice is the perfect finishing touch for this casserole, which is a handy way to use leftover chicken. If you don't have any cooked chicken breast on hand, see the Cook's Tip below for a quick way to prepare some.

SERVES 4 | 1 cup per serving

Preheat the oven to 350°F.

Prepare the rice using the package directions. Transfer to a medium bowl. Stir the cumin into the cooked rice. Spread the rice mixture in an 8-inch square baking pan. Drizzle with the oil. Using the back of a spoon, smooth the surface. Spoon the chiles over the mixture. Top with, in order, the cilantro, chicken, and cheese.

Bake, covered, for 15 minutes, or until the cheese has melted.

Serve with the lime wedges.

10 **ounces frozen brown rice**

1 **teaspoon ground cumin**

1 **tablespoon olive oil**

1 **4-ounce can chopped green chiles, undrained**

¼ **cup chopped fresh cilantro**

1½ **cups cubed cooked skinless chicken breast, cooked without salt (about 7½ ounces cooked)**

½ **cup shredded low-fat 4-cheese Mexican blend**

1 **medium lime, cut into 4 wedges**

per serving

calories 242	sodium 267 mg
total fat 8.5 g	carbohydrates 18 g
saturated fat 2.5 g	fiber 2 g
trans fat 0.0 g	sugars 0 g
polyunsaturated fat 1.0 g	protein 22 g
monounsaturated fat 3.0 g	dietary exchanges: 1 starch,
cholesterol 52 mg	3 lean meat

COOK'S TIP: For quickly cooked chicken to use in this recipe, discard all the visible fat from 10 ounces of boneless, skinless chicken breasts. Cut the chicken into bite-size pieces. Lightly spray a small skillet with cooking spray. Heat over medium-high heat. Cook the chicken for 3 to 4 minutes, or until no longer pink in the center, stirring constantly.

mini meat loaves

Making these single-serving meat loaves saves cooking time, and they're chock-full of veggies, so they're extra healthy, too. Save even more time by doubling the recipe and freezing the extras.

SERVES 4 | 1 meat loaf per serving

. . . .

Preheat the oven to 350°F. Line a baking sheet with aluminum foil. Lightly spray the foil with cooking spray. Set aside.

In a small bowl, whisk together the ketchup, Worcestershire sauce, and salt.

In a medium bowl, using your hands or a spoon, combine the beef, panko, green onions, bell peppers, corn, egg whites, and ¼ cup of the ketchup mixture until just blended. Divide the mixture into four parts. Transfer them to the baking sheet. Shape into four 3 x 4 x 1-inch loaves. Bake for 35 to 40 minutes. Remove from the oven.

Spoon the remaining ketchup mixture over the loaves. Bake for 2 to 4 minutes, or until the meat loaves register 160°F on an instant-read thermometer and are no longer pink in the center.

Cooking spray

½ cup no-salt-added ketchup

2 teaspoons Worcestershire sauce (lowest sodium available)

⅛ teaspoon salt

1 pound extra-lean ground beef

⅔ cup whole-wheat panko (Japanese-style bread crumbs)

½ cup chopped green onions

½ cup diced green bell pepper

½ cup diced red bell pepper

½ cup whole-kernel corn, thawed if frozen

2 large egg whites

per serving

calories 266
total fat 6.5 g
  saturated fat 2.5 g
  trans fat 0.5 g
  polyunsaturated fat 0.5 g
  monounsaturated fat 2.5 g
cholesterol 62 mg

sodium 228 mg
carbohydrates 24 g
  fiber 3 g
  sugars 11 g
protein 30 g

dietary exchanges: 1 starch, 1 vegetable, 3½ lean meat

pork tenderloin stuffed with spinach, pine nuts, and sun-dried tomatoes

This elegant main dish is sure to impress when the pork is sliced open to reveal its beautiful, bright filling. It may look complicated, but it's simple to prepare. Sweet sun-dried tomatoes, earthy spinach, and crunchy pine nuts provide a wonderful contrast to rosemary-scented pork. Have your oven do double duty by baking Acorn Squash Stuffed with Cranberry-Studded Quinoa (page 267) at the same time. *(See photo insert.)*

SERVES 4 | 3 ounces pork and 2 tablespoons sauce per serving

. . . .

Bring 1 cup water to a boil. Put the tomatoes in a small bowl. Pour in the boiling water. Let stand for 10 minutes, or until softened.

Preheat the oven to 375°F. Lightly spray a rimmed baking sheet with cooking spray.

Drain the tomatoes, discarding the soaking water. Squeeze them to remove any excess water. Coarsely chop the tomatoes.

Lay the opened pork on a cutting board. Sprinkle the tomatoes and pine nuts lengthwise over half of the pork. Sprinkle 1 tablespoon rosemary, the salt, and

½ cup dry-packed sun-dried tomatoes
  Cooking spray

1 1-pound pork tenderloin, all visible fat discarded, butterflied and flattened to 1-inch thickness

2 tablespoons pine nuts, dry-roasted

1 tablespoon chopped fresh rosemary and 1 tablespoon chopped fresh rosemary, divided use

¼ teaspoon salt

⅛ teaspoon pepper and ⅛ teaspoon pepper, divided use

4 cups loosely packed baby spinach

⅛ teaspoon pepper over the tomato mixture. Arrange the spinach in a single layer on top. Fold the half with no filling over the other half. Using kitchen twine, tie the pork at 2-inch intervals to secure it. Transfer the pork to the baking sheet. Lightly spray the pork with cooking spray. Sprinkle with the remaining 1 tablespoon rosemary and ⅛ teaspoon pepper.

Bake for 40 minutes, or until the pork registers 145°F on an instant-read thermometer.

Transfer the pork to a clean cutting board. Discard the twine. Let stand for 3 minutes before slicing.

per serving

calories 166
total fat 5.0 g
  saturated fat 1.5 g
  trans fat 0.0 g
  polyunsaturated fat 1.5 g
  monounsaturated fat 2.0 g
cholesterol 60 mg

sodium 218 mg
carbohydrates 6 g
  fiber 2 g
  sugars 2 g
protein 24 g

dietary exchanges:
1 vegetable, 3 lean meat

stuffed chayote squash

The pulp of the chayote squash is moist and tastes like a cross between an apple and a cucumber. The key to this recipe is not to overcook the vegetable filling. The tender-crisp texture is part of the charm of the finished dish.

SERVES 4 | 1 squash half per serving

Put the squash in a medium saucepan and fill the pan with enough cold water to cover by 2 inches. Bring to a boil over high heat. Reduce the heat and simmer for 30 minutes, or until the squash is tender when pierced with the tip of a sharp knife. Remove from the pan and plunge into a bowl of ice water to stop the cooking process. Let cool.

When the squash is cool, halve it lengthwise. Discard the seeds. Using a spoon or melon baller, scoop out the pulp, leaving a ½-inch border of the shell all the way around. Chop the pulp and set aside. Place the shells with the cut sides up on a rimmed baking sheet.

Preheat the oven to 375°F.

Meanwhile, in a small skillet, heat the oil over medium heat. Cook the celery, carrots, onion, and garlic for 2 to 3 minutes, or until tender-crisp (don't overcook). Stir in the soy

2   medium chayote squash (about 1 pound total)

1   teaspoon canola or corn oil

2   medium ribs of celery, diced

2   medium carrots, diced

1   medium onion, diced

2   medium garlic cloves, minced

5   ounces frozen soy crumbles, thawed

2   medium Italian plum (Roma) tomatoes, diced

2   medium green onions, thinly sliced

¼   teaspoon dried thyme, crumbled

⅛   teaspoon salt

⅛   teaspoon pepper

¼   cup whole-wheat panko (Japanese-style bread crumbs)

1   tablespoon plus 1 teaspoon shredded or grated Parmesan cheese

crumbles, tomatoes, green onions, thyme, salt, pepper, and reserved squash pulp. Cook for 30 seconds.

Spoon the soy crumble mixture into the squash shells. Sprinkle with the panko and Parmesan.

Bake for 15 to 20 minutes, or until heated through.

per serving

calories 142
total fat 2.0 g
  saturated fat 0.5 g
  trans fat 0.0 g
  polyunsaturated fat 0.5 g
  monounsaturated fat 1.0 g
cholesterol 1 mg

sodium 280 mg
carbohydrates 22 g
  fiber 7 g
  sugars 8 g
protein 11 g

dietary exchanges: ½ starch, 3 vegetable, 1 lean meat

COOK'S TIP: If you can't find chayote squash, you can use yellow summer squash or zucchini instead. Halve the squash lengthwise. Scoop out the pulp, leaving a ¼-inch border of the shell all the way around. Dice the pulp. Set aside. Place the shells with the cut sides down in a medium glass baking dish. Microwave, covered, on 100 percent power (high) for 4 to 6 minutes, or until just tender. Remove from the microwave. Uncover the dish carefully to avoid steam burns. Proceed as directed.

spinach lasagna

This healthier version of a classic dish boasts three kinds of cheese for a lasagna with decadent flavor but less sodium and saturated fat.

SERVES 8 | one 4 x 3½-inch piece per serving

. . . .

Preheat the oven to 350°F. Lightly spray a 13 x 9 x 2-inch baking dish with cooking spray.

Prepare the noodles using the package directions, omitting the salt. Drain well.

In a small bowl, stir together ¼ cup mozzarella and 2 tablespoons Parmesan.

In a medium bowl, stir together the spinach, ricotta cheese, and the remaining 1 cup mozzarella and ¼ cup plus 2 tablespoons Parmesan.

Spread 1 cup of the spaghetti sauce in a thin layer in the baking dish. Arrange about one-third of the noodles in a single layer on the sauce. Spread half the ricotta cheese mixture over the noodles. Repeat the layers. Top the second layer of ricotta cheese with 1 cup sauce, spreading it into a thin layer. Arrange the remaining noodles on top. Spread the remaining sauce over the noodles. Sprinkle with the mozzarella mixture. Bake for 30 to 40 minutes. Remove from the oven. Let stand for 10 to 15 minutes before slicing.

Cooking spray

- 1 pound dried whole-grain lasagna noodles
- ¼ cup shredded low-fat mozzarella cheese and 1 cup shredded low-fat mozzarella cheese, divided use
- 2 tablespoons shredded or grated Parmesan cheese and ¼ cup plus 2 tablespoons shredded or grated Parmesan cheese, divided use
- 3 cups chopped spinach
- 2 cups fat-free ricotta cheese
- 4 cups spaghetti sauce (lowest sodium available)

per serving

calories 345	sodium 439 mg
total fat 5.5 g	carbohydrates 52 g
saturated fat 1.5 g	fiber 8 g
trans fat 0.0 g	sugars 9 g
polyunsaturated fat 0.5 g	protein 23 g
monounsaturated fat 1.5 g	dietary exchanges: 3 starch,
cholesterol 15 mg	1 vegetable, 2 lean meat

tofu with orange and rosemary glaze

Tangy and sweet, these orange-glazed tofu slices are a great substitute for fish or chicken when you're topping a salad or making a sandwich.

SERVES 4 | 2 slices per serving

Put the tofu on a cutting board lined with four layers of paper towels. Cover it with four layers of paper towels. Place a large, heavy baking dish on top. Let stand for 30 minutes so the tofu releases its excess moisture, replacing the paper towels if necessary.

Preheat the oven to 350°F. Lightly spray a 13 x 9 x 2-inch baking dish with cooking spray.

In the baking dish, whisk together the remaining ingredients. Add the tofu, turning to coat. Arrange the slices in two rows, overlapping the slices if necessary. Bake for 45 minutes to 1 hour, or until golden brown, basting occasionally.

32 ounces light firm tofu, drained, patted dry, and cut into 8 slices

Cooking spray

2 tablespoons grated orange zest

½ cup fresh orange juice

2 tablespoons orange marmalade (optional)

2 tablespoons soy sauce (lowest sodium available)

2 tablespoons plain rice vinegar

2 tablespoons canola or corn oil

2 teaspoons finely minced fresh rosemary

¼ teaspoon pepper (freshly ground preferred), or to taste

per serving

calories 207
total fat 11.0 g
  saturated fat 1.0 g
  trans fat 0.0 g
  polyunsaturated fat 4.5 g
  monounsaturated fat 5.0 g
cholesterol 0 mg

sodium 273 mg
carbohydrates 8 g
  fiber 2 g
  sugars 4 g
protein 20 g

dietary exchanges: ½ other carbohydrate, 3 lean meat

creole eggplant

Unlike its Cajun cousin, Creole cuisine is flavorful but not spicy. Here, eggplant is layered with tomato sauce, then finished with a crunchy topping.

SERVES 10 | ½ cup per serving

In a medium skillet, heat the oil over low heat, swirling to coat the bottom. Cook the mushrooms, onion, and bell pepper for 5 minutes, or until the mushrooms and onion are soft and the bell pepper is tender, stirring occasionally. Stir in the tomatoes and pepper. Simmer for 30 minutes, stirring occasionally.

Put the eggplant in a large saucepan and fill with enough water to cover. Bring to a boil over medium-high heat. Boil for 10 minutes. Drain well in a colander. Set aside.

Preheat the oven to 350°F. Lightly spray an 11 x 7 x 2-inch baking dish with cooking spray.

Put half the eggplant in the dish. Spoon half the sauce over the eggplant. Repeat the layers. Sprinkle with the bread crumbs. Dot with the margarine. Bake for 30 minutes, or until bubbling.

2 tablespoons canola or corn oil

¼ cup sliced button mushrooms

2 tablespoons chopped onion

2 tablespoons chopped green bell pepper

2 cups canned no-salt-added stewed tomatoes or chopped tomatoes, drained

Pepper to taste (freshly ground preferred)

1 medium eggplant, sliced or cubed

Cooking spray

½ cup plain dry bread crumbs (lowest sodium available)

1 tablespoon light tub margarine

COOK'S TIP: If you prefer, substitute 1½ large yellow summer squash for the eggplant.

per serving

calories 79	sodium 56 mg
total fat 3.5 g	carbohydrates 10 g
saturated fat 0.5 g	fiber 3 g
trans fat 0.0 g	sugars 4 g
polyunsaturated fat 1.0 g	protein 2 g
monounsaturated fat 2.0 g	dietary exchanges: ½ starch,
cholesterol 0 mg	1 vegetable, ½ fat

cheesy kale chips

Reach for a serving of these crisp chips as a side to a sandwich or by themselves as a healthy snack.

SERVES 4 | ½ cup per serving

. . . .

Preheat the oven to 375°F. Put a wire mesh rack on a rimmed baking sheet. Lightly spray the rack with cooking spray.

Arrange the kale in a single layer on the rack. Lightly spray the kale with cooking spray.

In a small bowl, stir together the remaining ingredients except the Parmesan. Sprinkle over the kale. Bake for 28 to 30 minutes, or until the kale is crisp and the edges are browned. Sprinkle with the Parmesan. Bake for 1 minute, or until the Parmesan has melted.

Remove the baking sheet from the oven. Let stand for 5 minutes.

Olive oil cooking spray

1 bunch kale (about 4 ounces), ribs discarded and leaves torn or cut into 2-inch pieces

1 tablespoon sesame seeds

1 teaspoon dried minced garlic or garlic powder

1 teaspoon dried minced onion or onion powder

½ teaspoon smoked paprika

¼ teaspoon pepper

⅛ teaspoon salt

2 tablespoons shredded or grated Parmesan cheese

per serving

calories 45
total fat 2.5 g
  saturated fat 0.5 g
  trans fat 0.0 g
  polyunsaturated fat 0.5 g
  monounsaturated fat 1.0 g
cholesterol 2 mg

sodium 128 mg
carbohydrates 4 g
  fiber 1 g
  sugars 0 g
protein 3 g
dietary exchanges:
1 vegetable, ½ fat

COOK'S TIP: These chips can be stored in an airtight container for up to five days.

BAKING BONUS: *If you enjoy kale chips, try making chips out of brussels sprouts. Separate fresh brussels sprouts into leaves and put on a baking sheet in a single layer. Lightly spray with cooking spray or toss with a small amount of olive oil. Bake at 350°F for 7 to 10 minutes, or until crisp.*

sweet potato fries with curry dipping sauce

These are everything fries should be—crisp on the outside and tender on the inside. They're paired with a lightly sweetened, creamy curry sauce.

SERVES 4 | ½ cup fries and 2 tablespoons sauce per serving

Preheat the oven to 400°F. Lightly spray a baking sheet with cooking spray.

Put the sweet potatoes on the baking sheet.

In a small bowl, stir together the garlic powder, cumin, pepper, and salt. Sprinkle over the sweet potatoes, stirring to coat. Arrange in a single layer on the baking sheet. Lightly spray the fries with cooking spray.

Reduce the oven temperature to 350°F. Bake the fries for 40 to 45 minutes, or until golden brown on the outside and tender on the inside, turning once halfway through.

Meanwhile, in a small bowl, whisk together the sauce ingredients. Serve with the fries.

Cooking spray

2 **small sweet potatoes (about 1 pound total), peeled and cut into 4 x ¼ x ¼-inch strips**

1 **teaspoon garlic powder**

1 **teaspoon ground cumin**

¼ **teaspoon pepper**

⅛ **teaspoon salt**

SAUCE

½ **cup fat-free plain yogurt**

2 **teaspoons light brown sugar**

½ **teaspoon curry powder**

BAKING BONUS: *Root vegetables, including sweet potatoes, can also be baked into crisp chips. Thinly slice any combination of root vegetables such as beets, carrots, parsnips, sweet potatoes, jícama, radishes, or daikon radishes. Arrange in a single layer on a baking sheet. Lightly spray with cooking spray or brush with a small amount of olive oil. Bake at 350°F for 12 to 15 minutes, or until crisp.*

per serving

calories 129	sodium 161 mg
total fat 0.5 g	carbohydrates 28 g
saturated fat 0.0 g	fiber 4 g
trans fat 0.0 g	sugars 9 g
polyunsaturated fat 0.0 g	protein 4 g
monounsaturated fat 0.0 g	
cholesterol 1 mg	dietary exchanges: 2 starch

acorn squash stuffed with cranberry-studded quinoa

You'll really fall for this autumnal dish, which is baked in stages so that all the ingredients cook to perfection. *(See photo insert.)*

SERVES 4 | 1 stuffed squash quarter per serving

Preheat the oven to 375°F.

Line a baking sheet with aluminum foil. Put the squash quarters with the cut sides up on the baking sheet. Lightly spray the squash with cooking spray. Bake for 15 minutes. Remove from the oven.

In a small bowl, stir together the onion and oil. Arrange the onion around the squash. Bake for 20 minutes. Sprinkle the pecans over the onion. Bake for 5 minutes, or until the pecans are browned (watch carefully so they don't burn).

Meanwhile, prepare the quinoa using the package directions, omitting the salt. Fluff with a fork.

Transfer the squash to plates. Stir the onion mixture into the quinoa. Stir in the remaining ingredients. Spoon into the squash cavities.

- 1 **small acorn squash (about 1 pound), quartered, seeds and strings discarded**

   Cooking spray
- 1 **medium onion, coarsely chopped**
- 2 **teaspoons canola or corn oil**
- 1 **ounce chopped pecans**
- ¼ **cup uncooked quinoa, rinsed and drained**
- ¼ **cup sweetened dried cranberries**
- ⅛ **teaspoon ground cumin**
- ⅛ **teaspoon crushed red pepper flakes**
- ⅛ **teaspoon salt**

COOK'S TIP: For easier quartering, use a fork to pierce the whole squash in several places, then microwave it on 100 percent power (high) for 2 minutes. The heat will permeate the squash and soften it a bit. Carefully transfer it to a cutting board. Let it cool for about 3 minutes, or until it's easy to handle.

per serving

calories 179
total fat 8.0 g
  saturated fat 0.5 g
  trans fat 0.0 g
  polyunsaturated fat 2.5 g
  monounsaturated fat 4.5 g
cholesterol 0 mg

sodium 79 mg
carbohydrates 26 g
  fiber 4 g
  sugars 10 g
protein 3 g

dietary exchanges: 1 starch, ½ fruit, 1 vegetable, 1½ fat

cheddar cheese pub bread

Flecked with Cheddar cheese and subtly flavored with mustard, slices of this hearty loaf are the perfect partner for a bowl of steaming soup. Try a slice with Creamy Tomato-Basil Soup (page 59).

SERVES 8 | 1 slice per serving

In a small saucepan, stir together the green onions, water, and garlic. Bring to a boil over medium-high heat. Reduce the heat and simmer, covered, for 5 minutes. Stir in the milk, sugar, and salt. Heat or cool the mixture to 120°F to 130°F (use an instant-read thermometer to check).

In a medium mixing bowl, combine ½ cup flour, the yeast, and mustard. Add the green onion mixture and egg. Beat with an electric mixer on low to medium speed for 30 seconds, scraping the side of the bowl. Beat on high speed for 3 minutes. Using a spoon, stir in the Cheddar and as much of the 2 cups flour as possible.

Using the remaining 2 to 3 tablespoons flour, lightly flour a flat surface. Knead the dough for 6 to 8 minutes, adding enough of the remaining flour to make a moderately stiff dough that's smooth and elastic. Shape into a ball. Using cooking spray, lightly spray a large bowl and a piece of plastic wrap large enough to cover the top of the bowl. Transfer the dough to the bowl, turning once to coat all sides

⅓ cup sliced green onions

¼ cup water

2 medium garlic cloves, minced

¼ cup fat-free milk

1 teaspoon sugar

¼ teaspoon salt

½ cup all-purpose flour, 2 cups all-purpose flour, and 2 to 3 tablespoons all-purpose flour, divided use

1 ¼-ounce package active dry yeast

1 teaspoon dry mustard

1 large egg

⅓ cup shredded low-fat sharp Cheddar cheese

Cooking spray

with the cooking spray. Cover the bowl with the plastic wrap with the sprayed side down. Let the dough rise in a warm, draft-free place (about 85°F) until doubled in bulk (about 1½ hours).

Punch down the dough. Turn the dough out onto a lightly floured surface. Divide the dough into 16 equal pieces. Roll each piece into a ball.

Spray an 8 x 4 x 2-inch loaf pan with cooking spray. Arrange the dough balls in the pan. Cover with a clean dish towel. Let rise in a warm, draft-free place (about 85°F) until nearly doubled in bulk (about 45 minutes).

Preheat the oven to 375°F. Uncover the bread. Bake for 35 to 40 minutes, or until the bread is brown and sounds hollow when tapped on the bottom (remove it from the pan to test this).

Transfer the bread to a cooling rack. Let cool before slicing.

per serving

calories 172
total fat 1.5 g
  saturated fat 0.5 g
  trans fat 0.0 g
  polyunsaturated fat 0.5 g
  monounsaturated fat 0.5 g
cholesterol 24 mg

sodium 118 mg
carbohydrates 32 g
  fiber 2 g
  sugars 1 g
protein 7 g

dietary exchanges: 2 starch

three-cheese quiches

These veggie-studded crustless quiches are super simple to make.

SERVES 6 | 1 quiche per serving

. . . .

Preheat the oven to 350°F. Lightly spray a 6-cup muffin pan with cooking spray or use 6 cups of a standard 12-cup muffin pan. Fill the empty cups with water.

In a medium skillet, heat the oil over medium heat, swirling to coat the bottom. Cook the broccoli, carrot, zucchini, and green onions for 2 to 3 minutes. Spoon into the muffin cups.

In a medium bowl, whisk together the remaining ingredients. Ladle the egg substitute mixture into the muffin cups.

Bake for 25 to 28 minutes, or until a wooden toothpick inserted in the center of a quiche comes out clean. Transfer the pan to a cooling rack. Let stand for 10 minutes. Using a thin spatula or flat knife, loosen the sides of the quiches. Serve warm. Refrigerate leftovers in an airtight container for up to five days.

Cooking spray

- 1 teaspoon olive oil
- 1 cup chopped broccoli florets
- ½ cup shredded carrot
- ½ cup shredded zucchini
- 2 medium green onions, thinly sliced
- 1½ cups egg substitute
- ½ cup fat-free half-and-half
- ¼ cup shredded low-fat mozzarella cheese
- ¼ cup shredded low-fat Cheddar cheese
- 2 tablespoons shredded or grated Parmesan cheese
- ½ teaspoon dried oregano, crumbled
- ⅛ teaspoon pepper

per serving

calories 89
total fat 2.0 g
  saturated fat 1.0 g
  trans fat 0.0 g
  polyunsaturated fat 0.0 g
  monounsaturated fat 1.0 g
cholesterol 4 mg

sodium 249 mg
carbohydrates 7 g
  fiber 1 g
  sugars 4 g
protein 11 g

dietary exchanges: ½ starch, 1½ lean meat

easy peach crisp

This dessert couldn't be easier to prepare, and the results are delectable. Use fresh peaches when they're in season, but keep some frozen ones on hand for when they're not. This is a dessert you'll want to make again and again.

SERVES 4 | ½ cup per serving

Preheat the oven to 375°F.

Put the peaches in a nonstick 8- or 9-inch square baking pan. Stir in ½ teaspoon cinnamon and the cornstarch.

In a small bowl, using a fork, stir together the remaining ingredients, including the remaining ½ teaspoon cinnamon. Sprinkle over the peaches.

Bake for 30 to 40 minutes, or until the topping is golden brown and the peaches are heated through. Serve immediately.

4 medium peaches, peeled and sliced, or 2 cups frozen unsweetened peach slices, thawed

½ teaspoon ground cinnamon and ½ teaspoon ground cinnamon, divided use

½ teaspoon cornstarch

½ cup uncooked oatmeal

3 tablespoons chopped pecans

2 tablespoons light tub margarine

1 tablespoon light brown sugar

½ teaspoon ground nutmeg

¼ teaspoon ground ginger

per serving

calories 171
total fat 7.0 g
  saturated fat 0.5 g
  trans fat 0.0 g
  polyunsaturated fat 2.0 g
  monounsaturated fat 3.5 g
cholesterol 0 mg

sodium 47 mg
carbohydrates 26 g
  fiber 4 g
  sugars 16 g
protein 4 g

dietary exchanges: 2 other carbohydrate, 1½ fat

a heart-healthy pantry

Keeping healthy staples on hand makes cooking healthy meals at home easier and more convenient. Don't let the long list discourage you; most of these items aren't perishable or have a fairly long shelf life so you can acquire them over time to build up your pantry. If you keep some healthy basics in each category, you'll have more options for cooking nutritious meals at home. In fact, you'll be able to prepare most of the recipes in this book with the ingredients waiting in your well-stocked refrigerator, freezer, and pantry; for many other dishes, you'll need only a few additional items from the store.

FRESH

- garlic
- gingerroot
- lemons
- limes
- onions
- oranges
- shallots
- various chiles

FOR THE FRIDGE

- eggs
- egg substitute
- fat-free or low-fat feta cheese
- fat-free half-and-half
- fat-free milk
- fat-free ricotta cheese
- fat-free sour cream
- fat-free plain yogurt
- fat-free plain Greek yogurt
- light mayonnaise
- light tub margarine
- low-fat buttermilk
- low-fat Cheddar cheese
- low-fat mozzarella cheese
- Parmesan cheese, shaved, shredded, or grated
- queso fresco or farmer cheese

FOR THE FREEZER

- assorted fruits and berries
- assorted vegetables without added sauces
- brown rice
- chicken breasts
- extra-lean ground beef
- fish fillets
- ground skinless chicken breast
- ground skinless turkey breast
- lean steaks and chops
- seitan
- soy crumbles
- tofu
- turkey bacon

FOR THE PANTRY (NONPERISHABLES)

Rices (choose unseasoned)

- Arborio rice
- instant and/or regular brown rice

Beans and legumes

- dried beans, peas, and lentils
- no-salt-added canned black beans
- no-salt-added canned cannellini beans
- no-salt-added canned chickpeas
- no-salt-added canned kidney beans
- no-salt-added canned navy beans

PASTAS AND GRAINS

- assorted whole-grain and enriched pastas, including lasagna noodles
- barley
- corn tortillas
- farro
- instant, or fine-grain, bulgur
- quick-cooking oatmeal
- quinoa
- whole-wheat couscous

TOMATO PRODUCTS

- dry-packed sun-dried tomatoes
- no-salt-added diced, stewed, crushed, and whole tomatoes
- no-salt-added tomato paste
- no-salt-added tomato sauce
- spaghetti sauce (lowest sodium available)

DRY GOODS

- active dry yeast
- baking powder
- baking soda
- cornmeal
- cornstarch
- flour: all-purpose, whole-wheat, white whole-wheat, and whole-wheat pastry
- green tea bags
- plain dry bread crumbs
- salt-free instant bouillon: chicken and beef
- sugar: granulated, light brown, dark brown, and confectioners'
- whole-wheat panko (Japanese-style bread crumbs)

CANNED AND BOTTLED PRODUCTS

- 100% fruit juices
- boneless, skinless salmon canned or in pouches (lowest sodium available)
- canned very low sodium tuna, packed in water
- canned water chestnuts
- fat-free, low-sodium broths: chicken, beef, and/or vegetable
- fruits canned in water with no sugar added when possible or in their own juice
- garlic: minced, chopped, or whole cloves
- gingerroot, minced
- green chiles
- kalamata olives
- light beer
- no-salt-added canned vegetables
- red wine (regular or nonalcoholic)
- roasted red bell peppers
- sherry (not cooking sherry)
- unsweetened applesauce
- white wine (regular or nonalcoholic)

COOKING OILS

- canola or corn oil
- cooking sprays
- olive oil
- peanut oil
- toasted sesame oil

MISCELLANEOUS

- all-fruit spreads
- dried fruits, including raisins, cranberries, apricots, and plums (choose those with the least added sugar)
- honey
- low-sodium peanut butter
- molasses
- pure maple syrup
- unsalted nuts, including almonds, walnuts, peanuts, pecans, and pine nuts
- seeds, including sesame, anise, caraway, fennel, and pumpkin (unsalted)

CONDIMENTS (CHOOSE LOWEST SODIUM AVAILABLE)

- chipotle peppers canned in adobo sauce
- hot chili oil
- mustards
- no-salt-added ketchup
- red hot-pepper sauce
- soy sauce
- Thai sweet chili sauce
- vinegars, including cider, balsamic, red wine, white wine, and plain rice
- Worcestershire sauce

SPICES AND SEASONINGS

- black pepper
- cayenne
- chili powder
- crushed red pepper flakes
- curry powder
- dried herbs, including oregano, basil, thyme, rosemary, dillweed, parsley, sage, bay leaves, and saffron
- dry mustard
- garlic powder
- ground spices, including cinnamon, ginger, nutmeg, allspice, cumin, coriander, paprika, smoked paprika, and turmeric
- onion powder
- salt
- salt-free seasoning blends, including all-purpose, Creole or Cajun, Italian, and lemon pepper
- vanilla extract

cooking equipment and tools basics

APPLIANCES

- blender
- food processor
- grill (outdoor)
- microwave

- oven
- slow cooker
- stovetop

TOOLS

- basting brushes
- box grater
- can opener
- citrus reamer
- colander
- cooking parchment (or aluminum foil)
- cutting boards for vegetables, meats, and poultry
- fine-mesh sieve
- grill tools including wire cleaning brush
- instant-read thermometer
- kitchen shears
- kitchen twine
- knives: carving, chef's, paring, santoku, slicing, serrated, utility
- ladle

- mandoline
- measuring cups
- measuring spoons
- mixing bowls (glass)
- oven mitts and pot holders
- oven thermometer
- peeler
- rasp grater
- skewers (metal or wooden, bamboo)
- slotted spoon
- spatulas (regular and slotted, rubber and metal)
- timer
- tongs
- whisk
- wire rack
- wooden spoons

COOKWARE

- baking dishes, glass (9-inch square and 11 x 7 x 2-inch)
- baking pans, metal (8-inch square)
- baking sheets (rimmed and unrimmed, broiler-safe)
- broiler pan and rack
- Dutch oven with lid
- skillets with lids: small (8-inch, ovenproof), medium (10-inch), large (12-inch)
- pots with lids
- loaf pan (8 x 4 x 2-inch)
- microwaveable bowls, plates, casserole dishes with lids (1½-quart and 2-quart), baking dishes (8- or 9-inch round or square), pie pan (9-inch)
- muffin pan (12-cup)
- ramekins
- roasting pan and rack
- saucepans with lids: small (2-quart), medium (4-quart), large (6-quart)
- bamboo steamer or collapsible metal or silicone steamer basket
- wok (14-inch)

kitchen and food safety basics

GENERAL FOOD SAFETY

According to the United States Department of Agriculture (USDA), these are the four fundamental rules to keep food safe:

CLEAN: WASH HANDS AND SURFACES OFTEN.

- Wash hands with soap and warm water for 20 seconds before and after handling food.

- Use hot, soapy water and paper towels or clean cloths to wipe up kitchen surfaces or spills. Wash cloths in hot water in the washing machine.

- Wash cutting boards, dishes, knives, and countertops with hot, soapy water after preparing each food item and before you go on to the next item.

SEPARATE: DON'T CROSS-CONTAMINATE.

- Place raw meat, poultry, and seafood in containers or sealed plastic bags to prevent their juices, which may contain harmful bacteria, from dripping onto other foods both in your grocery cart and in your refrigerator or freezer.

- Liquid that was used to marinate raw meat, poultry, or seafood should not be used as a basting sauce or on cooked foods unless it is boiled just before using to destroy any harmful bacteria.

- Never place cooked food back on the same plate or cutting board that previously held raw food.

- If possible, designate one cutting board for fresh produce and bread and a separate one for raw meat, poultry, and seafood. Always use a clean cutting board.

COOK: COOK TO THE RIGHT TEMPERATURE.

Use a food thermometer inserted into the thickest part of the food (don't let it touch bone). Cook foods until they have reached the following safe minimum internal temperatures:

- All beef, pork, lamb, and veal steaks, chops, and roasts to a minimum internal temperature of 145°F. Allow the meat to rest for at least 3 minutes.

- All ground beef, pork, lamb, and veal to an internal temperature of 160°F.

- All poultry, including ground poultry, to an internal temperature of 165°F.

CHILL: REFRIGERATE PROMPTLY.

- Refrigerate perishable food within 2 hours (in the summer cut this down to 1 hour).

- Refrigerate or freeze leftovers within 2 hours (in the summer cut this down to 1 hour). Discard any food left out beyond this window.

- Be sure your refrigerator is set at and maintaining a temperature of 40°F or below and the freezer at 0°F or below. Monitor with an appliance thermometer.

COOKING SAFELY IN THE BLENDER OR FOOD PROCESSOR

When putting hot liquids into your blender or food processor, use the following safety guidelines:

- Always use a lid when using a blender or food processor.

- Process hot liquids in batches.

- Vent the lid so the steam can escape.

- Cover the open area with a kitchen towel to prevent spraying.

- *Don't* overfill your blender; always leave room for expansion of your ingredients. Blend the mixture in batches if needed.

COOKING SAFELY UNDER THE BROILER

Broiling is an intense technique because it uses high temperatures to cook food. Follow these safety guidelines when using your broiler:

- Never leave the room while broiling. Watch food carefully, because it can go from browned to burned very quickly.

- Check your oven's owner's manual to determine whether the door should be closed or left ajar while broiling.

- Vent the area well, especially if you have an electric oven. Splatters on the electric coils can cause smoke.

- If you're using cookware other than the broiler pan (when browning a casserole, for example), be sure the dish can handle high heat. Avoid using glass pans, which can crack or burst.

- Foods that are no more than 1 to 1½ inches thick are best for broiling, because only the surface of the food is cooked; the heat won't penetrate the food enough to cook the center of thicker foods.

- To avoid flare-ups, don't pour marinades and sauces over the food while broiling it.

COOKING SAFELY ON THE GRILL

According to the USDA, eating moderate amounts of grilled meats, poultry, and fish cooked—without charring—to a safe temperature does not pose a health problem. Follow these safety guidelines when using your grill:

- Completely thaw meat and poultry before grilling so it cooks more evenly. Use the refrigerator for slow, safe thawing or thaw sealed packages in cold water. For quicker thawing, you can use the microwave to defrost if the food will be grilled immediately.

- Always marinate food in the refrigerator, not on the counter.

- Always use a clean basting brush to avoid contamination.

- When taking food off the grill, use a clean platter. Putting cooked food on the same platter that held raw meat or poultry could contaminate it from the harmful bacteria in the raw meat juices.

- In hot weather (above 90°F), don't let food sit out for more than 1 hour.

- Cook food to a safe minimum internal temperature to destroy harmful bacteria (see "Cook to the right temperature" on page 279). Meat and poultry on a grill often browns very fast on the outside. Use an instant-read thermometer to be sure the food has reached a safe minimum internal temperature.

- When using a gas grill, avoid high temperatures. Food that is cooked on high heat for longer periods of time may produce unwanted carcinogens. Cut off any charred (burnt or black) parts before eating.

COOKING SAFELY IN THE MICROWAVE

Microwaves are convenient and safe appliances when used properly. Follow these safety guidelines when using your microwave:

- Arrange food evenly in a microwaveable dish and add some liquid if needed. Cover the dish with a microwave-safe lid or plastic wrap; loosen or vent the lid or wrap to let steam escape. The moist heat that is created will help destroy harmful bacteria and ensure uniform cooking.

- Microwave ovens can cook unevenly and leave "cold spots" where harmful bacteria can survive, so stir or rotate food midway through the cooking time to eliminate these.

- When partially cooking food in the microwave to finish on the grill or in the oven, be sure to transfer the microwaved food to the other heat source immediately. Never partially cook food and store it for later use.

- Remove food from packaging before defrosting it in the microwave.

- Use only cookware that is manufactured for use in the microwave oven. Glass, ceramic, and all plastics should be labeled for microwave use.

- Microwaveable plastic wraps, wax paper, cooking bags, cooking parchment, and white microwave-safe paper towels should be safe to use. Don't let plastic wrap touch food during microwaving; it may melt.

- The following should NOT be used in the microwave: plastic storage containers such as margarine tubs, take-out containers, and other one-time-use containers. These can warp or melt, possibly causing harmful chemicals to leach into the food. Also, never use thin plastic storage bags, brown paper or plastic grocery bags, newspaper, aluminum foil, or metal or foam containers.

- Never operate the microwave if it is damaged in any way, such as broken door seals or loose latches. Don't operate a microwave when it's empty, as this can damage the interior.

COOKING SAFELY IN THE SLOW COOKER

The direct heat from the crock, lengthy cooking times, and steam created within the tightly covered container combine to destroy bacteria and make slow cooking a safe process for cooking even on the low setting. Follow these safety guidelines when using your slow cooker:

- Become familiar with your cooker's temperature range so you can gauge cooking times accurately. Cooking temperatures of units from different manufacturers vary, and today's cookers may cook hotter than older models; your machine may cook a little hotter or cooler than the norm. If that's the case, the difference may affect not only the success of a recipe but also the safety of the food.

- To test the cooking temperature of your cooker, try this: Fill the crock one-half to two-thirds full of room-temperature water and heat the water, covered, on low for 8 hours. Uncover and immediately test the water temperature with an instant-read thermometer. (Act quickly because the temperature will drop when the lid is raised.) If the temperature is higher than 185°F, your cooker runs hot, and you should cook foods for slightly less time than recommended. If it is lower, foods may not reach an adequate cooking temperature quickly enough for safety. (If your cooker is not heating to a safe temperature, you should consider replacing it.) Altitude also will affect your cooker's performance, so modify your timing according to the manufacturer's instructions.

- Thaw frozen foods, especially meat and poultry, in the fridge or microwave—but not at room temperature—before you put them in the cooker. Frozen ingredients will keep the internal temperature lower than it should be, and the contents of the crock may not reach high-enough temperatures to cook properly.

- To prevent harmful bacteria from multiplying, don't leave food on the warm or off setting in your slow cooker for more than 2 hours.

- If you suspect that your cooker has been off for more than 2 hours because of a power outage, discard the food in the crock.

- Don't reheat leftovers in the crock because bacteria can grow in the time it takes for the food to reach a safe temperature. Instead, reheat food in a microwave or on the stove.

- Remove foods from the crock before refrigerating them. The crock is too thick to allow foods to cool quickly enough to prevent bacteria growth.

food groups and suggested servings

To get the nutrients you need, the American Heart Association recommends that you focus your diet on fruits, vegetables, whole grains, low-fat dairy products, poultry, fish, and nuts, while limiting red meat and sugary foods and beverages. Many diets fit this pattern, including the DASH (Dietary Approaches to Stop Hypertension) eating plan from the National Institutes of Health and diets suggested by the USDA and the American Heart Association. The DASH diet provides the average recommended number of servings of each basic food group, which are based on daily calorie intake and summarized on the following chart. The number of servings that is right for you will vary depending on your caloric needs. When shopping, compare nutrition facts panels and look for the products that are lowest in sodium, saturated fat, and trans fat, and that don't have added sugars.

SERVING RECOMMENDATIONS BY CALORIE LEVEL

FOOD GROUP	1,600 CALORIES	2,000 CALORIES	SAMPLE SERVING SIZES
VEGETABLES Eat a variety of colors and types.	3 to 4 servings per day	4 to 5 servings per day	1 cup raw leafy vegetable ½ cup cut-up raw or cooked vegetable ½ cup vegetable juice
FRUITS Eat a variety of colors and types.	4 servings per day	4 to 5 servings per day	1 medium fruit ¼ cup dried fruit ½ cup fresh, frozen, or canned fruit ½ cup fruit juice
FIBER-RICH WHOLE GRAINS Choose whole grains for at least half your servings.	6 servings per day	6 to 8 servings per day	1 slice bread 1 oz dry cereal (check nutrition label for cup measurements) ½ cup cooked rice, pasta, or cereal
FAT-FREE, 1% FAT, AND LOW-FAT DAIRY PRODUCTS Choose fat-free when possible and compare sodium levels to choose the lowest.	2 to 3 servings per day	2 to 3 servings per day	1 cup fat-free or low-fat milk 1 cup fat-free or low-fat yogurt 1½ oz fat-free or low-fat cheese
FISH* Choose varieties rich in omega-3 fatty acids.	6 oz (cooked) per week	6 oz (cooked) per week	3 oz cooked fish, such as salmon and trout

FOOD GROUP	1,600 CALORIES	2,000 CALORIES	SAMPLE SERVING SIZES
SKINLESS POULTRY AND LEAN MEATS **Choose lean and extra-lean.**	3 to 6 oz (cooked) per day	Less than 6 oz (cooked) per day	3 oz cooked poultry or meat
LEGUMES, NUTS, AND SEEDS **Choose unsalted products.**	3 to 4 servings per week	4 to 5 servings per week	½ cup dried beans or peas ⅓ cup or 1½ oz nuts 2 tbsp peanut butter 2 tbsp or ½ oz seeds
FATS AND OILS **Use liquid vegetable oils (such as olive, canola, or corn) and cooking sprays or light tub margarines most often. Choose products with the lowest amount of sodium.**	2 servings per day	2 to 3 servings per day	1 tsp light tub margarine 1 tbsp light mayonnaise 1 tsp vegetable oil 1 tbsp regular or 2 tbsp low-fat salad dressing (fat-free dressing does not count as a serving but does contain calories)
SWEETS AND ADDED SUGARS	0 servings per week	5 or fewer servings per week	1 tbsp sugar 1 tbsp jelly or jam ½ cup sorbet 1 cup lemonade

*If you are concerned about the mercury in fish and shellfish, remember that the health risks from mercury exposure depend on the amount of seafood eaten and the level of mercury in the individual fish. In most cases, the benefits of fish outweigh the risks. For more details, visit www.heart.org or www.fda.gov.

about the recipes

EACH RECIPE in the book includes a nutritional analysis so you can decide how that dish fits with your dietary needs. These guidelines will give you some details on how the analyses were calculated.

- Each analysis is for a *single* serving; garnishes or optional ingredients are *not* included unless noted.

- Because of the many variables involved, the nutrient values provided should be considered approximate. When figuring portions, remember that the serving sizes are approximate also.

- When ingredient options are listed, the first one is analyzed. When a range of amount is given, the average is analyzed.

- Values other than fats are rounded to the nearest whole number. Fat values are rounded to the nearest half gram. Because of the rounding, values for saturated, trans, monounsaturated, and polyunsaturated fats may not add up to the amount shown for total fat value.

- All the recipes are analyzed using unsalted or low-sodium ingredients whenever possible. In some cases, we call for unprocessed foods or no-salt-added and low-sodium products, then add table salt sparingly for flavor.

- We specify canola, corn, and olive oils in these recipes, but you can also use other heart-healthy unsaturated oils, such as safflower, soybean, and sunflower.

- Meats are analyzed as lean, with all visible fat discarded. Values for ground beef are based on lean meat that is 95 percent fat free.

- When meat, poultry, or seafood is marinated and the marinade is discarded, the analysis includes all of the sodium from the marinade but none of the other nutrients from it.

- If alcohol is used in a cooked dish, we estimate that most of the alcohol calories evaporate as the food cooks.

- Because product labeling in the marketplace can vary and change quickly, we use the generic terms "fat-free" and "low-fat" throughout to avoid confusion.

- We use the abbreviations *g* for gram and *mg* for milligram.

index

Bold page references indicate recipe has a photo in color insert.